Displacing Democracy

AMERICAN GOVERNANCE:
POLITICS, POLICY, AND PUBLIC LAW

Series Editors: Richard Valelly, Pamela Brandwein,
Marie Gottschalk, Christopher Howard

A complete list of books in the series
is available from the publisher.

DISPLACING DEMOCRACY

Economic Segregation in America

Amy Widestrom

PENN

UNIVERSITY OF PENNSYLVANIA PRESS

PHILADELPHIA

Published by
University of Pennsylvania Press
Philadelphia, Pennsylvania 19104-4112
www.upenn.edu/pennpress

Printed in the United States of America
on acid-free paper

10 9 8 7 6 5 4 3 2 1

Cataloging-in-Publication Data is available from the Library of Congress.
ISBN 978-0-8122-4659-9

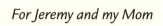

For Jeremy and my Mom

CONTENTS

Introduction: A Theory of Economic
Segregation and Civic Engagement

An African American middle and upper-middle class emerged in Atlanta in the early twentieth century, and after World War II these families increasingly sought homes away from the impoverished, decaying, and densely populated urban core. Additionally, and despite great effort by segregationists, residents of formerly all-white neighborhoods found it more difficult to maintain policies of racial exclusion as the civil rights movement gathered momentum. Beginning in the 1960s, middle- and upper-middle-class African American families moved into the formerly white neighborhoods west and southwest of downtown Atlanta, including the area known as West Manor.[1] The new residents of West Manor organized block clubs and civic groups, secured better city services, and voted at high rates; it was an economically, socially, and civically vibrant community, the type of community that forms when resources are abundant. Despite the fact that West Manor today remains an urban neighborhood that is nearly 100 percent African American—characteristics that many observers might associate with poverty and urban decay—the neighborhood has maintained its middle- and upper-middle-class identity and its vibrant and active civic life. Over the past forty years West Manor has remained a thriving community with good schools, safe parks, big homes, and high levels of civic engagement.[2]

Meanwhile, beginning in 1962, other black families moved into a newly completed housing development called Thomasville Heights across town in southeastern Atlanta. Families moved there as part of a relocation initiative designed to assist people displaced by urban-renewal projects in downtown Atlanta. City officials chose this area in the southeast for the relocation of predominantly low-income and working-class families because the land was available: until the 1960s there had not been a large enough population there to partition the land into smaller census tracts.[3] The new development was composed of single-family homes owned and occupied primarily by working-class African American families. The city assisted these first-time homebuyers in purchasing their homes, and throughout the 1960s and 1970s these homeowners behaved much the same way as their wealthier counterparts in West Manor: they organized civic clubs, secured postal and other city services for their neighborhood, advocated for and received city funds to build a library and recreation center, and actively participated in electoral politics.[4]

But Thomasville Heights began to change in the late 1970s and 1980s. The number of rental units in the neighborhood increased as low-income residents continued to move into the area owing to revitalization efforts throughout the city that displaced low-income, primarily black, Atlantans. Redevelopment efforts, including the construction of freeways and shopping centers, as well as venues for the 1996 Summer Olympics, prompted the relocation of thousands of poor citizens.[5] Over time this increased the concentration of high-poverty residents in this southeastern corner of Atlanta, creating a neighborhood that was increasingly isolated—and segregated—along economic lines. Today this community is plagued by persistent poverty, crime, and attendant economic and social problems. Another important result of this segregation is that residents are civically and politically inactive and largely neglected by political leaders.[6] Unlike West Manor, Thomasville Heights fits the stereotype of an urban neighborhood with a large African American population, and, not incidentally, the extent to which this neighborhood conforms to preconceptions, the harder it becomes to envision possible alternatives.

This community, which began as an initiative to help those in struggling inner-city neighborhoods, simply could not maintain its original character. Although the first wave of relocation in the 1960s seemed to work fairly well, subsequent waves of newly arrived impoverished residents gradually changed the character of the area. Starting in the 1970s, public officials too often seemed to take the view that because Thomasville Heights was already home to poor and working-class blacks, the neighborhood could serve as a landing spot for new waves of people being displaced by new redevelopment projects. Citywide policies targeting blight clearance, low-income housing construction, and relocation too often treated Thomasville Heights as a last stop for thousands of Atlantans. Over time a grim cycle developed: Thomasville Heights became known by policy makers and other city residents as a poor neighborhood, and it became a logical spot for public officials to shuttle more poor people, with scant concern about how those relocated might find their way in their new environs or what their arrival might mean for the future of the neighborhood.

The story of Thomasville Heights is a familiar one. Across the United States over the past several decades, low-income residents, usually racial and ethnic minorities, have become more likely to live in increasingly impoverished and blighted neighborhoods. That this has happened is not in dispute; the important questions are how and why this physical relocation of millions of people into these neighborhoods has occurred and what its effects have been.[7]

One popular theory focuses on public choice, arguing that as free agents, people can choose where they want to live and should "vote with their feet" if they are unhappy with their residential environments.[8] As enticingly simple as this theory may seem, this position does not adequately appreciate how our residential choices are shaped by two competing forces. One of these is political. There are numerous public policies that shape our lived environment, including housing and transportation policies, among others, and these interact with one another in complicated ways to circumscribe and modify the choices that individuals have regarding where they live. The other force is economic. The dynamism of local, national, and international economic forces combines with the individual motivations of people driven to improve their own economic well-being in ways that affect income distribution and inequality in society, which in turn can limit what some people, particularly poor people, can do to relocate to a better neighborhood.

Put simply, these political and economic phenomena—public policies and laws, and income and wealth distribution—combine with one another to have a profound effect on residential patterns in the United States, increasingly promoting residential segregation not by race but by class.[9] This is not to suggest that people are powerless and completely subject to the whims of large-scale political and economic forces, but to acknowledge that these phenomena matter and can circumscribe or modify the opportunities and options available to individual citizens. The stories of West Manor and Thomasville Heights exemplify this alternative understanding of residential patterns, which has not been sufficiently explored or appreciated by scholars. The evolution of these neighborhoods demonstrates that increasing economic segregation occurs for reasons that extend beyond simply the move-ment and concentration of individuals and resources as a result of their own choices. Instead, these brief narratives, which will be examined in greater depth in this study, highlight how residential segregation of different eco-nomic groups—like those in West Manor and in Thomasville Heights—or what we can call *economic segregation*, occurs. More important, the stories of how cities like Atlanta became more spatially divided along economic lines in the late twentieth century demonstrate the important civic and political consequences that emerge as a result of this residential economic segregation.

When explored further, these stories seem to suggest that economic seg-regation is not just a consequence of public policies and broad economic factors, it is also an underappreciated and understudied phenomenon shap-ing residential environments and the subsequent engagement of individual citizens. Economic segregation does this by contributing to the development of what we can call *civic environments,* or neighborhood contexts that do or do not contain the resources and capabilities to advocate for or fight policies that harm individual neighborhoods. From this perspective the well-documented trend in declining civic engagement among low-income citizens is not simply driven by individual low-income citizens opting out of political life.[10] Instead, the environments within isolated low-income neighborhoods create the circumstances that serve to diminish civic en-gagement among the least advantaged in society and those within high-income neighborhoods serve to promote engagement among the prosperous. Place matters, and the civic environment in which a person lives can affect the attitudes they develop about the political process and the likelihood that they will participate in civic life.

This book attempts to understand how economic segregation—the resi-dential segregation of low- and high-income individuals into spatially dis-tinct areas—affects civic engagement, including associational and political life in communities and, ultimately, voting behavior. The proposition here is that trends in voter turnout, particularly among low-income residents, are not simply attributable to individual choices and traits, and may be better explained by an examination of how neighborhoods segregated along eco-nomic lines create conditions that either inhibit or encourage political par-ticipation. This creates what we can call a *class gap* in political engagement and participation; different civic environments promote and encourage high levels of involvement among wealthier citizens while simultaneously discouraging and depressing levels of involvement among the poor. This gap is extremely important, as its existence helps perpetuate a virtuous cycle of engagement and responsiveness among the prosperous and a vicious cycle of isolation and disengagement among the impoverished.

Considered this way, developments in American politics in the late twentieth century become a story of citizens and resources sorting, not always entirely by choice, into economically segregated residential spheres, and today's levels of participation by different economic groups are a consequence that has emerged as a result. It is well known that certain resources and skills—time, money, and communication skills, among others—are vital assets in the political arena, and this investigation analyzes these assets at the neighborhood level. This does not mean that individual-level resources do not matter, but in order to complete our prevailing understanding of civic and political engagement it is important to acknowledge that neighborhood-level resources and attributes may also matter in significant and distinct ways not sufficiently appreciated in our current understanding of individual political behavior and American politics.

As economic segregation, that is the sorting of different economic classes into geographically distinct areas, occurs, the demographic and resource composition of neighborhoods changes, altering the environments of communities wherein citizens learn habits of civic engagement. In this way economic segregation does not simply aggregate individual characteristics within certain neighborhoods; it also produces contextual effects that alter civic engagement and political participation that are not driven by the socioeconomic status of individuals in neighborhoods but by the geographic isolation of communities, the concentration of poverty or wealth, and the physical conditions of neighborhoods.[11] These conditions combine to create civic environments that shape how low-income and wealthier citizens engage in the American polity.

In this study, civic environment means something specific and distinct from a more commonly used phrase in these types of studies: civic culture. Typically, we think of civic culture affecting engagement in one of three ways: influencing action by providing the values and goals that guide action; providing the "tool kit" from which people develop strategies of action; or shaping the patterns that govern day-to-day action.[12] Here we differentiate between civic environment and civic culture because the latter is a cognitive orientation held by citizens that either promotes or provides tools for certain behaviors, while civic environment conveys the context, physical conditions, and surroundings in which citizens develop that cognitive orientation, learn lessons of citizenship, and ultimately act. In this neighborhood environment, economic, social, and civic resources develop or dissolve through social networks, economic and business endeavors, and associational and organizational life. The dynamic interaction of these separate elements within neighborhoods creates a civic environment in which behaviors and attitudes vital to civic engagement and political behavior are learned or not and consequently in which participation is promoted or discouraged.

Research presented here suggests that these neighborhood elements hinder or promote civic engagement and political participation at the polls by altering civic and political mobilization within neighborhoods characterized by segregated poverty or wealth. Over time this creates a balance of political power that is dramatically skewed not only toward individuals with more economic resources but toward entire neighborhoods with more economic resources. In other words, it is not simply that there are a lot of poor or wealthy citizens in these neighborhoods; it is that the neighborhoods are isolated from other and different neighborhoods in the city, and this isolation allows them to take on certain contextual characteristics, altering the capacity of voluntary associations within these communities and enabling candidates and elected officials to focus resources and efforts on more highly resourced communities while ignoring the less advantaged ones. This means that the finite amount of time, money, and effort that these associations and public officials have is targeted in specific areas, and this targeting is made easier by the geographic isolation of these communities. Segregated, prosperous community residents are more easily mobilized and prompted to participate in civic life, while those in segregated, impoverished communities are discouraged or worse, ignored, creating and perpetuating virtuous and vicious cycles of segregation, mobilization-demobilization, and ultimately civic engagement and political participation in economically segregated communities.

The result is a gap, based on economic class, in overall engagement with the polity. We know that wealthier people participate more and receive more attention from public officials and the benefits of engagement while poor people participate less and are increasingly ignored and alienated. We need a better understanding of how economic segregation contributes to this phenomenon by creating civic environments within communities that promote or hinder engagement by the prosperous or the impoverished residents living in these neighborhoods.

The Political Origins of Economic Segregation

While much is made about the ability of Americans to choose where they live, residential choices are circumscribed by many factors, including economic resources, occupation, and, notably, public policy.[13] Indeed, neighborhoods and neighborhood choice have been directly shaped and altered by public policies in American cities throughout the twentieth century but most strikingly between 1945 and 2000. After World War II housing, economic renewal and revitalization, and transportation policies implemented by federal, state, and local officials in cities across the country worked to reorganize the spatial distribution of Americans in and around cities, contributing to increasing geographic segregation along economic lines in many urban areas.[14] This economic segregation not only affected individuals and families, as previous studies have shown; it also affected other aspects of the neighborhood environment by changing the physical arrangement of citizens and their resources, ultimately transforming the civic environment and civic lives of these neighborhoods.[15]

When considering patterns of segregation in American cities during the twentieth century, the most commonly discussed type of housing policies in the United States are those associated with racial exclusion, specifically federal housing programs, such as federal home-loan programs, restrictive covenants, and exclusionary zoning laws. After World War II returning veterans and growing families increased demand for housing. The Truman administration pushed for legislation to develop and expand the suburbs, in part by promoting financing options for returning veterans hoping to buy new homes being developed in Levittowns up and down the East Coast.[16] These policies encouraged movement out of the city and, because the majority of loans from the Federal Housing Authority and the Department of Veterans Affairs (then the Veterans Administration) went to white veterans, also encouraged white flight from urban centers.[17] This was particularly true for cities that had experienced rapid growth in their black populations as a result of the northward migration of Southern blacks in search of work in the early and middle part of the twentieth century.[18]

But it was not just loan programs that segregated blacks from whites in urban centers and the emergent surrounding suburbs. Restrictive covenants were agreements usually built into titles or deeds of property and most commonly used to prevent homeowners from selling (or renting) to specific racial and ethnic minorities in certain communities. As new developments were being built to keep pace with demand, in part as a result of new home-financing tools, some developers used restrictive covenants in their housing developments to prevent racial and ethnic integration if the homes were re-sold or rented. One of the most notorious developers known for using restrictive covenants was Jesse Clyde "J. C." Nichols in Kansas City, responsible for building the well-known Country Club Plaza, among other neighborhoods. These covenants most commonly targeted African Americans and Jews in the mid-twentieth century and were largely successful at maintaining racial and religious segregation in many U.S. cities.[19]

Exclusionary zoning laws at the local level were also key to maintaining racial segregation, particularly after fair housing laws went into effect.[20] Interestingly, though, most communities justified the use of zoning codes to keep out racial and ethnic minorities by using the language of private property. Although some white residents used explicitly racial justifications, neighborhood residents and local officials usually described residential racial integration as an affront to their freedom of choice and to their rights: as homeowners, they had the right to sell to whomever they would like; as taxpayers, they had the right to promote the kind of community in which they wanted to live; and, as responsible community residents they believed racial integration would devalue neighborhood property.[21] Through zoning codes communities were able to create, protect, and maintain their middle- and upper-middle-class nature by preventing the construction of certain types of buildings, such as multifamily housing, and certain types of businesses, including commercial enterprises targeting lower-income clientele, such as payday loan stores. Therefore, during the final decades of the twentieth century, residential divisions along economic lines became at least as pervasive, if not more so, than residential divisions along racial ones because the same tactics used initially to target racial and ethnic minorities were deployed against low-income citizens, and fair housing laws allowed wealthier members of racial and ethnic minorities to move into previously all-white, well-heeled communities, isolating the poor in specific neighborhoods.[22]

While housing policies play an important role in shaping cities in the second half of the twentieth century, deindustrialization and revitalization efforts were, and continue to be, another key feature of urban life. Although deindustrialization is commonly understood to be a late-twentieth-century phenomenon, as early as 1945 cities began to struggle financially as middle-class residents and businesses left.[23] This produced an urban environment that by the 1960s and 1970s was rundown, largely impoverished, and rapidly losing its population and remaining industry. Deindustrialization has not just translated into a loss of tax revenue and financial resources for cities; it has also meant higher unemployment rates and fewer jobs for residents, and it has meant that cities have had to deal with large swaths of vacant industrial land, which can have residentially dislocating effects as well.[24]

Those unable to leave during the suburban exodus, either because they were racially barred from communities or because they did not have the resources to move, found themselves in increasingly depressed neighborhoods with limited economic, educational, and social opportunities. This was made worse by the fact that banks in the 1950s, 1960s, and 1970s actively engaged in the practice of redlining: the explicit policy of not lending money for home purchases, improvements, or capital investments in specific communities, usually those that were low income and composed of racial or ethnic minorities.[25] Moreover, in an attempt to pursue urban renewal and economic revitalization, cities often engaged in wholesale blight clearance in an effort to prepare the land for future real estate and industrial investment, which inevitably swept up occupied housing along with vacant homes and industrial lots. This meant that those living in these increasingly depressed communities were often unwitting participants in urban-renewal programs that displaced these residents and required them to move to different neighborhoods, often also depressed and increasingly isolated.

Once land was available, cities and counties used tax incentives and favorable loan structures in an attempt to entice investors and industries back to urban cores.[26] This type of aggressive urban-renewal effort through economic revitalization included projects like the post–World War II Jefferson National Expansion Memorial (the Arch) in St. Louis, which required leveling forty square blocks of the city, and the development of the waterfront along Baltimore's Inner Harbor in the 1970s and 1980s. More recently, cities have turned to developing downtown entertainment or sports complexes in an effort to revitalize both inner-city neighborhoods and boost the tax base; one good example of this is the L.A. Live entertainment complex adjacent to the downtown Staples Center, where the Los Angeles Lakers and the Los Angeles Clippers play, and the more recent push to build a privately funded football stadium nearby. Ultimately, this type of urban renewal often produced two complementary trends, one of gentrification, in which residents of a community are essentially "priced out," and one of deliberate displacement and relocation as a result of blight clearance, each promoting the dislocation of urban poor. Accordingly, however well intentioned these redevelopment programs may have been, an unintended but troubling consequence has been a contribution to the growth of residential economic segregation.

Finally, transportation interests and federal transportation policy have dramatically shaped the physical layout of contemporary American cities.[27] Before major federal intervention during the first decades of the twentieth century, industries affiliated with auto, gasoline, and highway production purchased and dismantled nascent public-transportation systems, which encouraged consumer consumption of automobiles and the consequent road and highway development. In the 1950s the federal government, rather than promoting simultaneous development of mass transit and personal transportation, threw its weight behind the highway lobby and passed the Highway and Defense Act of 1956.[28] Moreover, urban politicians, investors, and boosters of downtowns in general saw the development of highways as promoting two beneficial ends: the destruction of blighted urban neighborhoods to make way for thoroughfares would get rid of blighted housing stock, and the construction of throughways would promote the movement of people and economic activity throughout the city and region. As a result, in 1956, there were 6,100 miles of federal-aid highways approved for urban areas, with 90 percent of the funds to pay for construction coming from the federal government.[29] And yet the proposed routes of these highways and expressways often ran straight through established neighborhoods.

Sometimes routing decisions were driven by cost, as it was cheaper to buy rights of way in poor neighborhoods, but many times they were driven by local activism, as residents in more prosperous neighborhoods were able to use their connections to halt road construction in their community.[30] So while antifreeway movements emerged and accelerated in cities across the country during the 1950s and 1960s, ultimately the consequences of freeway expansion were mostly felt in low-income and minority communities: by 1967, 330,000 families had been displaced by federal-aid highways in urban areas, a number that grew in the subsequent decades.[31]

Less residentially disruptive but no less economically dislocating was congressional legislation in the 1960s that encouraged cities to purchase their public-transit systems and legislation passed in the 1970s that provided federal transit subsidies to cities to operate and maintain these systems.[32] This federal assistance began to dry up in the late 1970s, leaving cities to shoulder the financial burden of running their own public-transit systems. With the simultaneous deindustrialization and the shuttering of factories in many cities, city governments had fewer funds with which to maintain public-transit infrastructure, and thus the conditions of systems declined and ridership dropped.[33] Faced with the choice of raising taxes or raising ticket prices, cities tended to shift the burden to riders, meaning that lower-income residents who depended upon public transportation had to pay more to get anywhere outside of their immediate neighborhood. This introduced another economic burden to already overburdened or economically inse-cure populations and further destabilized communities across the country as access to economic opportunities, which were moving beyond city bound-aries, dried up.

In short, housing, economic revitalization, and transportation policies all affected the development of neighborhoods in cities. These policies com-bined with a collapsing urban industrial base to create and exacerbate resi-dential economic segregation in American cities. Chapter 2 will discuss these policies at greater length, and provide specific examples of how these policies combined to create residential economic segregation in cities. Given the magnitude of this change, though, it is surprising that scholars have not spent more time examining the many and various consequences of this shift toward economic segregation for the civic and political life of segregated prosperous and impoverished neighborhoods.

The Economic Origins of Economic Segregation

It is important to understand the implications of economic segregation, as residential economic segregation is an important result and reflection of the growing income and wealth inequality in the United States. Rising economic inequality has received considerable attention from scholars and journalists in recent years, and it is well documented that economic inequality has in-creased dramatically over the last forty years, as measured by real wages and income and by wealth.[34] A key source of rising inequality as measured by income has been the stagnation of wages and salaries for families in the low-est quintiles compared with the rising income among families in the top

5 percent of the income distribution, and especially the top 1 percent of the income distribution. In fact, the share of income earned by the top 1 percent of wage earners has increased from 8 percent in 1974 to 18 percent in 2007, which goes up to 23.5 percent when income from interest on investments and dividends, otherwise called capital gains, is included. These numbers are even more staggering if you look at the incomes of the very, very rich: the top 0.1 percent, or the richest one-in-a-thousand households, take in collectively more than $1 trillion a year, including capital gains, which is 12.3 percent of the total income earned in the United States; the 0.01 percent, or the highest-earning 15,000 families, each earns more than $35 million a year, which is 6 percent of the total income earned in the United States.[35]

Moreover, wealth inequality, and non-home wealth inequality in particular, has increased as well.[36] In 2010 the top 1 percent of income earners in this country, about 300,000 people, held 42.7 percent of the non-home wealth, up from 38.4 percent in 1969. Notably, the share of income going to the top 1 percent was just 8 percent in 1974 compared with the 34.4 percent and 38.4 percent for net wealth and non-home wealth in 1969, respectively. These statistics tell us that wealth inequality has long been much greater than income inequality, but both have increased.[37]

These trends are particularly important for understanding the changing nature of economic segregation in the United States because rising income and wealth inequality have contributed to higher levels of economic segregation.[38] While urban policy determines where housing is located and what types of housing are available to residents in different neighborhoods, family income and wealth allow for residential mobility. Families with more income and accumulated wealth have more residential choices and freedom. Families earning middle-class incomes with no accumulated wealth and assets that would allow them to buy homes in middle-class neighborhoods find themselves living in communities that are changing around them, as the movement of poor individuals and families into increasingly low-income neighborhoods promotes economic segregation as well.[39] This has contributed to a residential landscape that has become more and more divided along economic lines. Indeed, two-thirds of metropolitan areas in America have experienced increasing residential economic segregation over the last three decades, with more than 85 percent of the urban population living in an area that was more economically segregated in 2000 compared with 1970.[40] While subsequent chapters focus more on how policies shaped urban areas, it is important to keep in mind that these broad, macroeconomic trends also influence individual economic resources and help shape the geographic distribution of people within the urban landscape more directly defined by urban policy.

Money, Economic Segregation, and American Politics

Taken together, over the past forty years the least advantaged in society have fared far worse in terms of wages and wealth. They have become more likely to live in poor and high-poverty neighborhoods, areas that were more and more likely to be spatially isolated and segregated from other communities and people of other economic classes. At the same time, wealthy citizens have also become more isolated in their own neighborhoods and communities, able to physically separate themselves from lower economic classes. This manifestation of economically segregated neighborhoods demands close consideration because it seems important for us to try to understand how these trends may have affected the civic and political life of neighborhoods and their residents, and how this increasing stratification and segregation may affect the American polity and American politics. Neighborhoods provide the context in which people learn and practice the skills and attitudes that ultimately determine their level of civic engagement, and isolation as a result of residential economic segregation creates distinctly different civic environments that encourage or inhibit that engagement.

In contrast to the proliferation of studies documenting the effects of racial segregation on economic, social, and political trends, few inquiries attempt to focus on class specifically and examine the civic and political effects of neighborhood change as a result of economic segregation.[41] Those studies that do focus on economic dynamics within neighborhoods typically do so by investigating the history of economic disparity or the influence of economic inequality or segregation, or both, on children, families, and health, or on social and neighborhood cohesion as a result of changes to community environments.[42] The contention here, though, is that the emergence of residential economic segregation is also a story of political development with specific political consequences. We know from previous studies that neighborhood and civic environments are built and altered through political decisions of citizens, policy makers, and elected officials, and that individual political attitudes and behaviors cannot be explained apart from the context in which they are learned and occur.[43] But unfortunately, those scholars best

poised to examine the consequences of economic segregation—political behavior scholars, American political development scholars, and urban politics scholars—have paid insufficient attention to the intersection of political
behavior, the political development of American cities, and residential economic segregation.

This is a crucial omission because the data demonstrate that segregation does in fact affect voter turnout (see Table I.1). One way to illustrate
this is to examine the simple bivariate relationship between segregation
and turnout, taking into account other factors that we know shape turnout, such as educational attainment, marriage, race, and institutional em-

Table I.1. The Effect of Economic Segregation on Voter Turnout in the
United States, 2000

Variables		Standardized (Beta) Coefficients (Standard Errors)		
	All Counties	Income <$32,000	Income >$62,000	Income >$73,000
White	0.40*	−0.87*	0.74*	0.65*
	(0.00)	(0.00)	(0.00)	(0.00)
Bachelor of Arts degree or higher	0.12*	−0.13	0.13**	0.18**
	(0.00)	(0.00)	(0.00)	(0.00)
Married	−0.28*	0.36	−0.11	0.24**
	(−0.00)	(0.00)	(0.00)	(0.00)
Per Capita Religious Institutions	0.06**	−0.08	0.09	0.06
	(3.4)	(8.3)	(16.9)	(33.8)
Economic Segregation	−0.44*	−0.67*	−0.15**	0.03
	(0.00)	(0.00)	(0.00)	(0.00)
Constant	0.62*	0.85*	0.31*	−0.01
N	1,050	51	171	71
R^2	0.37	0.73	0.55	0.57

Source: Neighborhood Change Database and the Voting and Elections Collection from CQ
Press; Urban Institute, and GeoLytics, *Neighborhood Change Database*, CensusCD
neighborhood change database (NCDB) [electronic resource]: 1970–2000 tract data: selected
variables for US Census tracts for 1970, 1980, 1990, 2000; CQ Voting and Elections
Collection from CQ Press (an imprint of SAGE Publications), http://library.cqpress.com/
elections/index.php (accessed on February 26, 2014).
*Significance at the 0.001 level
** Significance at the 0.05 level

beddedness. In other words, we know that voters who are more educated (which is highly correlated with income, and so education is used in the analysis here), who are married, who are not racial or ethnic minorities, and who are connected in some way to such community institutions as voluntary associations and churches vote at higher rates. In the aggregate then, county-level voter turnout should be shaped in part by the educational, marital, racial-ethnic, and institutional composition of a county. Based on the theory posited here, we should also expect that economic segregation will have a depressive effect on turnout but that segregated, prosperous neighborhoods find ways to overcome this effect while segregated, impoverished neighborhoods do not.

Table I.1 presents the relationship between voter turnout and economic segregation, controlling for a variety of factors, using ordinary least-squares regression analysis. Data are presented for all counties in the United States from the year 2000, as well as counties with average median income at different points along the income distribution: counties at 75 percent of the national median income, or $32,000 (there are insufficient observations to go below this threshold); counties at 150 percent of the national median income, or $62,000; and those over 175 percent of the national median income, or $73,000. Table I.1 presents standardized coefficients here because the goal is to understand the comparative effect of residential economic segregation when holding other factors constant, and the independent variables included in this analysis are calculated in different units, making it difficult to engage in this comparison.[44]

When examining the results, it is clear that economic segregation has a statically significant and negative relationship to voter turnout across all counties and that in all counties economic segregation has the greatest effect on voter turnout when compared with the effect of the other independent variables (i.e., the standardized coefficient of −0.44 is greater than the other coefficients).[45] This depressive effect is most pronounced in counties where residents earn less than $32,000 (a one standard-deviation change in economic segregation decreases voter turnout by two-thirds of a standard deviation), although in this case the effect is second to that of the size of the white population. Most important, though, is that the effect of economic segregation disappears in counties with an average median income of $72,000 or higher, where there is a positive relationship between economic segregation and voter turnout but one that is not statistically significant. These findings suggest that economic segregation has a significant effect on voter turnout but one that varies by economic context, and that at the upper ends of the income distribution the effect of segregation changes and may even be positive.

It is also surprising that scholars have not investigated the effects of economic segregation with greater vigor because of the role that money plays in politics and the role that political and policy decisions play in distributing income and wealth in the United States and in distributing people across geographic areas. In the first case, income and wealth are distributed not just through taxation and benefits, as people may be quick to assume, but also through the distribution of "market income," or income earned before taxes or benefits take effect. This includes all the laws that govern unions, minimum wage, corporate governance, and financial markets and institutions, to name a few. When considering this, we see that growing income and wealth inequality are not just natural outgrowths of a free market but rather that the rules of the market have an important effect on people's economic lives.[46] And in terms of the role that public-policy decisions play in income distribution, it is vital to appreciate how urban policy, especially housing policies, economic renewal initiatives, and transportation policies play a role in the geographic and residential distribution of people and resources, particularly in urban areas.

Of course, an important reason policies have developed to benefit the wealthy is because the wealthy have worked hard and applied political pressure to help drive the development of those policies. Given the importance of voting and civic engagement for political outcomes in American democracy, a great deal of research has been conducted examining who votes and why. One key finding that emerges from this research—and one that holds across numerous studies—is that while formal political rights are widely distributed in the United States, these rights are exercised far more often by those with higher socioeconomic status than by those with lower socioeconomic status, and that compared to wealthier citizens, lower-income Americans vote at lower rates, participate less in voluntary associations and advocacy organizations, donate to and volunteer less for political or issue campaigns, and write fewer letters to members of Congress and attend fewer protests, two strategies long considered tools of the disadvantaged.[47] Common explanations for these differences include differences in educational attainment, differences in the skills and resources needed to participate, and weaker connections to voluntary, social, and religious organizations among the least advantaged. In other words typical explanations for low participation among poor citizens and high participation among wealthy citizens focus on the *individual* assets and traits that these people possess.

This creates what scholars typically refer to as class bias in American politics, but a more precise way to phrase it might be to acknowledge that there is a *class gap* in terms of engagement and participation. There is a great deal of scholarship on "class bias," which focuses on how and why the political system is biased in favor of wealthier and more participatory citizens. Our investigation here focuses less on the existing bias in the system and more on delineating how this bias is produced. Because of this I use the phrase class gap throughout this investigation to refer specifically to the gap in participation between the prosperous and the impoverished, and the gap in representation and responsiveness to the prosperous and impoverished. In this way the phrase class gap is intended to focus us on the gaps that exist between the civic and political lives of the wealthy and the poor, so we can understand how ultimately the system has become biased in favor of the economic and political elite.

This gap has developed in part because over the past forty years people have become sorted and divided along economic lines, and this sorting includes physical location: rich people living surrounded by other rich people and poor people living surrounded by other poor people. It seems possible, however, that this geographic sorting does more than just group people together; residential segregation actually changes the character and context of the neighborhoods themselves, and these changes in turn contribute to the widening of the gap in engagement and participation. In other words, it is not simply the individual resources and attitudes, like educational attainment and income, that prompt rich people to engage more and poor people to engage less. Where they live also contributes to what they are likely to do, and the participation and representation gap becomes wider as segregation becomes starker. Indeed, in an analysis of class bias in American politics, Lawrence Jacobs and Joe Soss suggest that residential economic segregation might be the potential culprit in creating the class gap that produces class bias, and yet these scholars acknowledge that few good studies have explored this possibility specifically.[48]

When civic and political behaviors are examined through the lens of residential economic segregation, the question is not why do poor people not vote, but rather what has happened in economically segregated neighborhoods that has contributed to the widening class gap in political engagement and participation? Put another way, why do residents of segregated, impoverished communities vote at lower rates than residents of segregated, prosperous ones? Is it simply that individuals with lower socioeconomic status vote at lower rates, or is there something important about the isolation and concentration of economic, social, and civic resources that drives civic engagement and ultimately a class gap between participants in the American polity?

The answer to this question has serious implications for the future of democracy and social policy in America. If people in the least advantaged neighborhoods are going to the polls less, and this decline is caused or exacerbated by economic segregation, the capacity for residents of these neighborhoods to hold representatives accountable is severely diminished. This could produce political outcomes and policy decisions that represent a small segment of the population and that may perpetuate a vicious cycle of segregation and political alienation among those most in need of political attention and policy action.

Racial Versus Economic Segregation

While many urban cores and, increasingly, suburbs remain racially segregated, it is important to try and appreciate economic segregation as distinct from racial segregation, despite the fact that scholars and lay citizens alike typically think about segregation primarily as a racial phenomenon. In fact, the bulk of contemporary and historical research on segregation analyzes residential settlement patterns through the lens of racial segregation, including scholars who have expanded this perspective to include political repercussions of the economic and social isolation of low-income African American communities.[49] These and many other studies have shown that racialized politics and policies contributed to the current state of residential segregation in this country and that there are negative political consequences to residential racial segregation.

We know that throughout the post–World War II era, some whites used housing covenants, zoning laws, and racist lending practices to create entire urban and suburban communities that excluded African Americans.[50] As a result some neighborhoods within cities were populated exclusively by African Americans. However, as racial barriers to upward economic mobility and suburban housing have fallen, black families with the means to move out of historically black and often mixed-income or lower-income neighborhoods have done so in increasing numbers.[51] Coupled with trends in white flight, this has left those without means in increasingly poor neighborhoods, contributing to the rise in economic segregation.

This suggests that race and racial segregation may not be the only demographic and neighborhood-level factors shaping political outcomes. Indeed, scholars' focus on race and racial segregation and their subsequent conclusions about neighborhood life may overlook other factors shaping various civic and political phenomena.[52] Rather than designating race as the sole driver of social, economic, and political behaviors, economic segregation should be examined as another key factor in shaping neighborhood environments and behavior as well. This also makes sense because economic status and segregation carry with them an arrangement of resources (such as money, education, employment, and free time) that could be leveraged for political mobilization and participation, while race in and of itself does not. Race is highly correlated with economic segregation, and the history of racism in the United States plays a very important role in shaping residential patterns, particularly in urban areas. But the reliance on a racial analysis of segregation to understand urban geography, its political landscape, and its political outcomes has caused scholars to overlook the effects of important economic residential trends that have occurred since the 1970s. While acknowledging the very real racial bias that exists in America, this book focuses on *economic* segregation as a key factor in shaping community development and understanding political behavior.

We can see the effects of residential sorting along economic lines and the changing nature of inequality in the United States by comparing the socioeconomic characteristics of different types of neighborhoods—average neighborhoods, high-poverty neighborhoods, highly segregated neighborhoods, segregated poor neighborhoods, and highly segregated, high-poverty neighborhoods in 2000 (Figure I.1).[53] In segregated, impoverished census tracts educational attainment is lower and the percentage of welfare recipients and the unemployed are higher than in the average neighborhood. This situation is significantly worse in highly segregated, high-poverty neighborhoods— neighborhoods with an average poverty rate of 40 percent or higher and high levels of economic segregation—when compared with segregated, poor neighborhoods or neighborhoods with above-average poverty rates and above-average segregation, across all measures except for residential mobility.[54]

It is important to note, though, that these data show that residents in segregated, poor neighborhoods move more frequently than residents of

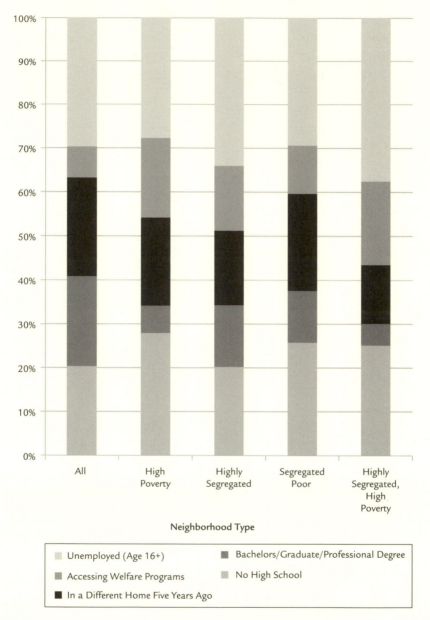

Figure I.1. Socioeconomic Characteristics by Neighborhood Type, 2000.

Source: Urban Institute, and GeoLytics, *Neighborhood Change Database*, CensusCD neighborhood change database (NCDB) [electronic resource]: 1970–2000 tract data: selected variables for US Census tracts for 1970, 1980, 1990, 2000.

any other type of neighborhood, including the residents in highly segregated, high-poverty neighborhoods, despite reports from community leaders in these types of communities.[55] It is also important to note that fewer people in highly segregated, high-poverty neighborhoods use public-welfare programs. This suggests that despite the need and slightly higher levels of residential stability, information about these programs may be limited or that residents in highly segregated, impoverished communities have lower levels of willingness to use government welfare programs.

Subsequent chapters examine the effect of this segregation on civic environments, civic engagement, and political participation within highly segregated environments in contrast to a focus on the economic and social lives of individuals and communities in similar economic situations.[56] Pursuing this line of inquiry is important because it is within these neighborhoods where citizens actually experience the effects of residential economic segregation. High levels of economic segregation should be troubling for those interested in robust civic and political engagement. If low-income citizens are doing worse individually, both in terms of income and wealth, and they are finding themselves increasingly living with others doing just as poorly, the possibility of advocating on their and their neighborhood's behalf—of having all the social and political resources necessary to build a vibrant, healthy neighborhood—may decline. This exploration is important for understanding the civic state of segregated urban America today.

A Theory of Economic Segregation and Civic Engagement

While no previous studies have examined the civic consequences of economic residential segregation in the way suggested here, there is a great deal of previous research that can be brought to bear on how to begin understanding the effect of neighborhood change on civic engagement. Most scholars studying political participation typically understand political behavior as a function of individual-level resources, in particular income and education, high levels of which are determinants of active civic engagement and political participation.[57] Other scholars examine the role of mobilizing institutions, such as political parties or voluntary associations, in encouraging and promoting political participation.[58] These studies have shown that mobilizing institutions are vital for promoting civic and political participation. Indeed, Steven Rosenstone and John Hansen make a very compelling case that people participate in politics because someone asks or encourages them to take part.[59] These contributions are important for the investigation here because individual characteristics that shape participation are still operational within certain contexts, and observations about mobilization help develop a more comprehensive theory of how economic segregation might shape civic engagement.

The few scholars who attempt to understand how residential context affects political behavior have found that levels of economic and political homogeneity and heterogeneity affect participation. In some cases we have learned that civic participation is lowest in homogeneous, affluent suburbs and highest in diverse, middle-income cities because of varying levels of local political interest and the consensus and conflict that emerge within homogeneous versus heterogeneous communities. In other instances both political homogeneity and heterogeneity promote high levels of different types of participation: conflict within politically heterogeneous communities promotes high levels of political participation (i.e., voting), and consensus within politically homogenous communities promotes high levels of civic engagement (i.e., group membership).[60] We also know that individuals purposefully develop social relationships with people who have similar political preferences but that opportunities for these relationships are hindered or promoted based on social contexts.[61]

These findings contribute to a theory about the civic consequences of residential economic segregation by suggesting how the context of economic segregation might shape civic engagement. A simple thought experiment might help illuminate the alternative theory of economic segregation and civic engagement proposed here. Imagine an economically heterogeneous but segregated city. Next, imagine a group of low-income citizens living together in a high-poverty neighborhood within this city so that they are both geographically isolated and living in high poverty. Much of the literature on low-income communities and the political ideology and preferences held by low-income citizens suggests that residents in this neighborhood would hold similar political positions.[62] However, faced with a city- or nationwide election in which they are the minority, they may be less inclined to advocate for their position(s) through group mobilization or voting for two reasons. First, the sociodemographic and neighborhood attributes—what I call the *civic environment*—of highly segregated and homogenous low-income neighborhoods may not be conducive to civic and political organization and mobilization, despite ideological consensus. Second, this lack of organization and mobilization may produce low levels of voter participation, despite the need for residents of this neighborhood to defend their position(s) in a contentious and heterogeneous city. Thus, economic homogeneity may not promote civic engagement, as some studies suggest, while conflictual relationships with other neighborhoods in the city may not promote political engagement, as others argue.

Economic segregation of neighborhoods may affect civic and political participation in ways not previously recognized or appreciated, particularly at the neighborhood level.[63] The premise of the examination offered here is that economic segregation has an important and distinct relationship to civic engagement, particularly associationalism, civic and political mobilization, and political behavior, specifically voting. This would be the case because higher levels of economic segregation within an area create isolated resource-deficient or resource-rich communities, which produces two interrelated trends that might affect civic engagement and political participation. First, the concentration and segregation of poverty or wealth alters the composition of residents within neighborhoods, producing "lower levels of collective efficacy" in impoverished communities due to diminished individual resources and higher levels of efficacy in prosperous ones.[64] And second, echoing Jacob Hacker and Paul Pierson's observation that politics is "organized combat," the segregation of wealth or poverty also concentrates a host of other neighborhood-level resources that are important for promoting civic engagement.[65] It is possible then that economic segregation affects political behavior by changing the nature of these resources and producing contextual effects that combine to heighten the effects of individual-level attributes and resources on civic engagement.

In this conception of civic engagement and political behavior, individual-level and mobilization explanations of voter participation are sufficient but not necessary for understanding civic and political mobilization and political participation. Consequently, the focus here is on how the context of residential economic segregation shapes civic engagement and political behavior. The theory guiding the investigation is that economic segregation alters the civic environment in which the segregated poor and the segregated wealthy live. This in turn affects the civic and political mobilization that occurs within these communities, and ultimately political participation, the results of which can be seen at the polls (Figure I.2).

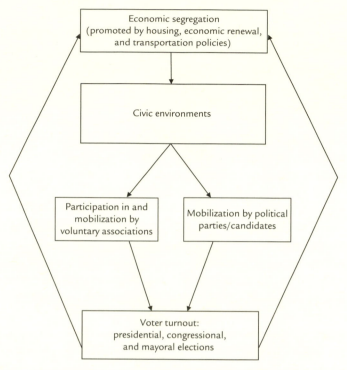

Figure I.2. Economic Segregation and Civic Engagement

Plan of the Book

Relying on this theory of economic segregation and civic engagement, the aim here is to gain a better understanding of how and why economic segregation affects civic engagement and specifically voter turnout. How does living in the context of segregated poverty or wealth shape the civic environment of citizens? How does this in turn shape civic and political mobilization and ultimately political behavior? To help us answer these questions, Chapter 1 outlines the methodology used to explore the dynamics of economic segregation and civic engagement in this study, specifically making the case for a case-study approach to these questions and articulating the selection criteria for the cities and neighborhoods used in this examination.

The following three chapters focus on distinct aspects of economic segregation, civic environments, and civic engagement. Chapter 2 first examines each identified case-study city to see how urban policy directly altered the residential patterns of thousands of city residents and how these policies shaped civic environments within the case-study neighborhoods of each city. This chapter also presents data on voter turnout within the segregated, impoverished and prosperous case-study communities examined here. The goal is to learn what we can about how economic segregation shapes engagement and participation in certain segregated contexts, and this chapter helps us set up the problem of participation so that subsequent chapters can address how and why we see these trends. This chapter ultimately suggests that the political development of cities is an important factor in shaping the political participation of their citizens.

Chapters 3 and 4 rely on evidence from eight case-study neighborhoods identified within Atlanta, Georgia; Kansas City, Missouri; Milwaukee, Wisconsin; and Rochester, New York, to investigate how economic segregation affects civic and political mobilization and political behavior. Chapter 3 investigates the relationship between economic segregation and patterns of associationalism and civic mobilization by civic and faith-based organizations, focusing on neighborhood associations, parent-teacher associations and organizations, and churches. In-depth interviews with presidents of community-based organizations and pastors of churches in this chapter reveal one part of the explanation for lower turnout in segregated, impoverished neighborhoods: the economic segregation of low-income populations undermines the capacity of and mobilization efforts by nonparty organizations in segregated, impoverished neighborhoods, while supporting capacity and efforts in segregated, prosperous communities. This appears to be due to the fact that certain, and specific, neighborhood attributes are necessary to support and sustain mobilization efforts, but these attributes are deeply affected by economic segregation.

In Chapter 4 we examine the relationship between economic segregation and political mobilization by political operatives, including political candidates and staff. Open-ended interviews with city council members and mayoral and city staff are used to explore how economic segregation affects the possibility and probability that politicians, their staff, and other public officials will contact and mobilize low-income constituents during (re)election campaigns, and whether or not elected officials contact and remain attentive to the needs of highly segregated, impoverished constituents between campaigns.

Evidence suggests that economic segregation alters the political calculations candidates, elected officials, and other city officials use when determining whom to contact and mobilize during campaigns and around issues, ultimately making it rational for candidates and officials to overlook entire neighborhoods and lavish attention and resources on others, but not because of the standard explanation that low-income voters do not vote. Rather, these public officials take into account the level of need within neighborhoods and the neighborhood resources residents can bring to bear on a problem, including those resources that make up the civic environment of the neighborhood, when deciding in which neighborhood(s) to engage and mobilize. The effect on voter turnout within specific neighborhoods, demonstrated in this chapter, shows that economic segregation ultimately alters the messages that elected officials and political candidates hear from constituents.

Indeed, voter-turnout data from neighborhoods in Atlanta, Kansas City, Milwaukee, and Rochester show that voter turnout in highly segregated, impoverished communities has declined significantly, in some cases by more than 40 percentage points, while turnout has remained high or increased in segregated, wealthy neighborhoods over time. Even more interesting, however, is the fact that in the 1970s voter turnout in these segregated, impoverished communities was often equal to or higher than that in their highly segregated, prosperous counterparts, particularly in local elections. This suggests that the commonly accepted notion that low-income citizens do not vote because of their individual economic status misses a significant point: low-income citizens are increasingly finding themselves living more exclusively with other low-income citizens, which means that individual disincentives for voting because of economic status are enhanced by an impoverished neighborhood context and social interactions with similarly disempowered citizens.

Chapter 5 concludes with a brief discussion about some political and policy implications of these trends. If increased segregation skews political mobilization and participation away from the least advantaged, the policy outputs at both the local and national levels may not be representative of all citizens. In this way the public policies that directly bear upon the segregation of low-income populations, such as housing, economic revitalization, and transportation, may continue to perpetuate not only the economic residential segregation of low-income populations that has emerged since the 1970s but their political alienation as well. Thus, a vicious cycle of demobilization and alienation occurs, displacing a more participatory and representative democracy with one serving the privileged and isolated few.

CHAPTER 1

Understanding Civic Engagement in Context: Methodology and the Logic of Case Study Selection

Understanding whether levels of civic engagement may have changed over time as a result of trends in economic segregation is vital for deepening our understanding of citizen participation in American politics. We know a great deal about national trends in voter participation and civic engagement, as well as about the factors that contribute to an individual person's sense of political identity, but our understanding of how local context—the neighborhoods where people spend their day-to-day lives—contributes to the development of civic disposition and, consequently, levels of civic participation remains incomplete. In order to understand this we need a research approach that draws out the historical evolution of neighborhoods and focuses on civic and political engagement at the neighborhood level. A historical approach appreciates how neighborhoods change over time and how public policies and local circumstances can shape and reshape civic environments. Studies of mass political participation typically do not take this kind of historical approach, in part because of a reliance on large survey and cross-sectional data. But such data-driven studies cannot tell us about all the ways in which local context contributes to citizen engagement; in order to do that we need to pay closer attention to specific neighborhoods.

Here I focus on urban neighborhoods, which is important because while scholars have meticulously documented the decline of cities in the post–World War II era, as of the year 2000, 68 percent of people still lived in urbanized areas, with 58 percent living in urbanized areas with a total population of

200,000 or more, and another 10 percent living in urbanized areas with 50,000 to 199,999 people. The number of urban dwellers actually increased to 71.2 percent in 2010.[1] In other words, despite the conventional wisdom that suggests deindustrialization and urban decay have decimated American cities, a significant majority of Americans still live in, around, or near urban areas. Using cities as case studies for unraveling civic engagement and demobilization thus makes sense because any relationship between local circumstances and civic life that can be demonstrated in an urban context necessarily affects tens of millions of citizens. Moreover, recent revitalization efforts by city governments, as well as shifts in demographic trends, have spurred movement back into cities by young professionals, including DINKs (dual-income [households], no kids) and families with small children, as well as retiring baby boomers. As the uptick in urban population between 2000 and 2010 indicates, cities remain relevant in regional economies and as ongoing sites of political contestation.[2] The findings presented here will help develop a more comprehensive understanding of how place matters, and how neighborhoods specifically matter, for civic engagement and political participation in the United States.[3] In order to explore the relationship between economic segregation and political participation, and civic engagement more broadly, we need to delve into specific cases that can illuminate how residential economic segregation shapes political behavior.

Identifying Case-Study Neighborhoods, Cities, and Counties

The specific neighborhoods used in this study were identified by using the Neighborhood Change Database (NCDB) to assess nationwide trends in economic segregation.[4] This database includes variables from the 1970, 1980, 1990, and 2000 censuses aggregated to and averaged at the census-tract level, allowing for an examination of how neighborhood environments changed over this thirty-year period. The NCDB data can be organized into a data set that provides economic, educational, residential, and employment data at the census-tract level for every tract in the United States from 1970 to 2000; crucially, this also makes it possible to calculate indicators of economic segregation. Another important feature of the database is that the data have been "normalized," allowing for comparison of census tracts over time.

Using census tracts as a proxy for "neighborhoods" is an imperfect but necessary accommodation for a couple of reasons. While certainly a neighborhood is more than a geographic boundary—it is a sense of community, a physical space, a place that residents identify with psychologically and emotionally—this complex notion is difficult to capture systematically. It is common, therefore, in studies of neighborhoods to use census tracts as proxies for neighborhoods because census tracts are "small, relatively permanent statistical subdivisions of a county"—usually having between one thousand and eight thousand residents, though four thousand is considered optimal—and, when first drawn, are designed to be relatively stable and homogeneous regarding population characteristics, income status, and living conditions.[5] This initial and often contemporary homogeneity captures some of the qualitative elements of neighborhood we are seeking to explore here, and given few other options, census tracts offer the best way to proceed in any neighborhood-level study. Therefore, in this examination I will use *neighborhood* and *census tract* interchangeably.

When considering neighborhoods in American cities, the word segregation is immediately problematic because of the long history of geographic isolation of peoples of different races and ethnicities.[6] Recognizing that the dynamics of race and economics are often intertwined, it is important here to try to focus on segregation along economic lines as separate and independent. In fact the concept of segregation is itself perhaps more complicated than some might think. Segregation has to be appreciated as a phenomenon with multiple interrelated yet independent dynamics that combine to create specific types of segregated neighborhoods and communities. Five distinct dimensions of segregation are generally recognized as organizing features of many communities, including evenness, concentration, centralization, clustering, and exposure; and understanding segregation in a multidimensional way allows for a more detailed and specific appreciation of how economic and racial minorities "may live apart from one another and be 'segregated' in a variety of ways."[7]

Evenness, typically measured by the dissimilarity index, is meant to capture the degree to which a minority is unevenly distributed over an area relative to another group. This measures in essence the proportion of a minority group that would have to change residence to create an even distribution of that group in a specific area. *Concentration* measures the amount of physical space occupied by a minority group, meaning that if a group resides in a relatively small area within the urban environment, they are said to be concentrated. While concentration measures the density of a group within a particular area, *centralization* measures the degree to which economic or racial minorities live near the center of a city. The extent to which this captures an important dimension of segregation seems questionable, given that it is certainly plausible that minority groups could cluster in other parts of the city or in inner-ring suburbs, but it does have some applicability to American cities in the late twentieth century because centralization has been a key component of segregation, confining minorities to central city areas. Another dimension of segregation is *clustering*, which describes the proximity of segregated neighborhoods to one another and the ways they adjoin another across a larger geographic area. While evenness is about the residential location of minorities relative to others, clustering is about the residential location of minorities relative to one another. Finally, *exposure*, usually measured by the isolation index, is the extent to which a group is exposed to members of their own group within a geographic unit.[8]

Douglas Massey and Nancy Denton, in their important article "The Dimensions of Residential Segregation," extensively examined the literature on residential segregation, including twenty separate indicators of segregation, and concluded that the dissimilarity and isolation indexes, used to measure the dimensions of evenness and exposure, respectively, capture useful and distinct aspects of segregation. Using both the dissimilarity and isolation indexes in this study to select economically segregated cases here will serve two purposes: first, relying on well-known and widely used indexes will help this study contribute to consistency across studies of segregation; and second, using two distinct measures of segregation to select cases from among the most segregated counties will ensure that the cases selected are not anomalous. In other words, if neighborhoods within case-study cities are considered segregated on two different dimensions—evenness and exposure—then it is likely that the populations living within those neighborhoods are truly spatially separate from one another.[9]

Using these two measures to select case-study neighborhoods also helps in a number of ways. It ensures that the word segregation is being applied here with a degree of specificity, which will hopefully make clear that any implications or conclusions drawn from this study are applicable in certain circumstances and not necessarily meant to suggest that every example of residential segregation will result in similar outcomes. Moreover, using the term segregation in this specific way allows for the conclusions drawn by scholars focusing on other types of segregation, including racial segregation, for example, to be considered in relation to or as distinct from the conclusions drawn here. Finally, as the purpose of this study is to examine the civic effects of isolating low-income individuals or exposing low-income citizens only to other low-income citizens, both evenness and exposure allow us to capture these aspects of segregation.[10]

The dissimilarity index, which measures evenness, is the proportion of a minority group within a specific area that would have to change residences in order to create an even distribution of their group across that area.[11] The dissimilarity index is calculated with the following formula:

$$D = \sum_{i=1}^{n} \left[\frac{t_i |p_i - P|}{2TP(1-P)} \right]$$

In this formula t_i and p_i are the total population and the low-income population, respectively, of area unit i, and T and P are the total population size and minority proportion of a county, which is subdivided into areal units. The minority population in this calculation is the number of people living below the federally determined poverty line, and the areal unit employed is the census tract. The dissimilarity index is calculated at the county level and then multiplied by 100 in order to state the percentage of people who would have to move from their census tract to another one in the same county in order to produce an even distribution of those living below the poverty line. A score of 0 means that no low-income residents would have to move to achieve an even distribution of low-income residents (no segregation), while a score of 100 means that all low-income people would have to move to achieve evenness (complete segregation).

The isolation index "measures the extent to which members of a particular group are *exposed*, in their neighborhoods, only to members of their group. In particular, for the poorer in any metropolitan area, the isolation index indicates how poor (e.g. 25, 50, 75 percent) the neighborhood of the average poor person is."[12] In other words the isolation index measures the degree to which individuals live in neighborhoods with other individuals like them. This isolation index for poverty is calculated with the following formula:

$$I = \sum_{i=1}^{n} \left[\frac{p_i}{P} \right] \left[\frac{p_i}{t_i} \right]$$

In this formula p_i is the number of low-income residents and t_i is the total population of area unit i, which in this case is a census tract. P is the total number of low-income citizens in the county. The low-income population in this calculation is the number of people living below the federally determined poverty line in a given areal unit.[13] The number resulting from this calculation is multiplied by 100 to express the isolation index as a percentage; a score of 0 indicates no segregation and a score of 100 indicates complete segregation.

Examining trends in the dissimilarity index, we see that the 1970s and the 1980s were the most segregated, and while the 1990s were less segregated, the levels of dissimilarity in 2000 were still quite high (Figure 1.1). In 1970 over 70 percent of U.S. counties housed residents that were unevenly distributed. For example, 20 to 40 percent of low-income residents in nearly 69 percent of all counties in the United States in 1970 would have had to change neighborhoods in order to achieve an even distribution of poor residents throughout their county. This number drops substantially by 2000, but even then, in 30 percent of all counties 20 to 40 percent of low-income county residents would have had to relocate to a different neighborhood to produce an even distribution of low-income residents within the county. In other words the data show that poor people were, generally speaking, very unevenly distributed throughout counties in the United States in the 1970s and 1980s, and while the situation improved somewhat in the 1990s, residential segregation along economic lines as measured by evenness remained significant in 2000.

In 1970, 21 percent of counties had isolation indexes between 20 and 40, which means that in 1970 low-income residents in one out of five counties in the United States lived in neighborhoods where 20 to 40 percent of the other residents of their neighborhood were also living below the poverty line. Most striking, though, is that by 1990 one-third of all U.S. counties housed low-income residents in neighborhoods where 20 to 40 percent of their neighbors were also poor (Figure 1.1). While the number in 2000 decreased dramatically, a curious trend that warrants study in its own right, the purpose of the study here is to examine civic life in the neighborhoods that experienced this heightened level of segregation throughout the 1970s, 1980s, and 1990s. Indeed, as will be shown, while segregation as measured separately by dissimilarity and isolation decreased between 1990 and 2000, the civic consequences of high levels of segregation along these two dimensions between 1970 and 1990 reverberated into the new century. Moreover, while

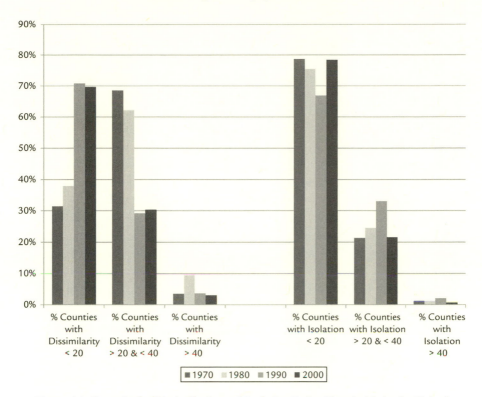

Figure 1.1. Counties by Dissimilarity and Isolation Index Thresholds in the United States, 1970–2000

Source: Urban Institute, and GeoLytics, *Neighborhood Change Database*, CensusCD neighborhood change database (NCDB) [electronic resource]: 1970–2000 tract data: selected variables for US Census tracts for 1970, 1980, 1990, 2000.

the dissimilarity and isolation indexes for 2000 were substantially improved, new data on poverty and inequality from the 2010 census may suggest a re-emergence of economic segregation, given the relationship between income inequality and economic segregation.[14]

It is interesting to note how these two dimensions of segregation behave differently between 1970 and 2000; dissimilarity was quite high in the 1970s and 1980s but was cut nearly in half by 1990, while isolation increased substantially between 1970 and 1990. Despite these differences the key point is that nearly one-third of all counties in 2000 had a dissimilarity index between 20 and 40 and nearly one-fifth of all counties had an isolation index between 20 and 40. This means that in 2000, 20 to 40 percent of residents in

30 percent of all counties would have had to move to achieve an even distribution, and 20 to 40 percent of low-income residents in 22 percent of counties
lived in neighborhoods with other impoverished individuals. Counties with
high levels of dissimilarity and isolation are therefore highly segregated residential areas.

Because the aim of this study is to understand the civic consequences of
residential economic segregation of poverty and comparative prosperity, the
case-study selection process began by first identifying neighborhoods that
have become deeply economically distressed within highly segregated counties. From here prosperous neighborhoods within each county were identified and paired with their impoverished counterpart so that we can explore
how economic segregation affects the civic lives of citizens living in different
economic contexts. The best way to identify case-study neighborhoods that
could demonstrate the role that economic segregation plays in shaping civic
environments, civic engagement, and political behavior was to begin by determining the neighborhoods that had become among the most impoverished neighborhoods in the nation. This was accomplished by rank ordering
all neighborhoods by their change in poverty rate from 1970 to 2000.[15] Once
these neighborhoods were identified, their level of segregation was determined by looking at the position they occupied in the rank ordering of the
most segregated counties in the nation. In other words I first identified very
poor neighborhoods and then selected neighborhoods from this list that
were also located in deeply segregated counties, as measured by both the dissimilarity and isolation indexes. This allowed for the selection of highly segregated, impoverished case-study communities.

One way to confirm the segregated nature of these counties was to look
beyond their position in the rankings and the values of their dissimilarity
and isolation indexes and to calculate the absolute difference between the
dissimilarity and isolation indexes for the counties that were home to the
poorest neighborhoods. In order to ensure selection of deep poverty within
deep segregation, it was important to select counties with high levels of segregation as measured by both dissimilarity and isolation but with a low absolute difference between these two measures of segregation; if the difference
is high, it would mean that the county is segregated along one dimension
but not the other, whereas counties with high levels of dissimilarity and isolation but low absolute difference between these two indicators are segregated across two dimensions. When we do this, we see some variance in the

dissimilarity and isolation indexes, but the absolute differences between the two indicators in the chosen case studies are among the lowest.[16]

A final factor considered was the presence of an urban area with stable census-tract boundaries from 1970 to 2000, which necessitated excluding many cities in the West and the Southwest because of problems with boundary stability.[17] These decision rules produced a case-study neighborhood in Atlanta, Fulton County, Georgia (census tract 13121, for example), that experienced a dramatic increase in poverty between 1970 and 2000—from almost 9 percent to 54 percent, a 45-point increase. Further, in 2000, Fulton County was the seventeenth most segregated county in the nation when measured by the dissimilarity index, with nearly 45 percent of impoverished residents needing to move to create an even distribution of the low-income population, and the twenty-seventh most segregated when measured by isolation, with 29 percent of low-income residents living in low-income communities, a difference of only 10 points. Thus, the neighborhood became increasingly economically distressed within a context of substantial economic segregation. The other impoverished case-study neighborhoods are in Kansas City in Jackson County, Missouri (census tract 29095); Milwaukee in Milwaukee County, Wisconsin (census tract 55079); and Rochester in Monroe County, New York (census tract 36055). The prosperous neighborhood counterparts in each city were identified by determining neighborhoods that experienced increasing wealth within these counties between 1970 and 2000, as measured by average family income.[18]

These case studies are suitable for comparison because they represent midsized cities in the United States that are geographically and historically diverse and, taken together, will help reveal the civic and political consequences of residential economic segregation. It is important, though, that these counties are not exactly the same, which is in some ways unavoidable and in some ways by design; it is nearly impossible to find census tracts with exactly the same levels of poverty and wealth within counties that have the same levels of segregation. So along these metrics the case studies naturally vary. In other ways, though, it is important for contextual factors to vary. Including Fulton County, for instance, as a case study allows for comparison with an urban case in the South, a region of the United States with a particular history and culture that is distinct from elsewhere in the country, as well as a region that has become much more populated in the late twentieth century.

Racial composition was another important factor that was considered when identifying the neighborhood pairs. It is difficult, possibly impossible, to talk about residential segregation in the United States and not grapple with the tortured and complicated history of race and racism that has certainly affected the lives of millions of residents in American cities. But as illuminating and useful as discussions about racial segregation can be, it is also important to try to determine the role that economic class plays in nurturing, or damaging, civic environments.[19]

For this study the racial composition of the case-study neighborhoods varies; in Atlanta both the prosperous and impoverished neighborhoods were 99 percent African American in 2000, while in Rochester the impoverished community was 66 percent African American and 33 percent Hispanic in 2000 and just 6 percent African American or Hispanic in the prosperous counterpart. This means that if similar civic and political trends emerge across similar economic contexts, whatever the racial or ethnic composition, we can say something specific about the effects of economic contexts separate and distinct from racial context. This is not to suggest that race is entirely removed as a factor that contributes to the shaping of a civic environment but to note that if similarities in civic and political mobilization and voting behavior can be determined across the case studies presented here, it seems as though economic factors may be more important than previously appreciated by scholars.

This research design—focusing on four cities in distinct regions of the United States that all have very high levels of residential economic segregation, and then on a wealthy and an impoverished neighborhood within each county—allows me to examine how economic segregation alters civic engagement by comparing two different economic contexts within high levels of segregation during the last decades of the twentieth century. It seems reasonable to suspect, especially given the data analysis in the preceding chapter, that economic segregation would diminish civic engagement and voter turnout in segregated, impoverished neighborhoods, while at the same time promote engagement and turnout in segregated, prosperous ones. If this is correct, it complicates our understanding of how economic inequality promotes a class gap in American politics; economic segregation is the physical manifestation of economic inequality, and in some contexts such segregation may actively circumscribe the opportunities for political participation in the polity in some communities while helping to provide a better, more nurturing environment for political participation in others. The case-study neighborhoods discussed here all have unique histories, and the local context is important to appreciate as we focus on the effects of residential economic segregation. But even allowing for other possible explanations for changing levels of civic engagement, it seems crucial that we understand the similar civic and political developments among the four impoverished case-study neighborhoods as well as within the four prosperous case-study neighborhoods and the ways in which residential economic segregation may have driven those developments.

Logic of Case-Study Selection

Comparing highly segregated, impoverished neighborhoods with prosperous ones allows for a focus on the effects of high levels of economic segregation, which is the goal of this study. This study employs some quantitative analysis but fundamentally is grounded in qualitative, case-study research. Unlike quantitative research, which typically relies on mathematical tools associated with statistics and probability theory, this type of qualitative research project is based on set theory and logic.[20] For this reason it is unnecessary to identify a mixed-income county and two mixed-income neighborhoods to compare with the highly segregated ones, as some may suggest. The purpose here is to examine what happens to the civic lives of communities when economic segregation is allowed to exist, not to attempt to compare what happens in highly segregated areas with what happens in minimally segregated areas. It also seems worth mentioning that for numerous reasons such theoretical mixed-income counties and neighborhoods are difficult to find within the United States.

But even if mixed-income case studies were available, including them in this study is beside the point. Because this is a qualitative study, there are two ways to think about case-study selection and analysis and the cases selected here. The first way requires us to think about key concepts of interest as categories in which our cases have membership and then to hypothesize associations between concepts relying on logical constructions of necessity or sufficiency or both.[21] In this analysis we are interested in explaining civic engagement and ultimately voter-turnout trends in segregated communities. Using the language of quantitative research, the dependent variable is voter turnout and the independent variable is economic segregation. Given the findings presented in the Introduction, which showed that the effect of economic segregation on voter turnout varies by context, we could refine this further and offer two hypotheses: segregated poverty produces lower rates of voter turnout, and segregated prosperity produces higher rates of voter turnout.

To frame these propositions in the language of necessity and sufficiency, it helps to visualize these conditions. In Figure 1.2A, being a member of X group is necessary to be in the Y group but is not sufficient because there are a lot of cases in the X group that are not Y. In Figure 1.2B, X is sufficient but not necessary to be in the Y group; X will be in Y, but there are other ways to fall into the Y group.[22] Applying this formulation to the hypotheses here, I suggest that segregated poverty is sufficient but not necessary for promoting low civic engagement and voter turnout, and that segregated prosperity is sufficient but not necessary for promoting higher levels of engagement. Put another way, there are other factors that also affect turnout (Y), but it is possible that economic segregation (X) does as well. To recast this formulation visually, Figures 1.3A and 1.3B show that economic segregation cannot be a

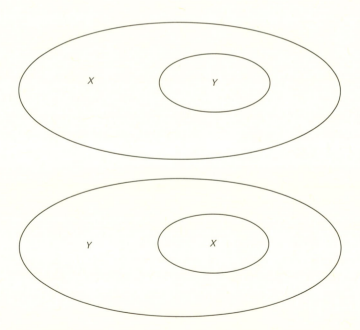

Figure 1.2
A. Necessary Conditions for Group Membership
B. Sufficient Conditions for Group Membership

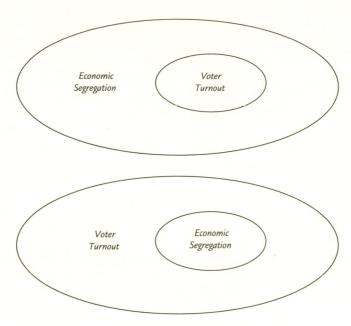

Figure 1.3
A. Economic Segregation as a Necessary Condition of Voter Turnout
B. Economic Segregation as a Sufficient Condition of Voter Turnout

necessary condition of voter turnout because being in a context of economic segregation is not necessary to produce an increase or decrease in voter turnout (Figure 1.3A) (this can happen for any number of reasons) but that it can be sufficient for affecting voter turnout (even if it is not the sole factor, economic segregation might increase or decrease engagement) (Figure 1.3B). In short, and removing the probabilistic reasoning of quantitative analysis, the premise here is that economic segregation is sufficient but not necessary for shaping civic engagement and political behavior.

What makes this puzzle—the relationship between economic segregation and turnout—challenging is that it is possible that some of the other factors sufficient for affecting voter turnout may also be shaped by economic segregation. To account for this dynamic case studies have to represent X, or economic segregation, within which we can investigate the various factors shaping voter turnout. A case-study analysis designed to investigate civic life and turnout in communities within the context of economic segregation

can tell us how and why a trend or relationship between economic segregation and turnout exists. While a quick quantitative assessment can show that
there is a relationship, a case-study analysis using qualitative research methods, focusing on specific instances of economic segregation, can show us the
nature of this relationship.

This suggests a second way to think about case-study selection and analysis. In statistical analysis "the most damaging consequences [of selection
bias] arise from selecting only cases whose independent *and* dependent variables vary as the favored hypothesis suggests, ignoring cases that appear to
contradict the theory."[23] And yet, moving away from the logic of quantitative
analysis and toward a logic of necessity or sufficiency, or both, "case studies
are much stronger at identifying the scope of conditions of theories and assessing arguments about causal necessity and sufficiency in particular cases."[24]
In this light there are several roles that case-study analysis can play:

- *Atheoretic/configurative idiographic* case studies provide good
  descriptions that might be used in subsequent studies for theory
  building . . .
- *Disciplined configurative* case studies use established theories to
  explain a case . . .
- *Heuristic* case studies inductively identify new variables, hypotheses, causal mechanisms, and causal paths. "Deviant" or "out-
  lier" cases may be particularly useful for heuristic purposes, as
  by definition their outcomes are not what traditional theories
  would anticipate. Also, cases where variables co-vary as expected
  but are at extremely high or low values may help uncover causal
  mechanisms . . .
- *Theory testing* case studies assess the validity and scope conditions
  of a single or competing theory . . .
- *Plausibility probes* are preliminary studies on relatively untested
  theories and hypotheses to determine whether more intensive and
  laborious testing is warranted.[25]

The case-study analysis in this book provides both heuristic and theory-
testing and -building leverage. They are a tool of heuristic analysis because
they help determine the causal mechanisms and paths through which economic segregation affects civic and political mobilization and voter turnout.
They offer theory-testing and -building heft because they contribute to a

theory of civic engagement by identifying a previously overlooked variable: economic segregation. And unlike an examination of a mixed-income county with mixed-income neighborhoods, the case studies used here provide these types of analysis by focusing on what happens when economic segregation is allowed to exist.

All of this said, some variance within these case studies is important; within the case studies there should be some variance along other factors that also contribute to voter turnout, such as income and race. If there is variance in these other factors across case-study counties and neighborhoods, and we see similar levels of voter turnout and trends in voter turnout over time, then in all similar case-study neighborhoods we can reasonably conclude that this may be the result of economic segregation because this is the one common feature across all cases. In this sense these cases represent "strong tests": "It is often argued that one should select cases that are representative or typical of the universe of cases. The 'extreme value on the IV [independent variable]' method of case selection argues the opposite, that cases that are atypical in their endowment with the independent variable teach us the most."[26]

This understanding of case-study selection only works if we move from a quantitative logic of probability to a qualitative logic of necessity and sufficiency, and understand that some of the core strengths of case-study analysis are heuristic causal mapping and theory building. Using this alternative, qualitative logic, the selection of four highly segregated counties that offer variance on income (segregated, impoverished and segregated, prosperous neighborhoods across the four counties, with different levels of poverty and prosperity in each) and race (both Atlanta neighborhoods are 99 percent African American while there is great variance across the other six) will help determine how and why economic segregation affects voter turnout and indeed civic engagement more broadly in urban America.

Voter Turnout and Economic Segregation in Context

Data presented in the Introduction illustrated that economic segregation significantly and negatively affects voter turnout in lower-income counties and positively, though not significantly, affects turnout in higher-income counties. The questions this study seeks to answer are how and why economic segregation may have this effect; this is fundamentally a problem-driven inquiry.[27] To set up the problem, though, it is important to explore voter-turnout trends in the types of case-study neighborhoods selected for analysis here. If there seem to be consistent patterns in turnout across segregated, impoverished and segregated, prosperous communities, allowing for the variance that exists across the communities, then further study into how economic segregation affects turnout will be warranted. It is worth attempting to understand the possible causal effects of economic segregation if we can be reasonably certain that segregation is creating similar turnout patterns in the case-study communities that have little else in common that would explain the similarity.

Unfortunately, there is no central repository of neighborhood-level turnout data, which means that the only way to understand local voting patterns is to rely on local records and sources. This presents numerous challenges, both in terms of developing a logical and consistent research design and in terms of logistical hurdles to overcome when attempting to conduct and analyze research. The first challenge concerns data collection at the local level, and correlating census-tract boundaries, which define where people live, to locally determined electoral districts, which determine where people vote. This requires locating ward and election district (ED) maps from 1970 to 2000 within the maze of city-level bureaucracies—a difficult task given that most cities do not require these records be kept or archived for any specified length of time so many cities have no archival system for these records.[28] With the appropriate maps ED boundaries can be compared and reconciled as best as possible with census-tract boundaries. In this step, local boards of elections, local and state archives, and local public libraries proved invaluable in helping locate election district and ward boundary maps, as well as voter-turnout records. In the end this boundary-matching process allows for the determination of the number of votes in any given election from each case-study neighborhood.

It is important to note, however, that the necessary reliance on local records creates two additional obstacles for scholars when matching election district boundaries to those of census tracts. The first is the fact that while at one time most board of election officials used the census tract boundaries as guidelines for election districts, the process of redistricting over time has produced election districts that in the majority of cases do not follow census tract boundaries. The second is that while most redistricting occurs following the decennial census, this is not always the case. In three of the four case-study cities—Atlanta, Rochester, and Milwaukee—there were at least two changes to local election district boundaries in at least one of the decades studied here. In order to determine accurate voter turnout, this redistricting had to be accounted for in all of the elections occurring between 1970 and 2000.[29] Election district maps in each city for each iteration of redistricting proved to be the only way to reasonably determine what percentage of the appropriate election districts covered the case-study census tracts used to approximate neighborhoods in this study.[30] Voter turnout was determined by counting the number of votes in each ward or precinct from the appropriate percentage of each ED covering each case-study neighborhood.

For example, one of the high-poverty neighborhoods studied here is census tract 12 in Milwaukee, Wisconsin, most of which falls in Aldermanic District 9 for all years included in this study, while a small portion lies in District 10. Analyzing voter-turnout data from 1970 meant using recorded voter turnout for all of ED 9 and 10 percent of ED 10, determined by calculating the percentage of blocks in census tract 12 that are included in ED 10. After 1983 the city of Milwaukee issued a new election district boundary map that spanned only two election years, 1984 and 1985—during which time there was a mayoral and presidential election, both in 1984—and issued a new map in 1986, whose boundaries held through 1992. This 1986 change did not affect the EDs covering census tract 12. Accordingly, it is possible to analyze voter turnout in census tract 12 for 1983 through 1992, using ED 172 and half of ED 173, again determined by calculating the percentage of blocks in census tract 12 that fall within the boundaries of ED 173. Finally, from 1993 to 2000, census tract 12 was covered by one-third of ED 166 and all of ED 167. (See Appendix A for calculations used for the remaining case-study census tracts.)[31]

Taking a percentage of an ED and attributing it to a particular census tract presents an ecological inference problem because to do so infers knowledge about individual voter behavior based on observations of aggregate data, from an area in which a voter may or may not actually reside. This is not an ideal solution, but owing to the fact that neither boards of elections nor any other city department collects or keeps voting data at the census-tract level, which would address this problem, this method is the only way to approximate voter turnout at the neighborhood level. As demonstrated in Appendix A, every effort was made to ensure that the voter-turnout data corresponded as closely as possible with the census-tract information in a given electoral year. It seems as though, given the nature of local record keeping, this is the only way we can hope to understand what turnout looks like on the local, neighborhood level over a period of decades. Since this study is seeking to ascertain the importance of neighborhood context with regard to civic engagement and voter turnout, all available maps and boundary guides were consulted when assessing turnout within a particular census tract. The resulting data, while perhaps less than perfect, is nonetheless more than reasonable to use as the basis for drawing conclusions, and because the results of this study seem to indicate that economic segregation does indeed shape civic environments and civic engagement, it is likely that future research will be able to improve upon data gathering and continue to solidify the conclusions reached here.

The second step in determining local patterns of voter turnout is to calculate voter turnout itself. Traditionally, voter turnout is calculated using the total number of ballots cast divided by the voting age population (VAP). This is usually the case because it is often difficult to determine the voting eligible population (VEP), which requires determining and then calculating the number of ineligible voters—noncitizens, the incarcerated or institutionalized, and convicted felons who reside in states where they cannot vote—and subtracting their numbers from the VAP with any accuracy.[32] Even among those scholars who argue that the difference between the VAP and VEP is significant and that VAP includes too many potential voters, thereby deflating actual turnout rates, calculating the VEP remains a major challenge at certain levels of governance.[33] At present most methods for calculating the VEP with any reasonable level of certainty can only be done with large units of analysis: the data required to calculate ineligible voters for small units of analysis, such as census tracts, is simply not available and certainly not consistently over time. VAP is for our purposes a useful approximation of the number of people who could vote in any given election.[34]

The following graphs (Figures 1.4 through 1.6) show aggregated voter turnout over time within each type of neighborhood, impoverished or prosperous, across all four cities for presidential, congressional or state (gubernatorial when congressional data was unavailable) and mayoral elections. The graphs display average trends in voter turnout across the four segregated, impoverished and four segregated, prosperous case-study neighborhoods. The bottom of each line in these graphs is the turnout rate in all four impoverished case-study communities, while the top of each line is the turnout in all four comparative prosperous neighborhoods. The length of the line between the two points represents the difference in turnout between the two communities. As a point of comparison these graphs also include the national turnout trends in presidential and congressional elections. Owing to the local nature of the data and the inability to gather large quantities of data, this analysis is limited but still instructive for illustrating the nature of voter participation in segregated, impoverished and segregated, prosperous communities in urban America.

As Figure 1.4 reveals, trends in presidential elections indicate that voter turnout across wealthy communities declined significantly between 1972 and 1980 but returned to pre-Watergate levels in 2000 by rebounding over

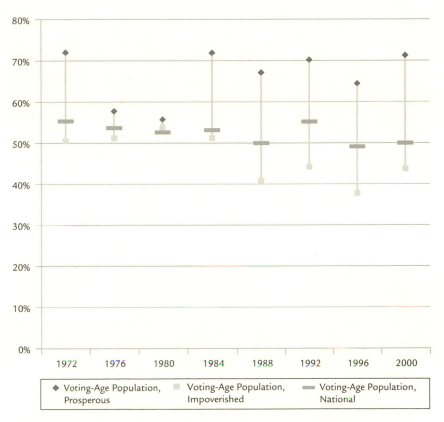

Figure 1.4. Average Impoverished and Prosperous Voter Turnout in Presidential Elections, 1972–2000: Atlanta, Kansas City, Milwaukee, and Rochester

Source: Author tabulations based on election return records from: Fulton County Registration and Elections, Elections Division, Fulton County, Georgia; Kansas City Board of Elections, Kansas City, Missouri; Kansas City Public Library, Kansas City, Missouri; Board of Election Commissioners, City of Milwaukee, Biennial Reports, 1970–2001; and, the Official Canvas of Monroe County, 1972, 1974, 1976, 1978, 1980, 1982, 1984, 1986, 1988, 1990, 1992, 1994, 1996, and 1997.

15 points from the low in 1980. Average turnout in the segregated prosperous communities was also well above the national average in 2000. Average turnout in segregated, low-income neighborhoods, however, declined since its high of 54 percent in 1980, which placed these communities above the national average, to 44 percent in 2000, a decrease of 10 points. Because turnout among residents in segregated impoverished neighborhoods continued to decline beyond 1980, while residents of segregated prosperous neighborhoods increasingly returned to the polls following 1980, on average the total difference between voter turnout in segregated, wealthy and segregated, impoverished neighborhoods grew from a low of 2 points in 1980 to 28 points in 2000.

This same trend holds for midterm congressional elections (Figure 1.5). The congressional election of 1974 was the lowest point of turnout for citizens living in prosperous neighborhoods. The drop in turnout of nearly 40 percentage points in both types of neighborhoods between the off-year congressional elections of 1970 and those of 1974 may be indicative of the general dismay and disillusionment citizens were feeling about the American political process as a result of Watergate and President Richard Nixon's resignation. Since the 1974 congressional election, however, average turnout among residents in the four segregated, prosperous neighborhoods rebounded by nearly 22 points on average, suggesting increased political participation among wealthy citizens living in economically segregated communities when compared with participation among impoverished citizens or the national average, even during off-year elections.

This was not the case for residents in the segregated, impoverished neighborhoods of Atlanta, Kansas City, Milwaukee, and Rochester. While turnout among the segregated, low-income population also plummeted in the 1974 congressional election, from 58 percent in 1970 to 27 percent in 1974, it fell even further to 17 percent in 1990. Despite a small increase between 1990 and 1998, the difference in voter turnout by residents of segregated, prosperous and segregated, impoverished neighborhoods grew from 6 points in the 1974 election to nearly 24 points in 1998. This is largely due to the fact that residents in segregated, poor communities continued to vote at much lower rates than segregated, prosperous citizens, while segregated, wealthy citizens have steadily increased their turnout since 1974, save for a small drop in turnout in 1990.

Figure 1.6 reveals trends in the average voter turnout in mayoral elections. Averaging turnout in mayoral elections is challenging because many

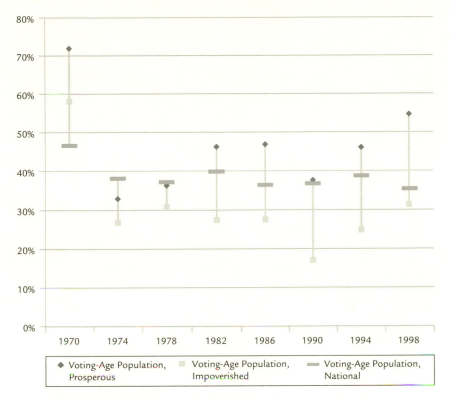

Figure 1.5. Average Impoverished and Prosperous Voter Turnout in Congressional Elections in Nonpresidential Years, 1970–1998: Atlanta, Kansas City, Milwaukee, and Rochester

Source: Author tabulations based on election return records from: Fulton County Registration and Elections, Elections Division, Fulton County, Georgia; Kansas City Board of Elections, Kansas City, Missouri; Kansas City Public Library, Kansas City, Missouri; Board of Election Commissioners, City of Milwaukee, Biennial Reports, 1970–2001; and, the Official Canvas of Monroe County, 1972, 1974, 1976, 1978, 1980, 1982, 1984, 1986, 1988, 1990, 1992, 1994, 1996, and 1997.

mayoral elections occur in off-off-years. In other words many years between 1970 and 2000 had only one mayoral election across all four cities. For example, in 1971, Rochester and Kansas City had city council and mayoral elections, while in 1972 only Milwaukee held a mayoral election and that was in April. The only years between 1970 and 2000 when more than one mayoral election was held across Atlanta, Kansas City, Milwaukee, and Rochester were 1971, 1975, 1979, 1983, 1985, 1989, 1993, and 1997. As a result these years were used to create an average turnout in mayoral elections. Due to the difficulty

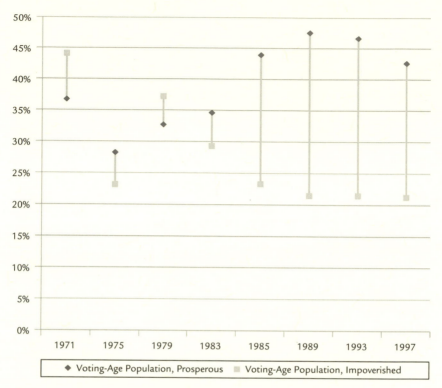

Figure 1.6. Average Impoverished and Prosperous Voter Turnout in Mayoral
Elections, 1971–1997: Atlanta, Kansas City, Milwaukee, and Rochester

Source: Author tabulations based on election return records from: Fulton County Registration and
Elections, Elections Division, Fulton County, Georgia; Kansas City Board of Elections, Kansas City,
Missouri; Kansas City Public Library, Kansas City, Missouri; Board of Election Commissioners,
City of Milwaukee, Biennial Reports, 1970–2001; and, the Official Canvas of Monroe County, 1972,
1974, 1976, 1978, 1980, 1982, 1984, 1986, 1988, 1990, 1992, 1994, 1996, and 1997.

in averaging mayoral election results, there are no available data for national
voter-turnout trends in these elections.

The trend remains of declining participation of residents in segregated,
low-income communities and increasing participation of residents in segregated, wealthy communities. Perhaps most striking about this graph,
however, is the fact that throughout the 1970s, on average, residents in
impoverished neighborhoods often voted at similar or higher rates than
residents of prosperous neighborhoods. Indeed, in 1971 and in 1979, residents in segregated, low-income neighborhoods voted 7 and 5 percentage

points higher than residents in segregated, prosperous neighborhoods, respectively.

Figure 1.6 also reveals that the increase in the difference between voter turnout rates has grown more in mayoral elections than in other types of elections. In 2000 the difference in turnout rates in presidential elections between prosperous and impoverished communities was 27.5 points, up 26 points since 1970, while the increase in difference in congressional elections was smaller, at 18 percentage points. The absolute difference is greater in presidential elections, but in mayoral elections the difference between turnout in prosperous and impoverished communities grew by 29 points between 1970 and 2000, the largest increase among all three elections. This is even more notable precisely because average turnout in segregated, impoverished communities was regularly higher than turnout in segregated, prosperous communities throughout the 1970s.

Together these graphs indicate that the difference between voter-turnout rates in segregated, prosperous and segregated, impoverished neighborhoods has increased in all types of elections between 1970 and 2000, though particularly between 1980 and the mid-1990s, the decades during which economic segregation increased the most. In fact, between 1970 and 1980 the difference in voter turnout between impoverished and prosperous neighborhoods largely disappeared, reflecting a broader trend toward economic and civic equality in American society that had begun in the 1950s.[35] Beginning in the late 1970s and early 1980s, however, economic segregation began to grow, and these graphs indicate that political inequality simultaneously grew during this period as well. It is important to note that key sources of this trend are stagnated or declining voter-turnout rates in segregated, poor neighborhoods and rebounding and increased turnout in segregated, wealthy communities.[36]

The results across all eight case-study neighborhoods illustrate a larger phenomenon concerning voter participation and economic segregation in urban America. The case-study cities and neighborhoods within those cities are in different regions of the country, have different racial and ethnic compositions, and have their own history of civic life and participation. And yet the fact that all of the case studies demonstrate a similar trend in voter participation in segregated, impoverished and segregated, prosperous communities seems to strongly suggest that economic segregation is an important factor that can help explain these results.

While provocative, these graphs raise two important questions. Are the differences between these two types of neighborhoods real and significant? And is declining turnout in segregated, poor neighborhoods simply the result of wealthier citizens moving out of these neighborhoods, taking their active political participation with them? To test the first query about difference in turnout rates, I created three data sets composed of cross-sectional time series data, where observations from each neighborhood were compiled by type of election, between 1970 and 2000. The question here is whether or not average turnout rates in impoverished communities are significantly different from average turnout rates in prosperous ones. A series of simple one-way analysis of variance (ANOVA) tests were able to answer this question.[37] These tests allow for the investigation of whether the mean turnout of one population (turnout in segregated, poor neighborhoods) is significantly different from the mean turnout of another (turnout in segregated, wealthy neighborhoods). In this case the null hypothesis, or the hypothesis that is being tested, is that there is no difference between the two turnout rates, with the corollary being that there is a difference. If the null hypothesis can be rejected, then we can claim that there is a significant difference in turnout between these two neighborhoods over time.

In all presidential elections from 1972 to 2000 mean turnout in segregated, impoverished communities was 47 percent, while mean turnout in segregated, prosperous communities was 66 percent. In congressional elections over the period analyzed, average turnout was 28 percent in segregated, poor neighborhoods and 46 percent in segregated, wealthy neighborhoods. In mayoral elections over this period average turnout was 28 percent and 40 percent in segregated, impoverished and segregated, prosperous communities, respectively. Thus, in all types of elections average turnout in segregated, impoverished communities was substantially lower than turnout in segregated, prosperous ones. Is this difference significant?

Table 1.1 summarizes the findings of the ANOVA analyses conducted for presidential, congressional, and mayoral elections separately, and presents the systematic effect of the independent variable of interest (economic segregation) on the variable of interest (average turnout) within two categories of neighborhoods (segregated poverty and segregated wealth). The test for whether the mean turnout rates are the same is the F-ratio, which is the variation due to experimental treatment or effect divided by the variation due to experimental error. The F-ratio was 32.93 for presidential turnout, 21.01 for congressional turnout, and 10.59 for mayoral turnout. The signifi-

Table 1.1. One-Way Analysis of Variance of Presidential, Congressional, and Mayoral Voter Turnout in Selected Case-Study Neighborhoods, 1970–2000

Presidential Turnout

Source	Sum of Squares	Degrees of Freedom	Mean Square	F-ratio	Significance
Segregated Wealth	5547.53	1	5547.53	32.93	0.000
Error	10106.51	60	168.44		

Congressional Turnout

Source	Sum of Squares	Degrees of Freedom	Mean Square	F-ratio	Significance
Segregated Wealth	3863.66	1	3863.66	21.01	0.000
Error	9195.41	50	183.91		

Mayoral Turnout

Source	Sum of Squares	Degrees of Freedom	Mean Square	F-ratio	Significance
Segregated Wealth	2059.77	1	2236.48	10.59	0.002
Error	11705.99	60	195.10		

Note: The segregated wealth variable is a dummy variable with segregated poverty coded 0 and segregated wealth coded 1.

Source: Data to determine the segregated nature of neighborhoods is from the Neighborhood Change Database; Urban Institute, and GeoLytics, *Neighborhood Change Database*, CensusCD neighborhood change database (NCDB) [electronic resource]: 1970–2000 tract data: selected variables for US Census tracts for 1970, 1980, 1990, 2000; Voter turnout tabulated by author based on election return records from: Fulton County Registration and Elections, Elections Division, Fulton County, Georgia; Kansas City Board of Elections, Kansas City, Missouri; Kansas City Public Library, Kansas City, Missouri; Board of Election Commissioners, City of Milwaukee, Biennial Reports, 1970–2001; and, the Official Canvas of Monroe County, 1972, 1974, 1976, 1978, 1980, 1982, 1984, 1986, 1988, 1990, 1992, 1994, 1996, and 1997.

cance columns in all cases indicate how likely it is that *F*-ratios of these sizes would have occurred if there were no difference between the mean turnout rates. Therefore, the extremely low probabilities (0.000, 0.000, and 0.002, respectively) indicate that it is very unlikely that the *F*-ratios shown here could have occurred without the mean turnout rates being significantly different.

While trend and ANOVA analyses demonstrate that there is a significant difference between voter-turnout rates in economically segregated prosperous and impoverished neighborhoods, it is possible that wealthier residents at one time lived in these segregated, low-income communities and that they voted. As they left, they may have taken their voting habits with them, causing voter turnout in these neighborhoods to decline and turnout in other parts of these cities to increase. This would reflect a change in neighborhood composition and may be what is driving turnout trends in segregated, impoverished communities.

To address this possibility we first need to calculate the proportion of households in each impoverished case-study neighborhood that earned the national median income or higher for each decennial census year and use linear interpolation to determine the proportion for intercensus years.[38] Then we need to calculate a change score from one year to the next. In most cases the change score is negative, indicating that nonpoor households were leaving these segregated, impoverished neighborhoods, though in some years there is no change at all. We also need to determine a change score for voter turnout by calculating the difference in turnout between election years for presidential elections, congressional elections, and mayoral elections separately. Finally, with these data a series of correlational analyses can be performed to assess the relationship between the changing proportion of nonpoor households and changing voter turnout in each impoverished case-study neighborhood. Because we are interested in the one-to-one relationship between the nonpoor composition of a neighborhood and voter turnout in a neighborhood, the strength of the relationship between change in proportion and change in voter turnout is the most important aspect of this analysis. The correlation coefficient should be 1 if there is a direct relationship between the changing proportion of nonpoor households and a change in voter turnout.

Table 1.2 shows that there is no clear pattern of a strong relationship between the change in proportion of nonpoor households and a change in voters at the polls. Indeed, in three cases there is no relationship at all, and in two other cases the relationship is very weak. In all other cases there is great variation in the strength of the relationship and no clear trend regarding positive or negative correlations. Although the number of cases in each correlational analysis is small, across all case-study cities in presidential, congressional, and mayoral elections there seems to be no clear indication that a relationship exists between the proportion of nonpoor residents in segre-

Table 1.2. Correlation Between Change in Proportion of Nonpoor Households and Change of Voter Turnout at the Polls in Impoverished Neighborhoods

	Atlanta	Kansas City	Milwaukee	Rochester
Presidential elections	0.06	−0.01	−0.22	0.69*
	(7)	(8)	(8)	(8)
Congressional elections	−0.78	−0.69	−0.74*	0.00
	(5)	(6)	(8)	(7)
Mayoral elections	0.00	0.11	0.35	0.00
	(7)	(8)	(8)	(8)

Source: Data to determine the national median income, and therefore neighborhoods above the median income, for each decennial census year are from the Neighborhood Change Database; Urban Institute, and GeoLytics, *Neighborhood Change Database*, CensusCD neighborhood change database (NCDB) [electronic resource]: 1970–2000 tract data: selected variables for US Census tracts for 1970, 1980, 1990, 2000; Voter turnout tabulated by author based on election return records from: Fulton County Registration and Elections, Elections Division, Fulton County, Georgia; Kansas City Board of Elections, Kansas City, Missouri; Kansas City Public Library, Kansas City, Missouri; Board of Election Commissioners, City of Milwaukee, Biennial Reports, 1970–2001; and, the Official Canvas of Monroe County, 1972, 1974, 1976, 1978, 1980, 1982, 1984, 1986, 1988, 1990, 1992, 1994, 1996, and 1997. *Note:* The number of elections in each city is noted in the parentheses.
* Significance at the 0.10 level

gated, impoverished neighborhoods and the change in voter turnout in these neighborhoods.

This suggests that changes in political behavior within segregated, impoverished communities may be the result of contextual effects beyond aggregate compositional effects within neighborhoods. While one can never make too much of statistical analysis conducted with such a small number of cases, it appears that the difference in turnout between the types of neighborhoods is significant and that it is not driven solely by wealthier residents leaving segregated, impoverished neighborhoods. The project then becomes figuring how and why residential economic segregation has this effect on the civic life of segregated, impoverished and segregated, prosperous communities.

Solving the Puzzle

The evidence presented here suggests that economic segregation affects voter turnout, negatively in segregated, impoverished communities and positively in segregated, prosperous neighborhoods. While the data reveal the phenomenon, they do little to reveal the nature of the relationship between economic segregation and political participation or the mechanisms through which economic segregation affects turnout. The case-study neighborhoods will help reveal these mechanisms, which will help us better understand how economic segregation affects civic engagement and political participation at the local level. Specifically, subsequent chapters investigate the role that economic segregation plays in shaping civic environments. These civic environments are the physical and social worlds that create the conditions for active or weak civic engagement and political participation within communities. In other words an individual's decision to vote is supported by a number of factors, some of which are individual but many of which include the streets and buildings that make up a neighborhood as well as the attitudes and beliefs that percolate within the shared space of that neighborhood and the relationships formed within this context. The civic environment of a particular neighborhood helps drive civic and political awareness, mobilization, and participation.

The following chapters will focus on how voluntary associations, churches, and political operatives are able to mobilize citizens and encourage them to feel as though they have a stake in their local polity, and subsequently to participate in elections.[39] Ultimately, we see that residential economic segregation affects the success or failure of these mobilizing institutions to maintain civic awareness and participation among neighborhood residents. Within economically segregated, prosperous neighborhoods associations, churches, and political operatives have an easier time reaching the citizenry, communicating with them, and acting to address common concerns. Conversely, within economically segregated, impoverished neighborhoods the work done by these associations and organizations is made more difficult because of the scarcity of resources, the transient and unstable nature of the citizen population, and a vicious cycle of disengagement with and alienation from the political process that is made worse over time.

It is important to take the time to understand specifically how economic segregation affects the mobilization process in the eight case-study neighborhoods studied here. Doing so will not only tell us more about political participation in the United States, but it will also perhaps suggest ways to begin to address the class gap seen in American politics today. If wealthy citizens vote at higher rates, it seems reasonable for politicians to address their concerns; conversely, if poorer citizens vote at lower rates, it also seems reasonable for politicians to ignore their concerns.[40] But to see that poorer citizens did vote at higher levels in the 1970s, and to understand that their declining participation is not solely a function of individual apathy or apolitical attitudes but rather can be attributed in part to growing economic segregation and isolation, means that perhaps the slide toward a greater class gap in participation and representation and resulting policies could be mitigated or reversed by the concerted action of civic and political leaders.

Before we can begin exploring the machinations of economic segregation and mobilization in context, though, the next chapter introduces each of the case-study cities and neighborhoods, offering a brief history of how each became the segregated cities they are today. Although the stories of Atlanta, Kansas City, Rochester, and Milwaukee share some common themes and ultimately created similar situations of residential economic segregation within those cities, the unique and specific histories and cultures of these cities remind us of Tolstoy's famed quote about unhappy families: every segregated city has become segregated in its own way.

CHAPTER 2

Public Policy and Civic Environments
in Urban America

The story of urban decline and attempted renewal in the United States has been told and retold, and the broad contours are well known. But the effect of urban development policies implemented in the mid-twentieth century needs further examination, especially the degree to which those policies reconfigured the spatial arrangement of city dwellers along economic lines. Policy makers in Atlanta, Kansas City, Milwaukee, and Rochester, and many other cities, enacted policies that effectively created neighborhoods of segregated and concentrated poverty as well as neighborhoods of segregated and concentrated wealth, even if their stated goals were to promote a more general public good by revitalizing crumbling urban centers.

This chapter briefly summarizes the origins of the midcentury "urban crisis" and the three types of public policies that federal, state, and local officials in cities across America most often used to address that crisis. The case-study cities of Atlanta, Kansas City, Milwaukee, and Rochester are discussed in detail, demonstrating how similar policy initiatives were implemented within local contexts, although to different degrees and in different ways, and produced the same outcome of increased residential economic segregation. Later chapters will explore the effect that this segregation had on the capacity of civic organizations, churches, and political parties and operatives to organize and mobilize the citizenry, but this chapter focuses on how economic segregation affected the civic environments of impoverished and wealthy neighborhoods.[1]

American cities grew and changed tremendously during the twentieth century. Immigration in the late nineteenth and early twentieth centuries prompted astonishing population growth in cities, beginning on the East Coast but gradually expanding across Midwestern states and elsewhere in the nation. The huge swell of immigrants, primarily from Eastern and Southern Europe, strained the infrastructure and forced residents, businesses, and local officials to adapt. During this time, Progressive Era political reform initiatives transformed these cities by developing extensive water and sewage systems; instituting refuse collection and electrical wiring; investing in public schools, parks, and other shared spaces; introducing new modes of transportation like streetcars and trolleys; and establishing building and health codes that coincided with the development of new housing stock.[2] Within the American tradition of local control this growth occurred somewhat haphazardly, allowing different cities and municipalities to confront problems and create solutions in particular ways.

Although the initial population growth began with European immigration, the outbreak of World War I helped kick-start the "Great Migration" of African Americans from the rural South to the urban North, and black migration into cities continued even after federal restrictions implemented in the 1920s stemmed the flow of immigrants. By the time of the stock market crash in 1929, 56.1 percent of Americans lived in or near areas considered "urban" by the U.S. Census, and during the Depression the figure increased as Dust Bowl refugees and others hard hit by the economic downturn found their way into cities.[3] The rapid growth of American cities, first fueled by European immigrants and later by African American migrants, put tremendous strain on urban infrastructure, particularly housing stock. Indeed, the relocation to urban areas during the twentieth century by millions of African Americans in search of economic opportunities had profound and long-lasting effects on urban politics and policy.[4] As these millions of residents moved into cities, dwellings were constructed hastily, often with speedy construction prioritized over quality craftsmanship. And, of course, America's ongoing struggle with the "dilemma" of racism prompted many city dwellers to look upon African American arrivals with suspicion.[5]

Following World War II Americans began to move to the suburbs, although the flight from the chaos of urban life had actually begun decades before.[6] The streetcars and trolleys that made it easier to get around the city also made it easier to live farther and farther from the downtown area and to commute to work, and pent-up demand for automobiles following the lean war years increased rates of automobile ownership and served to hasten the flow of residents to the immediate suburbs. Postwar policies, especially the G.I. Bill, served as a powerful mechanism for relocating millions of families to Levittown-type housing developments in suburban areas across the country. American cities meanwhile were showing growing pains brought on by the previous decades of population growth and hasty infrastructure expansion. In the 1940s and 1950s politicians and local leaders confronted a confluence of problems: insufficient and blighted housing stock, a rapidly accelerating exodus to the suburbs (especially by white, middle-class families), and, perhaps most alarming of all, decreasing revenues from a shrinking commercial base, as businesses followed populations out of the city.[7] These were national problems that affected nearly every American city in the decades following World War II, and although the precise ways in which the "urban crisis" developed were particular to individual cities, the shared sense of crisis was inescapable.

In response lawmakers at the national, state, and local levels developed a series of policies, working in concert with private developers and under pressure from real-estate associations, to advance "urban redevelopment" in the Housing Act of 1949, which became "urban renewal" in the Housing Act of 1954. These acts provided federal funds for local governing authorities, primarily redevelopment authorities, to acquire and clear blighted land and to sell that land to private developers and housing authorities.[8] Blight clearance and the acquisition of land for the development of private and public housing and new commercial enterprise radically reshaped urban centers beginning in the 1940s and in some cases extended well into the 2000s.

Additionally, federal-aid highway programs that dated back to 1934 but had expanded during the postwar decades also provided funds for land acquisition to create new roads and highways in order to develop connections between emerging suburbs and commercial centers, to promote mobility across the country, to provide extended shipping routes to commercial interests to farther-flung markets, and to provide a highway system that supported national security efforts in case of foreign attack.[9] Urban renewal, which encompassed housing redevelopment and economic revitalization, and transportation policy in the 1950s and 1960s provided funds for local redevelopment authorities to compensate those whose land was acquired by the state or federal government under the principle of eminent domain (the authority of a government entity to take private property for public use with just compensation), and aid these individuals, families, and businesses in their effort to relocate.[10] Together these three distinct but interrelated sets of policy—housing, economic revitalization, and transportation, along with the relocation efforts coordinated in response—combined to create new urban environments in post–World War II American cities.

The idea behind uniting these three types of policy proceeded logically in the minds of urban-renewal proponents. Improving the housing stock seemed like a straightforward way to stanch the flow of people to the suburbs and encourage people to remain in cities while possibly attracting new residents. Strengthening the central business district would attract commercial investment while providing services and employment opportunities to city and suburban dwellers alike, and the new roads and highways would provide access and promote the flow of people as well as goods and services within and around cities. Ideally, the policies would overlap and promote urban growth and improve the quality of city life while also developing the city as a place where suburbanites could work and in their leisure time perhaps visit for recreational purposes as well.

Of course, one of the goals of urban renewal was also to improve housing for and the general welfare of those living in substandard conditions within the city. Many politicians and business leaders recognized the dilapidated housing stock but were less attentive to the people who were living inside these crumbling homes. City officials seemed to have their eyes trained on the suburbs and the exodus of middle-class (and mostly white) residents as they considered how to address the urban crisis. Rather than focus on ways to make better the lives of people already living in the city but struggling to succeed, urban redevelopment was undertaken to try and remake the city to entice people who were not already enamored of urban life to return. The result of this prioritization, playing itself out in city after city across the United States during the later decades of the twentieth century, meant that revitalization efforts failed to address or ameliorate some of the problems associated with overcrowding and segregation, and indeed served to continue or even exacerbate these conditions.[11]

Segregation, as discussed in the previous chapter, is a multidimensional phenomenon that has to be defined specifically in order to be a useful and descriptive term. Certainly, it is most commonly employed when discussing racial exclusion, and policy makers in midcentury America were well aware of the fact that many of the people fleeing for the suburbs were white while many of the city dwellers living in poor conditions were black. It is certain that race and racism affected the types of urban redevelopment policies undertaken in many cities, a point that has been well documented and discussed in numerous important books and articles.[12] But even if the segregation patterns that existed within cities when urban renewal began in the 1940s were organized by skin color, it is important to note that the outward movement of middle-class blacks from low-income and overcrowded conditions, a flight that intensified during the 1970s and 1980s after the effects of urban redevelopment had a chance to take hold, indicates that economic segregation emerged as a new and distinct problem.[13]

This is not to discount the role that race plays in the development of civic environments, but the examination here does attempt to isolate and focus on the particular effects of concentrated poverty and wealth segregated into specific geographic locations. Each of the four case-study cities selected for analysis sheds light on how these three policy areas—housing, including not just housing provision but zoning as well, economic revitalization, and transportation—combined to deepen economic segregation in American cities. A second related and important point is to appreciate how patterns of residential segregation were not simply the result of city residents choosing housing options in a free market; rather residential choices were explicitly shaped by urban policies that promoted certain kinds of real-estate and residential options, which often displaced and relocated low-income residents in particular neighborhoods, creating patterns of neighborhoods segregated by class even after explicit racial segregation was discontinued.[14]

American cities have, of course, been made and remade throughout American history. Growth, migration, public and private investment, decisions made by public officials and private citizens, actions taken and not taken, and the whims of nature in the form of natural disasters combine in particular ways and over time push and pull cities to grow and change. Unfortunately but unsurprisingly, dynamics like racial and ethnic and class difference have always played some role in determining the ways that cities have developed and where people lived and worked. However, even if cities have always been (and always will be) segregated, the post–World War II combination of urban renewal and housing policies, transportation policies, and relocation initiatives created a particular dynamic that resulted in a new kind of urban segregation. While racial and ethnic differences continued to play a role in defining the characteristics of particular enclaves and neighborhoods in cities across America, the effects of the post–World War II urban redevelopment policies created residential segregation along economic lines within cities in ways that had not occurred previously and that are to date not fully appreciated.

Concurrent with the largely voluntary relocation from cities to suburbs undertaken by many mostly white and middle-class or middle-class-aspirant families, within cities themselves there were numerous instances of typically involuntary relocation of residents—usually impoverished but not always, often African American but not exclusively so—into particular neighborhoods. This spatial reorganization of citizens along economic lines occurred gradually, and the effects of this reorganization, including effects on the civic environment of individual neighborhoods, would not be seen for decades. But the policies instituted in the immediate post–World War II decades decidedly circumscribed future opportunities for political engagement for millions of low-income citizens.

One way to better understand the evolution and effect of urban renewal and transportation policies is to examine them in context. This chapter explores how public and private actors in Atlanta, Kansas City, Milwaukee, and Rochester each confronted similar problems by using similar policy solutions, but they did so in ways that reflected the history and circumstances unique to each city. The post–World War II "urban crisis" in each city manifested itself in similar but distinct ways, and the redevelopment strategies to confront the crisis were likewise similar but not identical. However, the consequences of urban redevelopment policies undertaken in Atlanta, Kansas City, Milwaukee, and Rochester were the same: increased residential segregation along economic lines. In each instance, and very likely in many other cities across America, urban-renewal policies had dramatic effects on the spatial arrangement of and residential patterns of citizens along class lines.

It is important to keep in mind that although different policies figured more prominently in each city, and that the way the policies came together was always shaped by the particular circumstances within each city, the resulting segregation remains a constant. Put another way, the cities each took slightly different paths to reach the same destination. The policies required to undertake urban renewal necessitated the relocation of thousands of city residents, and they directly altered who lived with whom and where. Indeed, by 1962, 1,665,000 people were involved with federal urban-renewal programs, with 609,000 of those slated to be relocated by the end of 1963. The remainder were scheduled to be relocated by the end of 1965.[15] In addition to individuals and families, by 1962, 44,000 businesses and nonprofits were also displaced by federally funded renewal and highway programs, and yet only 50 percent of families, 49 percent of individuals, and 53 percent of businesses and nonprofits received payment to assist in relocation. And in 1965 there was no sign of letting up; the Urban Renewal Administration estimated that by 1972, an additional 1 million families would be displaced by renewal, and the Advisory Commission on Intergovernmental Relations further estimated that 136,000 businesses and nonprofits would be affected between 1963 and 1971.[16] This meant that authorities at the time believed that nearly 4 million people and 180,000 businesses would be displaced by urban renewal by 1972, a staggering number by any account.

Further, 26.4 percent of the displaced families between 1949 and 1963 were relocated to federally aided public housing or substandard housing, indicating that forced relocation as a result of urban-renewal and highways policies in many instances produced the (probably unintended) consequence of increasing economic segregation in many cities, including those examined here.[17] The funneling of low-income residents to particular neighborhoods served to both isolate them from others and increase the segregation and population density of poor people within specific areas. As a result certain neighborhoods experienced general decay, despite renewal efforts in other parts of the city, which was physical as well as economic and social. While these trends have been documented by other scholars in other contexts, this chapter aims to reveal how urban-renewal policies helped create residential economic segregation in the specific case-study cities of interest here and how this segregation helped depreciate the civic environments of some neighborhoods while strengthening the civic environments in others.[18] In order to make sense of civic and political mobilization as well as voter-turnout results from the eight case-study neighborhoods in the last decades of the twentieth century, we first have to understand the public policies enacted in the mid-twentieth century intended to address the urban crisis in Atlanta, Kansas City, Milwaukee, and Rochester.

Atlanta, Fulton County, Georgia

Atlanta emerged as the capital of the "New South" in the late nineteenth and early twentieth centuries because its geographic location made it an ideal city to serve as a hub of rail transportation and goods transport. Like many Northern cities that had established themselves during the 1800s as railroads crisscrossed the country, Atlanta grew after the Civil War because agricultural tools and products needed across the South could be shipped through the city. Unlike most other cities in Georgia and elsewhere in the South, Atlanta was not itself an agricultural center but rather grew as the connection point between other regional agricultural centers; also as the capital of Georgia, Atlanta was the political center of the state, and local officials were quick to realize how transportation infrastructure development could help promote the city's development. This booming transportation industry spurred population and economic growth: the population of Atlanta grew from 37,400 in 1880; to 65,533 in 1890; to 89, 872 in 1900; and to more than 150,000 in 1910.[19]

This rapid growth attracted commercial and other interests, and Atlanta's expanding middle and upper-middle classes soon wanted newer, nicer neighborhoods beyond the increasingly populated downtown. As early as the 1880s, Atlanta experienced "intense" residential development and growth in areas expanding outward, away from the city center.[20] Significantly, this migration included African Americans as well as white residents. Although racial segregation and Jim Crow laws made intermingling of the races impossible, a black middle class was able to develop in Atlanta in the late nineteenth century that in many ways mirrored the emerging white middle class. The presence of Spelman and Morehouse colleges helped ensure an educated and ambitious cohort of black Atlantans who became well-known and prominent citizens within the African American community. Black-owned newspapers, banks, and other businesses ensured that an entirely separate and all-black commercial center developed, as did pockets of black middle-class residential neighborhoods, essentially establishing two cities—one black and one white—by the 1930s.[21]

Atlanta's location in the Deep South cannot help but distinguish the city from the other cities examined in this study. The history of *de jure* racial discrimination made possible by Jim Crow laws, and the complicated and tortured history of race relations in the South dating back to slavery is something that Kansas City, Milwaukee, or Rochester never experienced, although those cities certainly had their own levels of racial hostility and prejudice. But if Atlanta is unique because of its Southern location, it is also unique among Southern cities because of the development of this stable and thriving black middle and upper class in the late nineteenth and early twentieth centuries. It is important to appreciate how following World War II city officials and policy makers had to confront the "two cities" dynamic; the black elite could not simply be pushed aside and ignored. In fact, one important consequence of economic segregation, particularly in Atlanta, was the de-mise of economically integrated black communities, a sentiment expressed by civic leaders I spoke with in Atlanta. A result, as has been already noted, is that both the impoverished and prosperous case-study neighborhoods ex-amined in this study are 99 percent African American, and the prosperous neighborhood of West Manor exists in part because the black middle class was well established even before the civil rights movement compelled the discontinuation of legal racial segregation and they took advantage of resi-dential opportunities that allowed them to move away from the urban poor.

But if the "two cities" of Atlanta were thriving as World War II drew to a close, the city nevertheless confronted some of the same problems that many other cities in America faced. City infrastructure and housing stock needed to be refurbished and improved, and the Great Migration of rural African Americans to urban centers saw thousands of poor blacks continuing to move to the city.[22] According to a report by the housing coordinator in Atlanta's Bureau of Planning, four phenomena changed the cityscape of Atlanta in the 1950s and 1960s, both in terms of residential patterns and race relations: the poor condition of existing housing available to African Americans (especially newly arrived, poor rural migrants), the displace-ment of hundreds of families for expressway and urban-renewal policies, the unprecedented growth of the black population inside the city limits, and the rising income level of blacks and the concurrent push for more middle-class black housing in a region that was still strictly geographically segre-gated along racial lines.[23]

These trends in housing and demographic shifts produced a familiar story of blockbusting, redlining, population relocation, and rising racial tensions in part because the white population viewed black "encroachment" on their neighborhoods as a threat to their safety, property values, and com-munity. But race was not the only motivating factor in the reorganization of Atlanta's residents. Although whites were apprehensive about blacks mov-ing into previously all-white neighborhoods, middle-class blacks were also eager to move away from the overcrowding and poverty in the city center. Dealing with overcrowding in the city center was in fact the priority in the 1940s and 1950s, along with the economic revitalization of the downtown, which had become increasingly blighted and densely populated with low-income residents.[24] There were opportunities on the horizon to develop parts of downtown, but something would need to be done about the "sore thumb" of inner-city Atlanta.[25] Atlanta would have to take major action "if the city [was] to handle a predicted two million citizens by 1980."[26] This meant that public officials had to take an active role in urban planning by identifying neighborhoods for renewal, relocation, and development in order to alleviate overcrowding as well as the racially tinged social tensions emerging in the city.

In order to accomplish blight clearance and economic revitalization, two types of policies needed to be engaged simultaneously: the city needed to provide incentives to attract new businesses and industries downtown while also demolishing centrally located, blighted neighborhoods, which would require building new housing elsewhere and providing assistance to secure temporary and, later, permanent housing for those displaced by renewal.[27] These were important goals for city planners at the time, but numerous reports from the Bureau of Planning also suggest two other factors city officials considered regarding the relocation of populations as part of urban renewal.

The first was concern over the possible effects of concentrated poverty. While many blacks experienced an increase in income in the late 1950s and early 1960s, instances of poverty, single-parent households, and unemployment in black neighborhoods were much higher than in white neighborhoods. Thus, when planning new neighborhoods for those displaced from the blighted downtown, city planners hoped to disperse poverty and address accompanying social concerns through city programs and services.[28] The plan was to relocate black and low-income families away from the blighted urban core into single-family homes or newer apartments. City planners hoped that the development of mixed-income communities in new parts of town would accomplish three goals: deconcentrate poverty, attract black families whose income allowed them to move away from the blighted urban core without relocation assistance, and with financial assistance from the city provide home-ownership opportunities for low-income individuals and families displaced as a result of urban renewal and expressway development. In this way the city hoped to create stable, mixed-income black communities similar to those that existed before racial desegregation and urban-renewal efforts, which generated the middle-income push to flee urban poverty.

The second and more troubling factor motivating city officials in the development of urban-renewal plans was concern over the political implications of low-income and black residential patterns in the 1950s and 1960s.

In 1957 an anonymously written memo to the Metropolitan Planning Commission, which was established to determine a comprehensive development plan for the City of Atlanta and Fulton County more broadly, questioned the wisdom of "creat[ing] class neighborhoods characterized by age, education, politics, or income thru zoning standards," suggesting planners were concerned about concentrated poverty separate from concentrated racial or ethnic groups. Moreover, to combat the expected effect of a "political[ly] active people mov[ing] from central city" as a result of relocation policies, Jim Parham, the outgoing housing coordinator for urban-renewal projects in Atlanta, further promoted the idea that the "dispersion of Negro communities throughout the area will help to avoid the high densities conducive to so many social problems, [and] *will make exploitation of Negro voters less likely.*"[29] In other words, city officials were nervous about the organization and mobilization of black voters in Atlanta—both as an economic and a racial voting bloc—and about the possibility that this population could gain power in the political system. Therefore, city planners in Atlanta aimed to disperse the low-income and the black population throughout Atlanta in order to deconcentrate poverty and to deconcentrate African Americans so that potential political power within either class or racial groups could not develop.

In order to accomplish these goals, however, city council members and the mayor had to come to an agreement about what type of revitalization would occur downtown, and, more important for our purposes here, elected officials had to determine what type of housing would be provided for those relocated and where this housing would be built. There were essentially two possibilities for determining the location of housing for the displaced: housing could be built close to the existing neighborhoods or in new open areas further removed from the city center.[30] Within these two options urban-renewal programs and housing sites were hotly contested issues in Atlanta in 1960. Many wealthy and white Atlantans did not want low-income, predominantly black residents moving into their neighborhoods, while advocates for new housing and economic opportunities for those living in the center-city slums argued that "there's a great moral issue at stake as well as economic and political issues. . . . The brains of youth are going down the drain of Atlanta's slums."[31] Yet, simply rebuilding low-income housing in the inner-city area seemed undesirable because it would not necessarily address the problems associated with segregated, concentrated poverty and overcrowding.

Thomasville Heights was developed in 1962 for families displaced by urban renewal. When conceived, the land—southeast of downtown—was
largely open, though a medium-security federal prison is close by, and when
the roads were built, they were not paved and few services reached the
community. Initially Thomasville Heights thrived as a community of single-
family homes, owned by their residents with the assistance of city homeownership programs. Leroy Perkins, former president of the Thomasville
Heights Civic Club, explained the history of the community: "This was a
early one [a development for those displaced] . . .'62. Well, for the good of it,
this was the last housing was built before integration." He went on to describe
the neighborhood as having "little nice houses," saying that residents were
"so proud of this community."[32] Initially, at least, the plan to relocate lower-
income, predominantly black residents away from the city center and into a
new area sowed the seeds for a thriving neighborhood.

In 1963 President John Kennedy issued executive order 11063 that effectively ended the practice of developing racially segregated housing with federal funds. Kennedy's executive order, coupled with the civil rights movement
and other new political and policy developments, paved the way for broad
neighborhood transition along economic lines, as policy makers could no
longer specify housing developments designated for black people, producing
stark economic differentiation and segregation within the black community;
blacks who could afford to move out of the center city moved to the western
and southwestern side of Atlanta, including to West Manor, which became
increasingly black and increasingly wealthy. Indeed, "one resident of the area
[said], a listing of of those who live off Cascade Road reads like a 'Who's
Who' of black Atlanta."[33]

Consequently, economic class, not race, became the explicitly stated reason
for housing construction and resistance to new housing, and this presented
a problem. Middle- and upper-class residents were wary about low-income
housing, concerned that such developments could negatively affect the value
of their own property as well as possibly bring more crime closer to their
homes. In response, successful activism against low-income housing throughout the 1960s and 1970s in nonpoor neighborhoods and pressure by private
developers forced the city to situate new low-income housing in or near already
existing working-class and low-income neighborhoods rather than consider
sites for low-income housing in nonpoor neighborhoods. The initial hope
among city officials of creating mixed-income communities was unfulfilled,

in large part because of pressure from wealthier citizens. Instead, the relocation moved impoverished citizens into already poor areas of the city, the far
northwest and south-southeast areas of downtown.[34]

Ironically, in the 1970s the residents of Atlanta's "renewed" midtown, a
revitalized neighborhood occupied by "enlightened" and "progressive" citizens, and residents of wealthier black communities long familiar with "not-
in-my-back-yard," or NIMBY, attitudes presented some of the greatest
resistance to low-income housing development in their neighborhoods.
Officials had successfully lured people back to some parts of the downtown
area, but these same people were not interested in seeing housing for low-
income residents built in their new backyard. A meeting about a proposal to
build new housing in midtown "was full of pro-civil rights activists who have
carried banners across the South," and "there were numerous elected
officials—including the local state representative and the local state senator—
who campaigned for office on liberal-progressive platforms." But "not a word
of encouragement reached the ears of the mayor from these old friends. In
the meantime, a petition being circulated in Midtown opposing the subsidized
housing, had picked up a load of signatures."[35]

Additionally, concerns over where to locate Atlanta's poor and largely
black populations grew, even as a wealthy black enclave was emerging across
town.[36] Indeed, in many cases these emergent middle-class and wealthier
black communities were just as wary as their white counterparts of housing developed for the urban poor, in part because of similar concerns
about property values and safety and in part because their stable communities were a hard-fought victory. Thus, urban-renewal and housing policies
in the 1950s through the 1980s, as well as the successful resistance to subsidized housing in prosperous neighborhoods and the subsequent economic
sorting within the black community, increased economic segregation in
Atlanta. By the 1970s the two case-study neighborhoods examined in this
study were already beginning to exhibit the characteristics of clearly segregated communities.

Mapping neighborhood poverty rates in Fulton County between 1970
and 2000 helps demonstrate how this segregation of poverty increased over
time.[37] Figures 2.1 through 2.4 show the geographic patterns of neighborhood poverty rates and the black population in Fulton County in 1970 and
2000. Circles drawn around the impoverished Thomasville Heights neighborhood in the southeast and the prosperous West Manor neighborhood in
the west highlight the impoverished and prosperous case-study communi-

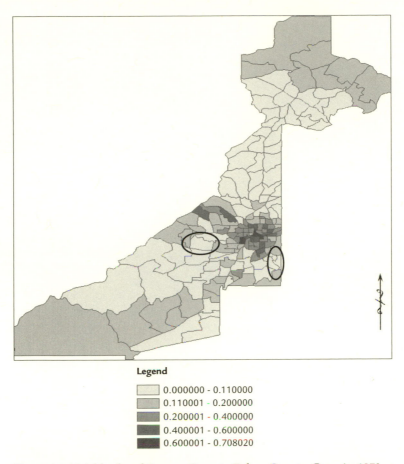

Legend

☐ 0.000000 - 0.110000

▨ 0.110001 - 0.200000

▨ 0.200001 - 0.400000

▨ 0.400001 - 0.600000

■ 0.600001 - 0.708020

Figure 2.1. Neighborhood Poverty Rates in Fulton County, Georgia, 1970

Source: Urban Institute, and GeoLytics, *Neighborhood Change Database*, CensusCD neighborhood change database (NCDB) [electronic resource]: 1970–2000 tract data: selected variables for US Census tracts for 1970, 1980, 1990, 2000.

ties. As Figures 2.1 and 2.2 show, not only was there an increase in the number of poor and high-poverty census tracts in Atlanta, the pattern of these census tracts in 2000 runs from the northwest through the urban core to the southeast, precisely where the city targeted its urban renewal and relocation housing with the goal of dispersing poor and high-poverty populations. Instead of economically integrating the city, the policies created a clear band of poverty through the city and incentivized movement out of high-poverty neighborhoods for those who could afford it. This occurred even as the black

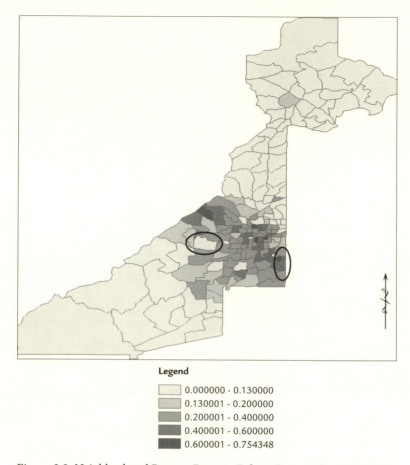

Legend

☐	0.000000 - 0.130000
☐	0.130001 - 0.200000
☐	0.200001 - 0.400000
☐	0.400001 - 0.600000
☐	0.600001 - 0.754348

Figure 2.2. Neighborhood Poverty Rates in Fulton County, Georgia, 2000

Source: Urban Institute, and GeoLytics, *Neighborhood Change Database*, CensusCD neighborhood change database (NCDB) [electronic resource]: 1970–2000 tract data: selected variables for US Census tracts for 1970, 1980, 1990, 2000.

population became more dispersed throughout the southern part of the county between 1970 and 2000, suggesting a decrease in racial segregation (Figures 2.3 and 2.4).[38]

These maps show that poverty became more segregated and concentrated, while racial residential patterns grew more diffuse in Atlanta over time. Coupling these trends with the historical narrative of Atlanta, it is clear that political decisions, particularly about housing, altered residential patterns of low- and high-income Atlantans. It is crucial to understand how

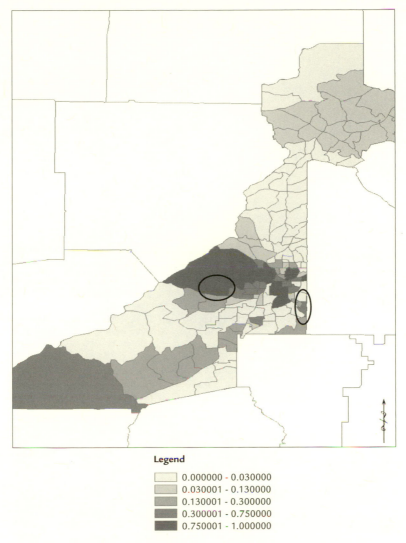

Legend

☐	0.000000 - 0.030000
▦	0.030001 - 0.130000
▦	0.130001 - 0.300000
▦	0.300001 - 0.750000
■	0.750001 - 1.000000

Figure 2.3. Neighborhood Percentages of African American Residents in Fulton County, Georgia, 1970

Source: Urban Institute, and GeoLytics, *Neighborhood Change Database*, CensusCD neighborhood change database (NCDB) [electronic resource]: 1970–2000 tract data: selected variables for US Census tracts for 1970, 1980, 1990, 2000.

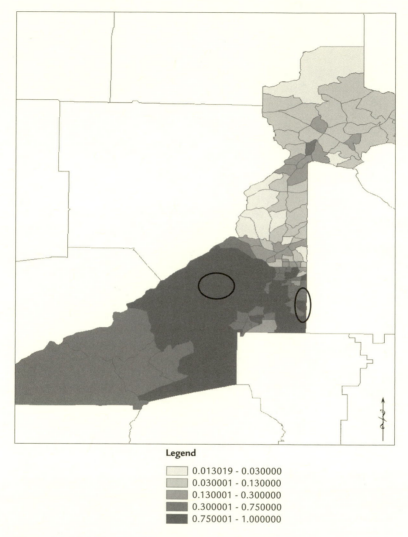

Legend

▢	0.013019 - 0.030000
▢	0.030001 - 0.130000
▢	0.130001 - 0.300000
▢	0.300001 - 0.750000
▢	0.750001 - 1.000000

Figure 2.4. Neighborhood Percentages of African American Residents in Fulton County, Georgia, 2000

Source: Urban Institute, and GeoLytics, *Neighborhood Change Database*, CensusCD neighborhood change database (NCDB) [electronic resource]: 1970–2000 tract data: selected variables for US Census tracts for 1970, 1980, 1990, 2000.

this residential segregation served to modify the civic environment within these newly segregated neighborhoods. Table 2.1 shows trends in neighborhood characteristics, including poverty rates, housing and demographic trends, educational attainment, and unemployment in the impoverished Thomasville Heights and prosperous West Manor case-study communities between 1970 and 2000. This comparison reveals how these neighborhoods have changed over time.

In 1970 the Thomasville Heights and West Manor neighborhoods were not much different, but between 1980 and 2000 the neighborhood poverty rate was much higher in Thomasville Heights, as was the percentage of the population aged sixteen and older with no high school diploma and the percentage of people living in a different home than they did five years ago. There were also three-and-a-half times as many renter-occupied units and twice as many female-headed households by the year 2000. This suggests that in 2000, familial, social, and economic resources were weak and residential stability low, and therefore potential civic and political activists few. The Thomasville Heights community had significantly fewer neighborhood resources—fewer people with a high school degree, less disposable income, more overburdened single-parent households, and higher unemployment. Coupled with the aging housing, higher crime rates, and fewer economic opportunities, the combined effect of these trends is an entire neighborhood with fewer civic resources, which diminished the civic environment and undermined support for the mobilizing capacity of voluntary associations or any subsequent civic or political efforts. Residential segregation thus decidedly inhibited the maintenance of a supportive civic environment by segregating and concentrating people together who were less likely to have the resources necessary to be engaged and active.

Conversely, by 2000 in West Manor, a neighborhood composed of ambitious middle-class African Americans, educational attainment was much higher, with 42 percent of the population holding bachelor's, graduate, or professional degrees; homeownership was prevalent, with 88 percent of residents owning their home; and there were relatively fewer female-headed households. Moreover, the average household income in West Manor in 2000 was 14 percent higher than the national average of $56,604, while in Thomasville Heights the average income was half of the national average. As a result, by 2000 there were more resources, including skills, money,

Table 2.1. Economic, Housing, Demographic, Educational, and Unemployment Trends: Thomasville Heights and West Manor, Atlanta, Georgia

Category	Thomasville Heights				West Manor			
	1970	*1980*	*1990*	*2000*	*1970*	*1980*	*1990*	*2000*
Total Population, Census Tract	4,054	4,925	4,442	3,923	4,558	5,067	4,416	4,389
% Below Poverty Line	8	49	54	54	6	6	6	6
% In High Poverty	2	43	48	47	2	5	4	4
Average Wages and Salaries	$8,503	$15,161	$19,346	$26,225	$13,923	$24,749	$53,968	$64,476
Neighborhood Income Percentile	55	35	10	5	95	85	95	90
% Age 16+ Without High School Diploma	55	55	47	41	23	18	14	12
% With Bachelor's/Graduate/Professional Degree	2	3	4	4	36	38	39	42
% African American Population	73	98	99	99	82	97	98	98
% Latino Population	N/A	0	0	0	N/A	1	1	1
% In Different House from Five Years Ago	29	15	32	32	49	11	12	15
Number of Renter-Occupied Units	154	631	722	708	71	176	151	208
% Female-Headed Households	12	69	76	86	13	24	49	40
% Age 16+ Unemployed	23	50	45	44	23	26	23	36

Source: Urban Institute, and GeoLytics, *Neighborhood Change Database*, CensusCD neighborhood change database (NCDB) [electronic resource]: 1970–2000 tract data: selected variables for US Census tracts for 1970, 1980, 1990, 2000.

* High poverty is determined by calculating those living below 74.99% of the poverty line.

and time, in West Manor that could be leveraged to support the kind of civic environment conducive to a vibrant civic life, including robust civic organizations, contact with candidates and elected officials, and active get-out-the-vote drives.

Finally, it is important to remember that both case-study neighborhoods in Atlanta are 99 percent black, which makes the comparison of Atlanta with the other case-study cities particularly interesting in subsequent chapters. The discussion about economic segregation in this study is meant to complement, not replace, the massive scholarly literature about the effects of residential segregation along racial lines, and the case-study neighborhoods of Thomasville Heights and West Manor help highlight the role of economic class in the development of civic environments.

While urban-renewal and residential patterns in Atlanta were affected by racial animus and tension, local officials had hoped to deconcentrate poverty, in part to minimize the effects of concentrated poverty but also as a political ploy to break up political power among the least advantaged.[39] Unfortunately, as the urban-renewal, transportation, and housing policies were implemented, the consequence was to segregate and isolate low-income populations. As a result, the neighborhood and civic contexts in Thomasville Heights and West Manor developed in vastly different ways. Economic segregation had distinct effects in each neighborhood, inhibiting a thriving civic environment in one case while promoting it in another. The concentration of individuals with particular incomes, levels of educational attainment, familial stability, and other characteristics is the first way that segregation begins to modify the civic environment; as we will see in later chapters, the organizational capacity of voluntary associations is also affected, as is the level of engagement of local politicians.

The diminished civic environment in Thomasville Heights has weakened the political voice of its residents, while the strong civic environment in West Manor has amplified the political voice of its residents. While a few citizens in Thomasville Heights continue to organize and vote to address community concerns, the low-income population that continues to reside in this neighborhood is largely unaffiliated with any neighborhood or community organization; they no longer vote at high rates (as will be discussed in subsequent chapters), and, as one Atlanta City Council member said when discussing the difficulty of organizing segregated, low-income citizens, "There's a feeling out there that local governments don't care about them."[40] On the other hand, the highly engaged citizenry in West Manor continues to enjoy attention and responsiveness from local officials, creating a virtuous cycle of involvement and participation.

Kansas City, Jackson County, Missouri

The development of Kansas City is much like other cities in the United States, except for two distinct features. First, the current greater Kansas City area straddles two states and lies within eleven counties. The historical development of Kansas City, Missouri, was complex, requiring interstate and intercounty cooperation. The second feature that helped shape Kansas City and its surrounding areas is the location of the city within the United States, which is near the geographic center of the country. Owing to its location the city has always been a hub of transportation systems, connecting the West to the East and the North to the South, with no fewer than five interstates and U.S. routes running through it; it still ranks the third busiest rail hub in the United States.[41] These two distinctive features combined with more traditional historical trends—including population increase and subsequent infrastructure development in the early twentieth century, followed by a midcentury "urban crisis" characterized by population loss and a crumbling city center—to create the conditions for reform and revitalization following World War II.

Transportation systems were a major feature in the Kansas City region and in the city itself long before its incorporation in 1853. The Missouri and Kansas rivers were major thoroughfares for trading in the region before the opening of the Kansas territory, at which point Kansas City became a hub of activity for those traveling to the new territory. Railway speculation in the region began shortly after the beginning of the Civil War, and federal incentives for railway development brought construction of tracks and bridges to the region. This development facilitated the transportation of goods throughout the region, especially serving as a hub for cattle ranchers throughout Texas and the Great Plains to ship their livestock to the meatpacking center of Chicago. Similar to most other American cities, the establishment of public transit and trolleys in the early twentieth century allowed some residents of Kansas City to move beyond the then urban boundaries into the "suburban hinterland" of Kansas and Missouri that had once been farmland, while rural migrants looking for work and opportunities continued to strain the housing stock in the city center.[42]

Three interurban streetcar lines helped spur the first wave of suburbanization in Kansas City in the 1920s. As with other cities, "the interurbans
were supposed to bring the countryside closer to the city, but they tended to
spread the city into the countryside."[43] A great deal of housing development
also occurred in Kansas City at this time, primarily in what were then suburban communities outside of the central city and primarily for wealthier
residents of Kansas City. The upscale communities of Armour Hills and the
Country Club Plaza, developed by prominent real-estate developer J. C.
Nichols, renowned for prolific development and his use of exclusionary zoning and racially restrictive covenants, provided opportunities for wealthier
citizens to move far away from what Kenneth Jackson referred to as the "fes-
tering metropolis."[44] Meanwhile, investment in urban housing and infrastructure was spotty and uneven, setting the stage for the midcentury urban
crisis.

The Great Migration of African Americans from the rural South to urban areas decidedly changed the population demographics of Kansas City,
beginning in the 1920s and continuing over the next several decades.[45] The
decline of sharecropping in the South and increasing industrial opportunities in Kansas City, primarily in the rail industry, lured rural blacks from
Texas, Louisiana, and Arkansas to the city. After World War II the trickle
of migration from the city to the suburbs swelled to a flood, as thousands
of (mostly white) middle-class residents sought to escape the overcrowding
and deteriorating conditions in the downtown area.

Movement into the suburbs was slowed, however, because the boundaries of Kansas City began expanding (whites were trying to move to the suburbs even as the urban boundaries were growing to accommodate this
movement); the city was trying to sustain population and a revenue base by
annexing these new suburbs. Therefore, the flow of whites out of the city
and suburbanization in general were partially stemmed in Kansas City not
because people stopped moving but because city officials expanded the
boundaries of the city itself to include the surrounding areas: "During the
1940s and 1950s, Kansas City, Missouri, indeed looked something like a
monster devouring everything in its path." Kansas City's city manager, L. P.
Cookingham, "sought between 1947 and 1963 to extend the city's limits
south. . . . By the time this plan was fully in place, Kansas City, Missouri,
included over 310 square miles within its limits. The 1947 number had been
63 square miles."[46] As a result, the population decline experienced in so
many cities has not been felt to as great a degree here because the city grew

to incorporate the rapidly moving population.[47] Indeed, "in the year 2000, Kansas City, Missouri, was the largest city in the state of Missouri by more than 100,000 persons. St. Louis declined from its highest population of 857,000 in 1950 to just under 340,000 in 2000."[48]

Although wealthy and white residents did not move outside of the city boundaries in high numbers because of this expansion, residential differentiation and economic segregation still occurred and has continued to occur. The redistribution of citizens along both racial and, crucially, economic lines proceeded in ways similar to what occurred in Atlanta but with a particular emphasis on transportation policy driving this shift, which makes sense given Kansas City's unique history as a railway nexus and the particularities dictated by the rapidly expanded city boundaries. While both Atlanta's and Kansas City's aims with urban renewal were primarily to promote downtown economic revitalization, they did so in different ways. Kansas City's renewal plan was in some ways the inverse of Atlanta's: Atlanta promoted economic revitalization as a way to develop communities and infrastructure, while Kansas City sought to use housing renewal and infrastructural development as a way to spur economic revitalization.[49]

Three distinct factors complicated the process of renewal and worked to increase economic segregation in Kansas City: the lack of a long-term commitment to and vision of comprehensive urban renewal and sound housing policy by a city council more concerned with transportation; the intricacy of expressway development politics; and the ongoing struggles of the relocation authority in Kansas City. In contrast to Atlanta, where city officials seemed to have had a better understanding of urban redevelopment dynamics but had to contend with NIMBY activism, in Kansas City local officials were ambitious but seemed to generally lack a long-term vision for those displaced by renewal, which made it difficult to move forward efficiently with policy implementation. And yet despite the fact that the situations in Atlanta and Kansas City were quite different, the result of midcentury urban renewal efforts was the same: creation of distinct patterns of economically segregated neighborhoods in both cities.

Though Kansas City was heralded by the American Institute of Architects and *Look* magazine, among many others, for its slum clearance efforts in the 1950s, throughout the 1960s and early 1970s citizens and policy experts frequently called for local officials to adopt a more comprehensive urban-renewal plan.[50] They were frustrated by the lack of vision, lack of clear policy guidelines for officials and private developers, and lack of political will demonstrated by elected officials as Kansas City struggled to deal with a blighted city center and the populations displaced by urban renewal. Federal resources of various types were available to help address the problem of displacement—4,415 individuals, 52 percent of whom were white and 48 percent of whom were black, and 755 businesses between 1954 and 1969— and yet city leaders in Kansas City deployed these resources to build only public housing for those uprooted by urban renewal instead of applying the available resources to promote the public good.[51] Specifically, there seemed to be a consensus among citizens and consulted experts about the need for long-term goals and a master plan focusing on land-use analysis and projections, population forecasts, economic analysis, and parks, playgrounds, schools, and other types of community facilities and services.[52] Instead, the Housing Authority of Kansas City, Missouri, built public-housing developments, all within six miles of each other, ensuring that urban renewal and relocation would remain controversial topics throughout the 1960s and 1970.[53] This is important for the evolution of economic segregation in the city because while these housing projects were segregated by race—there were white public-housing projects and black public-housing projects—they were clustered so closely together that poor city residents all lived in the same part of town, regardless of skin color.

The lack of long-term planning and vision demonstrated by officials meant that projects throughout the 1960s, 1970s, and 1980s were often initiated without adequate funding; other projects were funded but later had money rescinded, and still other projects were indefinitely delayed.[54] And these local struggles were exacerbated by federal policies and state agencies as well. Some of the funding difficulties that municipalities experienced during this time were due to changes in funding provided by the federal government and to the inability of state legislators to agree on tax exemptions that would help businesses moving into redeveloped areas. For instance, President Richard Nixon implemented a shift from categorical grants to cities, which were used for specific projects, to block grants, which were lump sums of money provided to cities to be used as necessary and at the discretion of city officials.[55] This seemingly small decision had profound effects in cities like Kansas City, where the major problem was inefficiency of local planning and use of resources. (Nixon also decreased the amount each city received under the new block-grant system.)

Moreover, in the mid-1980s city and state officials began to question the use of Missouri's 353 law and the city's own version of this law, which allowed the municipality to give eminent domain and tax-abatement advantages to private developers.[56] Indeed, by 1986 both the state and city versions had been revised to require greater communication between private developers and affected area interests.[57] As a result of this economic and political tumult, land-clearance initiatives that had begun earlier found their funding sources dried up, and the ongoing funding for land-clearance and relocation programs became more precarious and often contentious.[58] The situation was made all the more difficult by the lack of clear policy guidance from state and local officials, resulting in poorly implemented renewal projects.[59]

Urban renewal in Kansas City was not just focused on housing and large-scale redevelopment projects. Transportation also played a significant role in revitalization efforts. Major expressways were developed through most American cities in the 1950s and 1960s owing in large part to the Interstate Highway Act of 1956. This freeway construction, funded through the Highway Trust Fund, decidedly remade the entire United States, especially urban areas, during the second half of the twentieth century. Kansas City's long history as a railway hub prompted local officials to conceive of the city in a particular way, with its geographic location near the center of the country making it seem as though the city was naturally suited to being the country's crossroads. Thus conditions that prompted highway development across the country were compounded by a particular zeal among Kansas City officials to maintain their city as a major nationwide transportation center. Their efforts were eagerly supported by special interests like tire manufacturer and dealers, auto suppliers, oil companies, road builders, and land developers, although these special interests were never the stated reason for highway investment; the "public good" was always trotted out as the primary concern.[60] City officials in Kansas City suggested that improved access to the economic center of the city and better mobility throughout the region would expand economic opportunity. Expressways would theoretically connect the expanding residential area to the center city, where jobs and cultural activities were located. Moreover, the new expressways would also make it easier for industries and the city to deliver goods and services to an ever-widening area of residential settlements, particularly important to Kansas City's residents who were spread out over 310 square miles.[61]

But the process of developing freeways in Kansas City was made more difficult because of the incompetence of the Kansas City Land Clearance and Redevelopment Authority. Time after time the authority demonstrated an inability to anticipate and eventually address the needs of citizens displaced by freeway construction, of which there were many: 8,642 households, or 31,543 people by Martin Anderson's calculation, were displaced between 1950 and 1975 as a result of highway right-of-way land acquisition.[62] This seemingly obvious problem was met with ongoing apathy and resistance by authority officials. Public hearings were packed with citizens complaining about payment delays, substandard housing options, lack of assistance finding new homes, and numerous other problems, none of which should have surprised officials.[63] The lack of vision that plagued urban redevelopment in Kansas City thus had two interrelated components: city officials more concerned with transportation above other concerns, and ineptitude when it came to implementing transportation policies.

Another problem was, of course, race and racism. As poorly designed and implemented as Kansas City's urban-redevelopment projects may have been, particularly in the 1960s and 1970s, the familiar dynamic of white flight to the suburbs (or in the case of Kansas City, to the outer regions of the city) coinciding with an increasing African American population in the city center, affected the way that Kansas City was remade in the postwar decades. Blacks occupied some of the most blighted areas of the city, areas that were often identified as prime locations for freeway construction.[64] Whether Land Clearance and Redevelopment Authority officials were motivated by racism or by simple color-blind incompetence, relocating black citizens from these areas routinely resulted in major problems for the affected citizens; indeed, between 1954 and 1969, 52 percent of those displaced by urban renewal were black so that "urban renewal became the synonym for 'black removal.'"[65] By 1975 families organized and filed a class-action lawsuit against the U.S. Department of Housing and Urban Development for their local office's relocation practices, arguing that the substandard housing opportunities for the displaced were shaped by the race of those being relocated.[66]

Ultimately, however, the role that race may have played in the implementation of urban redevelopment policies is somewhat beside the point. This is not to suggest that the role that race and racism played in the creation and implementation of public policy is unimportant, but to say that this particular study is focused on investigating the effects that these policies had on promoting economic segregation and the civic environments of the neighborhoods it has helped produce. In Kansas City urban-renewal policies, especially the location of public-housing development and highway construction, created pockets of segregated poverty, including the case-study Ivanhoe community on the east side of the city. Ivanhoe, a neighborhood that was directly in the projected path of the South Midtown Freeway and eventually suffered large-scale dislocation because of land acquisition and clearance, ultimately became more densely populated with lower-income residents because families were provided minimal compensation for blighted houses and very little assistance in finding new housing. City officials were only concerned with getting the freeways constructed, not with what happened to the people displaced by their construction. Those with the means to do so moved to farther-flung, wealthier areas of the city, but those without became more and more concentrated on the east side of the city in neighborhoods like Ivanhoe.[67]

Figures 2.5 and 2.6 bear this story out and show the patterns of the neighborhood poverty rate in 1970 and 2000. The case-study neighborhoods are circled, with the impoverished Ivanhoe neighborhood in the east and the prosperous Union Hill neighborhood in the west. These maps reveal that in 1970 poverty was clustered near the river in the northern part of the city, a once thriving industrial area. This indicates a residential pattern of low-income residents living near their place of employment, while wealthier residents were able to live farther away from inner-city life and commute into their white-collar jobs downtown. In 2000, however, poor and high-poverty neighborhoods were clustered on the east side. Indeed, a clear dividing line between east and west—Troost Avenue—can be seen running north and south through the city.

Figures 2.7 and 2.8 show the residential patterns of African Americans living in Kansas City in 1970 and 2000. They show a dramatic increase in the number of high-percentage African American neighborhoods on the east side of the city, and again there is a clear north–south boundary dividing the east side of the city from the west along Troost Avenue. While in Atlanta some poor and high-poverty neighborhoods overlap with predominantly black neighborhoods without being synonymous with them—there are many non-poor, all-black neighborhoods in the west and southwest of Atlanta—in Kansas City these populations almost exactly overlap: the primary concentration of poor and high-poverty populations and populations of African Americans in Kansas City clearly fall to the east of Troost Avenue. In this instance race and class are intertwined, as they often are in the United States, but seeing Kansas City in context with the other case-study cities in this project illustrates how the economic nature of this segregation may be more important in shaping the civic environment of Ivanhoe than the racial aspect.

Table 2.2 shows some of the economic, demographic, educational, and employment trends that have occurred within neighborhoods as a result of

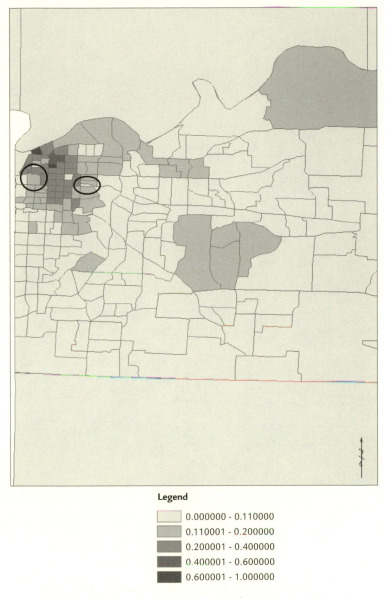

Legend

▢	0.000000 - 0.110000
▢	0.110001 - 0.200000
▢	0.200001 - 0.400000
▢	0.400001 - 0.600000
▢	0.600001 - 1.000000

Figure 2.5. Neighborhood Poverty Rate in Jackson County, Missouri, 1970

Source: Urban Institute, and GeoLytics, *Neighborhood Change Database*, CensusCD neighborhood change database (NCDB) [electronic resource]: 1970–2000 tract data: selected variables for US Census tracts for 1970, 1980, 1990, 2000.

Legend

- 0.000000 - 0.110000
- 0.110001 - 0.200000
- 0.200001 - 0.400000
- 0.400001 - 0.600000
- 0.600001 - 1.000000

Figure 2.6. Neighborhood Poverty Rate in Jackson County, Missouri, 2000

Source: Urban Institute, and GeoLytics, *Neighborhood Change Database*, CensusCD neighborhood change database (NCDB) [electronic resource]: 1970–2000 tract data: selected variables for US Census tracts for 1970, 1980, 1990, 2000.

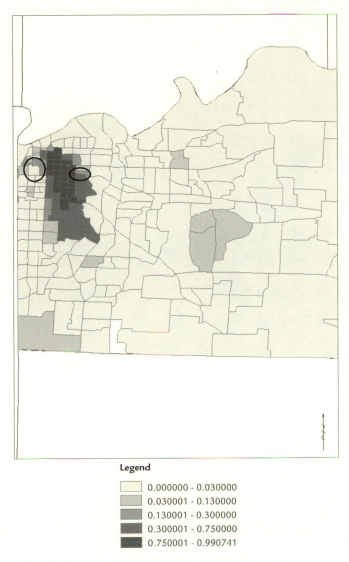

Legend

☐	0.000000 - 0.030000
☐	0.030001 - 0.130000
☐	0.130001 - 0.300000
☐	0.300001 - 0.750000
☐	0.750001 - 0.990741

Figure 2.7. Neighborhood Percentages of African American Residents in Jackson County, Missouri, 1970

Source: Urban Institute, and GeoLytics, *Neighborhood Change Database*, CensusCD neighborhood change database (NCDB) [electronic resource]: 1970–2000 tract data: selected variables for US Census tracts for 1970, 1980, 1990, 2000.

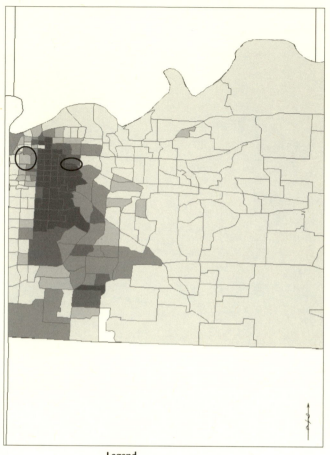

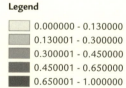
Figure 2.8. Neighborhood Percentages of African American
Residents in Jackson County, Missouri, 2000

Source: Urban Institute, and GeoLytics, *Neighborhood Change Database*,
CensusCD neighborhood change database (NCDB) [electronic resource]:
1970–2000 tract data: selected variables for US Census tracts for 1970, 1980, 1990,
2000.

Table 2.2. Economic, Housing, Demographic, Educational, and Unemployment Trends: Ivanhoe and Union Hill Neighborhoods, Kansas City, Jackson County, MO

Category	Ivanhoe				Union Hill			
	1970	1980	1990	2000	1970	1980	1990	2000
Total Population, Census Tract	1,079	916	838	731	1,013	1,039	885	1,098
% Below Poverty Line	11	23	38	52	19	25	21	17**
% In High Poverty*	52	57	56	100	—	—	—	—
Average Wages and Salaries	$8,135	$14,599	$17,925	$25,152	$4,893	$23,105	$50,629	$55,521
Neighborhood Income Percentile	45	30	5	5	5	80	95	85
% Age 16+ Without High School Diploma	56	49	44	26	51	29	21	12
% With Bachelors/Graduate/Professional Degree	3	5	0	0	7	21	37	57
% African American Population	36	53	54	66	2	9	25	24
% Latino Population	N/A	1	12	2	N/A	5	4	5
% In Different House from Five Years Ago	19	31	32	35	18	35	37	34
Number of Renter-Occupied Units	138	135	147	140	389	362	266	461***
% Female-Headed Household	8	35	52	43	25	15	35	3
% Age 16+ Unemployed	39	44	40	47	34	33	35	24

Source: Urban Institute, and GeoLytics, *Neighborhood Change Database*, CensusCD neighborhood change database (NCDB) [electronic resource]: 1970–2000 tract data: selected variables for US Census tracts for 1970, 1980, 1990, 2000.

* High poverty is determined by calculating those living below 74.99% of the poverty line.

** This relatively high number represents a group of low-income families that have since been relocated as a result of new condo development in this neighborhood, making the neighborhood of Union Hill even wealthier today.

*** Part of the rise in rental units in Union Hill is the result of high-end condominium and row-house development, many of which are rental units.

the shifting residential patterns prompted by the urban-renewal policies, including in the two selected case-study neighborhoods. These neighborhood-level characteristics are vital for understanding the formation and maintenance of civic environments because these environments are created by the sum total of conditions in a neighborhood that would promote or hinder active civic engagement, such as social networks, residential stability, and permanent skilled volunteers. Table 2.2 demonstrates that residential stability, educational attainment, and familial and social networks are low and weak in the Ivanhoe community when compared with those characteristics in Union Hill.

Much like Atlanta, economic, familial, and social well-being and educational attainment declined between 1970 and 2000, while unemployment and residential mobility grew in the segregated, impoverished Ivanhoe neighborhood. The opposite occurred in Union Hill, as more prosperous, better-educated, and more stable families relocated and clustered together. Subsequent chapters will explore how once-thriving civic associations in Ivanhoe wilted over time owing to increased economic segregation, as well as how city officials and other political operatives gradually paid more and more attention to Union Hill while ignoring Ivanhoe, creating feedback loops of engagement and disengagement, respectively.

The effect of residential economic segregation on the organizational capacities of associations and politicians has to be considered alongside changes to the basic demographic composition of the neighborhoods. The correlation of income and educational levels with civic engagement and voting is well established, but it remains important to draw attention to how residential segregation along economic lines clusters people who are already less likely to be engaged with other such people. In Union Hill this clustering is a good thing: being surrounded by other engaged citizens helps reinforce levels of engagement. But in Ivanhoe it makes it that much harder for the rhythms and patterns of civic involvement to be maintained.

Milwaukee, Milwaukee County, Wisconsin

As with Kansas City and Atlanta, the geographic location of Milwaukee, on the shore of Lake Michigan, is vital for understanding the development of the city. Milwaukee grew in large part because of its ideal location—with connections to the East but on the edge of the West, the burgeoning "frontier" in the mid-nineteenth century. The city was incorporated in 1846 by French and German missionaries, fur traders, and frontiersmen, making it a destination for new German immigrants who would arrive in droves in subsequent decades, swelling the city's population to over twenty thousand by the time of the Civil War.[68] The 1860s saw an influx of Irish, Polish, British, Scandinavian, Dutch, Italian, and Russian arrivals, and each immigrant group settled into separate parts of town, started their own organizations—civic, recreational, and political—and began various businesses and industries, giving Milwaukee a particularly diverse and vibrant society and culture.[69] By 1875 the population had grown to nearly one hundred thousand; by 1900 it had reached over a quarter of a million people; and by the 1920s over a half million people lived in Milwaukee, with a population density of eighteen thousand people per square mile, the second most densely populated city in the nation next to New York City.[70] Immigration was a clear driver of this growth, and it is key to understanding the city's development later in the twentieth century and indeed for its current state of affairs.

The rise of the railroad industry also played a major role in Milwaukee's growth and establishment as a hub for the transportation of goods across the nation. By the late nineteenth century Milwaukee was the terminus for both of Wisconsin's railroads—ideally located for its ports on Lake Michigan—and thanks to increased industrialization and production because of the Civil War, the city had replaced Chicago has the country's primary shipper of wheat. Milwaukee was poised to become a major industrial center in the early twentieth century owing to the large population increase and the development of transportation infrastructure. In fact, in the early twentieth century Milwaukee was home to Harley-Davidson and Miller Brewing, two companies in distinct industries that gradually grew to become national brands. During this time Milwaukee was second among the twenty largest cities in the nation for employing workers in manufacturing jobs, and World War II, which brought wartime industrial growth, expanded Milwaukee's manufacturing sector and increased demand for workers.[71]

As was the case elsewhere, Milwaukee's growth attracted African American workers during the Great Migration. Before World War I, Milwaukee had fewer than 9,000 African American residents, but by 1960 there were 62,548 African Americans living in the city.[72] Legal forms of racial segregation, including restrictive housing covenants and redlining, combined with racist attitudes to help segregate the city along racial lines, which caused the economic and social characteristics of Milwaukee's low-income communities to change (i.e., to become predominantly black).[73] This establishment of black enclaves close to the city center reverberates with the experience of dozens of other cities that received black arrivals during the Great Migration, who clustered in available but already deteriorating housing in the city center, and likewise makes Milwaukee's reaction to the post–World War II urban crisis similar to what occurred elsewhere.

Neglected and dilapidated housing at the center of the city and just northwest of downtown Milwaukee coupled with a general housing shortage drove those who could afford it beyond the city limits and often into the suburbs. Families, mostly white, experienced increased economic prosperity and access to federal loan programs like the G.I. Bill following World War II, which spurred additional movement from the city. And Milwaukeeans, much like residents of other cities, were recovering from the lingering effects of the Depression and the war. A fifteen-year lull in consumer spending and the lack of urban investment meant that Milwaukeeans with means had a pent-up desire to spend, and the gritty urban environment caused them to seek out new, more spacious housing options beyond the city limits: "With so many forces at work, the explosion on the fringe was absolutely predictable, but its intensity was still a shock."[74]

Thus, by the 1950s Milwaukee's inner city was in a state of crisis. The inner core was rundown, but the parts of town where African Americans had been allowed to settle just north and west of the city center were in far worse shape. During this decade more than 67 percent of homes occupied by African Americans were considered "unfit for use" or "in need of major repairs."[75] The African American community in Milwaukee also experienced dramatically higher rates of infant mortality, poverty, crime, and unemployment.[76] To escape these problems, those who could move did so, but owing to housing restrictions on African Americans the path of black movement out of the city was constrained. Many American cities were segregated racially, but Milwaukee was extremely so; some scholars have argued that the city was (and continues to be) "hyper-segregated" along racial lines.[77] This history of hostility to blacks meant that geographic racial segregation was acute, and there was not a lot of political capital to be earned by attending to the wants and needs of the black community.

One field director of the Milwaukee Social Security Administration warned that this stark segregation and the conditions within the black community would make urban revitalization particularly costly and complex in this city.[78] Yet revitalization of downtown was necessary for the same reasons considered by policy makers in other cities: a revitalized downtown could attract and retain businesses and industry, while better transportation to and from the city could promote economic activity, thereby boosting the tax base and vibrancy of the city.

In the mid-1950s urban renewal began under the guidance of socialist mayor Frank Zeidler, who warned against relocating minority groups from one "slum" area and crowding them into available housing only to create another "slum" in an effort to improve the city.[79] He also "expressed hope . . . that 'the conscience of the community' would not permit Milwaukee's urban renewal program to be stalled either because of hostility from 'special interest groups' or by fears that minority group problems would be increased."[80] Zeidler's foresight and concern were admirable, but, when it came time to actually implement redevelopment policies, familiar fights about land acquisition and relocation of those displaced by urban renewal yielded results similar to Atlanta, Kansas City, and other cities.[81]

Housing clearance policies proved instrumental in cementing the segregation of low-income black residents in the northwestern section of the city, which includes the case-study Silver Spring neighborhood.[82] Similar to what occurred in Kansas City, poor relocation assistance for displaced families was a key factor in limiting the opportunities for people to move elsewhere. But, and also similar to Kansas City, city officials chose to construct two very large public-housing developments in this part of the city, serving to further isolate and concentrate impoverished citizens.[83] Concurrently, people with the means to do so self-segregated on the east side of the city, including in the case-study Murray Hill neighborhood. Housing policy in Milwaukee repeated a familiar pattern of wealthy (mostly white) people relocating voluntarily, while poorer (mostly black) people faced compelled relocation with minimal assistance or concern shown by public officials regarding the locations where those displaced wound up.

Transportation policy also wound up exacerbating economic segregation in Milwaukee, as well as serving as a great source of frustration for residents in low-income neighborhoods. In the 1950s and 1960s, neighborhood residents waged intense battles over land acquisition for expressway projects. Prior to a Wisconsin State Supreme Court ruling in 1959, the City of Milwaukee was taking land from property owners, claiming it was vital for redevelopment, without any due process or process of complaint or inquiry into the request for the landowner. The ensuing legal battles over land use and acquisition slowed urban renewal plans to a near halt in the late 1950s and early 1960s.[84] Eventually, however, as had been the case in Kansas City, the supporters of highway development generally got the land that they wanted, while the former residents were left under-compensated and unsupported in their efforts to reestablish themselves elsewhere. Moreover, unlike the expansive boundaries of Kansas City, Milwaukee's city borders were not moved, and white flight to the suburbs was reinforced by freeway construction around the city designed to accommodate suburban commuters.[85]

Finally, the trend of concentrating poor and high-poverty African American families was accelerated in the 1970s due in large part to a general collapse of Milwaukee's industrial base and the general shift from heavy to service-based industries. This was a major economic realignment that was particularly hard for industrial cities like Milwaukee, in part because deindustrialization in heavily industrial cities decimated the tax base of the city, and made much of Milwaukee's subsequent urban renewal efforts focused on economic and community revitalization. Due to the continued economic struggles the urban-renewal policies that began in the 1950s in response to the "urban crisis" have continued throughout the twentieth century, as the "crisis" never abated.[86] Unlike Atlanta and Kansas City, neither of which primarily featured heavy industry as their economic base, cities like Milwaukee experienced tremendous economic decline that required constant attention to urban redevelopment. The city has struggled to attract new industries, coping with a relatively paltry tax base that has hamstrung policy makers as they have tried to revive the city.[87] Indeed, Milwaukee representatives continue to work at economic and community revitalization today, attempting to attract new economic powerhouses to their city and region.

Urban redevelopment policies and economic circumstances have concentrated high-poverty populations in neighborhoods north and west of the city. As with Kansas City, and unlike Atlanta, from the beginning the high-poverty and black populations of Milwaukee overlapped—or were perceived to overlap—and therefore the concentration and segregation that have occurred follows both racial and economic lines to a certain extent. Figures 2.9 and 2.10 show patterns of neighborhood poverty in the city, while Figures 2.11 and 2.12 demonstrate the residential patterns of African Americans. These maps reveal clear patterns of movement from the city center out

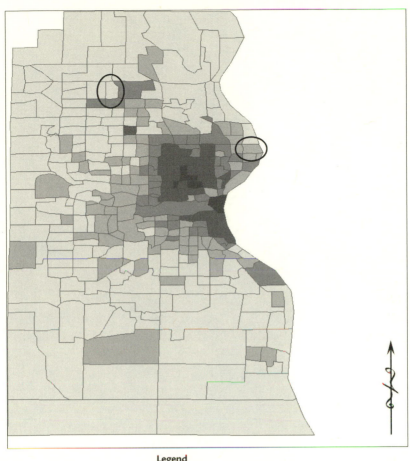

Figure 2.9. Neighborhood Poverty Rates in Milwaukee County, Wisconsin, 1970

Source: Urban Institute, and GeoLytics, *Neighborhood Change Database*, CensusCD neighborhood change database (NCDB) [electronic resource]: 1970–2000 tract data: selected variables for US Census tracts for 1970, 1980, 1990, 2000.

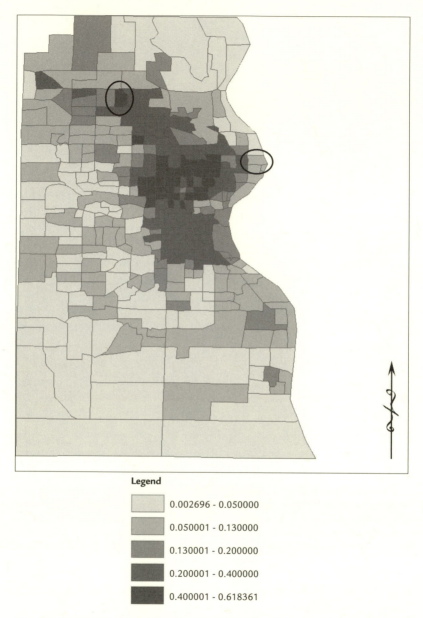

Legend

- 0.002696 - 0.050000
- 0.050001 - 0.130000
- 0.130001 - 0.200000
- 0.200001 - 0.400000
- 0.400001 - 0.618361

Figure 2.10. Neighborhood Poverty Rates in Milwaukee County, Wisconsin, 2000

Source: Urban Institute, and GeoLytics, *Neighborhood Change Database*, CensusCD neighborhood change database (NCDB) [electronic resource]: 1970–2000 tract data: selected variables for US Census tracts for 1970, 1980, 1990, 2000.

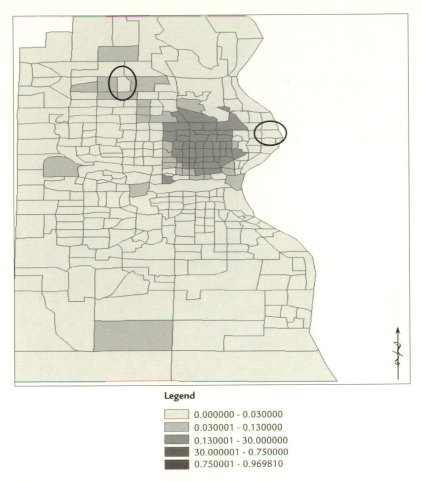

Legend

☐	0.000000 - 0.030000
▨	0.030001 - 0.130000
▨	0.130001 - 30.000000
▨	30.000001 - 0.750000
▨	0.750001 - 0.969810

Figure 2.11. Neighborhood Percentages of African American Residents in Milwaukee County, Wisconsin, 1970

Source: Urban Institute, and GeoLytics, *Neighborhood Change Database*, CensusCD neighborhood change database (NCDB) [electronic resource]: 1970–2000 tract data: selected variables for US Census tracts for 1970, 1980, 1990, 2000.

to the north and west of the urban core; though the populations do not overlap as neatly as in Kansas City—poverty encircles the city to the west, while the African American population is largely northwest of the city. The two case-study neighborhoods within this city are circled: the prosperous Murray Hill neighborhood is on the east side, and the impoverished Silver Spring neighborhood is in the northwest.

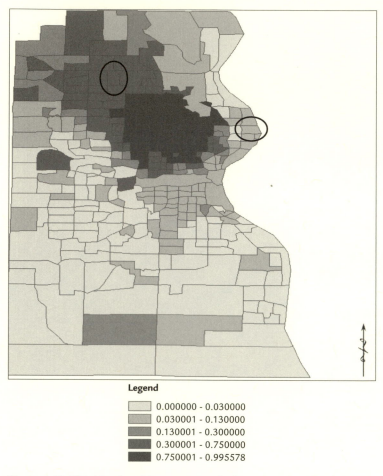

Legend

▢	0.000000 - 0.030000
▨	0.030001 - 0.130000
▨	0.130001 - 0.300000
▧	0.300001 - 0.750000
▪	0.750001 - 0.995578

Figure 2.12. Neighborhood Percentages of African American Residents
in Milwaukee County, Wisconsin, 2000

Source: Urban Institute, and GeoLytics, *Neighborhood Change Database*, CensusCD
neighborhood change database (NCDB) [electronic resource]: 1970–2000 tract data: selected
variables for US Census tracts for 1970, 1980, 1990, 2000.

This economic segregation has had dramatic effects on the civic environment of the low-income Silver Spring neighborhood as well as in the
prosperous Murray Hill. Table 2.3 details the economic, demographic, educational, and housing trends that have occurred within these case-study
neighborhoods. As is the case in the other case-study neighborhoods, eco-

Table 2.3. Economic, Housing, Demographic, Educational, and Unemployment Trends: Silver Spring and Murray Hill Neighborhoods, Milwaukee County, Wisconsin

Category	Silver Spring				Murray Hill			
	1970	1980	1990	2000	1970	1980	1990	2000
Total Population, Census Tract	3,633	3,005	3,079	3,193	2,151	3,183	3,495	3,306
% Below Poverty Line	4	21	35	48	5	3	2	6
% In High Poverty*	2	10	27	37	0	0	0	0
Average Wages and Salaries	$10,427	$16,364	$24,302	$24,596	$8,012	$29,442	$88,475	$113,350
Neighborhood Income Percentile	75	45	35	5	45	90	95	95
% Age 16+ Without High School Diploma	38	37	27	39	8	1	2	1
% With Bachelors/Graduate/ Professional Degree	3	4	6	2	51	62	71	77
% African American Population	3	29	64	75	2	6	4	5
% Latino Population	N/A	2	2	3	N/A	4	2	3
% In Different House from Five Years Ago	40	57	49	60	27	18	19	15
Number of Renter-Occupied Units	737	679	734	696	205	228	221	205
% Female-Headed Households	15	48	59	74	6	14	13	2
% Age 16+ Unemployed	21	22	32	29	25	15	10	11

Source: Urban Institute, and GeoLytics, *Neighborhood Change Database,* CensusCD neighborhood change database (NCDB) [electronic resource]; 1970–2000 tract data: selected variables for U.S. Census tracts for 1970, 1980, 1990, 2000.
* High-poverty is determined by calculating those living below 74.99% of the poverty line.

nomic status and educational attainment was very low and residential instability high in the Silver Spring neighborhood by 2000, while the opposite
was the case in Murray Hill. In 2000 the Silver Spring neighborhood had a 48
percent poverty rate, 39 percent of the people had not finished high school,
and 74 percent of the households were headed by single mothers. It is important to note that 75 percent of the Silver Spring neighborhood is black, but it
is also important to appreciate how economic indicators contribute to the
overall health of the civic environment.

The development and redevelopment that occurred in Milwaukee was
uneven and convoluted, and proceeded in fits and starts as in Atlanta and
Kansas City, which often introduced new and additional problems rather
than solving the problems policy makers set out to address.[88] And while
there were critics of Atlanta's and Kansas City's urban-renewal programs,
Milwaukee's urban-renewal efforts throughout the 1950s, 1960s, and 1970s
were widely regarded with suspicion by many city residents.[89] A large part of
this was undoubtedly driven by the perception that racial prejudice animated
urban policy decisions: African American arrivals during the Great Migration were severely constrained in their residential and employment opportunities owing to legally sanctioned racism. This is not to suggest that white
Milwaukee residents were more racist than whites in other cities but to note
that white racism in Milwaukee was especially effective at concentrating
poor blacks in particular areas, and the rapid decline of heavy industry had
a devastating effect on black workers and consequently on their neighborhoods. City officials choosing to erect large public-housing developments
in areas that were already densely populated with low-income residents only
increased the problem of economic and racial segregation in the city.

Milwaukee's particular history of racial exclusion may have shaped the
urban redevelopment projects, but the results remain the same as in Atlanta
and Kansas City: urban-renewal policies, especially regarding housing and
transportation, served to codify and later exacerbate the levels of segregation along economic lines. This concentrated more prosperous residents in
specific neighborhoods and made it easier for them to share and leverage
their resources, attitudes, and behaviors regarding civic engagement. Conversely, this also segregated and isolated poor people in separate and distinct
neighborhoods, which in theory could also have made it easier for them to
leverage resources, attitudes, and behaviors, but unfortunately in the latter
instance such close proximity serves to diminish rather than encourage

political awareness and participation, despite a clear need for concerted political action.

Rochester, Monroe County, New York

Founded in 1812 by Colonel Nathaniel Rochester, the city of Rochester, New York, quickly became a significant way station and port for trade in the growing region of upstate New York. Rochester grew into an industrial center, despite lacking access to traditional industrial resources, such as coal, or serving as a transportation hub, as the other cities examined here.[90] Instead, Rochester was able to grow based on the development of a few key businesses and industries. John Jacob Bausch, a German immigrant, started the Bausch and Lomb optical and eye-health company in 1853, while George Eastman patented his dry-plate photography process and founded the Eastman Kodak Company in 1888; finally, the Haloid Company, now Xerox, was founded in Rochester in 1906.[91] The presence of these successful companies helped attract immigrants, particularly skilled laborers, and to a certain extent growth begat growth; as more people arrived, the city grew to accommodate them, projecting an aura of a city on the rise.

Like countless other cities in America, immigrant groups from throughout Europe, especially Southern and Eastern Europe, arrived in Rochester in the late 1800s, followed by rural Southern blacks in the early decades of the twentieth century. Although cities like Detroit and Chicago attracted larger numbers of African Americans, Rochester's growing industrial base was attractive to black migrants. These new arrivals tended to settle just north of East Main Street and on the east side of the river, with large numbers of Italians settling there in the 1890s followed by African Americans in the 1920s and 1930s. At this time these neighborhoods were full of single-family homes, housed active commercial districts, and supported vibrant communities. Meanwhile, in an unfortunately familiar development, some of Rochester's "native" white residents resented the arrival of both Europeans and blacks, and by the 1930s suburbanization had begun to segregate the city along lines of race and ethnicity as well as class.[92]

As the housing stock began to age and as more African Americans moved in during the 1930s and 1940s, whites and also white ethnic residents began accelerating their flight to the surrounding suburbs as well as to other parts of the city. The swath of land north and northeast of the city became increasingly dilapidated, but restrictive housing covenants and legalized racial segregation made similar movement nearly impossible for black families who could afford it. Soon the number of people in the area strained the capacity of the neighborhood's single-family homes, and many were converted into apartments or multifamily units. In addition to living in this area of the city blacks were also concentrated in the Third Ward in the southwest quadrant of the city, but the population in the Third Ward had higher rates of homeownership, higher incomes, and higher levels of educational attainment, similar to the well-to-do blacks of Atlanta, and provided a striking early example of economic segregation even within the black community.[93] But even housing stock in the Third Ward began to show signs of strain by the late 1930s, and, like so many American cities, after World War II the urban core of Rochester needed renewal assistance.

As with Atlanta, Kansas City, and Milwaukee, the post–World War II era in Rochester was also a time of transition. Demographic shifts occurred in neighborhoods because African Americans continued to come to Rochester, drawn there by its still-thriving industrial base. This further strained aging housing stock, and new financial opportunities allowed those with means, white and black, to move to the expanding suburbs. The 1950 census found that "more than 72% of the dwellings in the City of Rochester were built before 1920," while this applied to just 14 percent of homes in the suburbs.[94] Moreover, the city lacked rental housing catering to moderate-income families, usually workers employed by factories in the area, which forced these families to move into already overpopulated, largely low-income neighborhoods and housing.[95] The key issue facing city officials in the 1940s and 1950s was housing: there was an overall shortage of housing, with much of the existing stock rundown and in need of repair, and there was inadequate housing for low-income residents in particular.

Early actions taken by officials focused on tearing down dilapidated single-family homes across the city and in particular in the Third Ward and neighborhoods north of the city, areas that form the shape of a crescent.[96] In addition to slum clearance Rochester embarked upon its first expressway development project during this time. Renewal and relocation policies helped middle-income families by providing homeownership incentives and opportunities to leave or rebuild blighted neighborhoods, which meant that a small percentage of middle-income African American families in these neighborhoods were able to secure housing for themselves, often moving to or remaining in the southwest, which developed into a stable community with higher housing values and a racially diverse population.[97]

But as in other cities, relocation of displaced families was dependent on the type of housing they could afford. For those families without already accrued resources, urban-renewal policies only served to concentrate them into one area by clustering new low-income housing options for poor, relocated families. In Rochester the near north and northeast became the site of this housing, most notably with the city's first high-rise public-housing project. Hanover Houses, which was located in the northeastern Baden-Ormond neighborhood, was often the final home for displaced low-income families from the southwestern and other northeastern neighborhoods during this time.[98] In 1952 Hanover Houses "was heralded as a milestone" for "exchanging dilapidated, under-heated, over-crowded and convenience-lacking quarters in a blighted area for a fine, new apartment with every facility at a much lower cost."[99] City leaders professed that the new housing development would improve the lives of low-income citizens and lead to a better neighborhood in the future.

Yet six years later, on June 8, 1958, the Citizens Advisory Committee to the Rehabilitation Commission published the Report of Survey of Hanover Houses and its residents. This report stated that not only had this neighborhood taken on harmful characteristics but that these were detrimental to residents: "Hanover Houses can scarcely escape the impact of its neighborhood and many of its problems arise from the environment, an observation substantiated by social workers, teachers and police representatives."[100] The most common comments in interviews with 326 tenants included poor maintenance, poor landscaping, unfair services or charges, uncontrolled vermin, poor tenant selection and regulation, unsatisfactory guard service, noisy tenants, no playground, overcrowded schools, and inadequate health care.[101] While these stories primarily document the physical conditions of Hanover Houses, one third of those interviewed by the Citizens Advisory Committee said they were dissatisfied with the neighborhood, suggesting the important relationship between physical environment and sense of community.

The conclusion of the Hanover Houses report stated that the Baden-Ormond neighborhood had become a problem that needed to be addressed. Not only were some tenants of the project critical of the area, but many residents of the neighborhood were critical of the project: "Of the 708 families surveyed in the area of the Rehabilitation Project, about 50% are probably eligible for public housing, but only 32 families or less than 10% of [those] eligible indicate[d] a willingness to move into Hanover Houses."[102] Despite these findings, the northeast quadrant, and increasingly the neighborhoods in the near north and northwest, remained the primary location of low-income, predominantly black housing in Rochester.[103]

This would continue to be the case throughout the twentieth century, as once Hanover Houses established the area as low income in the minds of city residents, people with other opportunities sought to live elsewhere, leaving behind a neighborhood that was geographically segregated along economic lines. Indeed, on January 24, 1970, a reporter from the *Democrat and Chronicle*, one of the two major newspapers in Rochester at the time, followed top city officials as they visited Hanover Houses and the surrounding community, reporting that they "wandered through the neighborhoods, down dark hallways lined with overflowing trash bags, into dingy apartments that hung heavy with cooking odors and sometimes the faint smell of urine."[104] Six months later the *Times-Union* editorial page articulated the crux of the problem in Rochester: the construction of affordable rental units did not keep pace with demand in the 1960s, and so low-income residents, racial minorities, and the elderly have been kept out of more suitable housing in the suburbs through exclusionary zoning as a result of "economic and/or racial discrimination."[105]

The advisory report on and journalistic accounts of Hanover Houses and the broader neighborhood throughout the 1950s, 1960s, and 1970s are particularly illuminating as they call attention to some of the ways that housing policy advanced not just racial exclusion but economic exclusion as well and to the way economic segregation affects a neighborhood beyond the aggregative effects of many low-income individuals living in one place. The social and physical environments are altered by the sheer volume of attendant consequences associated with concentrated poverty, which compose the civic environment necessary for promoting political mobilization and participation.[106] Figures 2.13 and 2.14 show the emergence of segregated poverty over time. There is a very clear pattern of segregated and concentrated poverty in the shape of a crescent, encircling the city to the north, which is why citizens and elected officials alike refer to the poverty-stricken area north of downtown as "the Crescent." The impoverished case-study neighborhood selected for analysis is in the Crescent and is referred to by itself as the Crescent in following chapters, while the comparatively

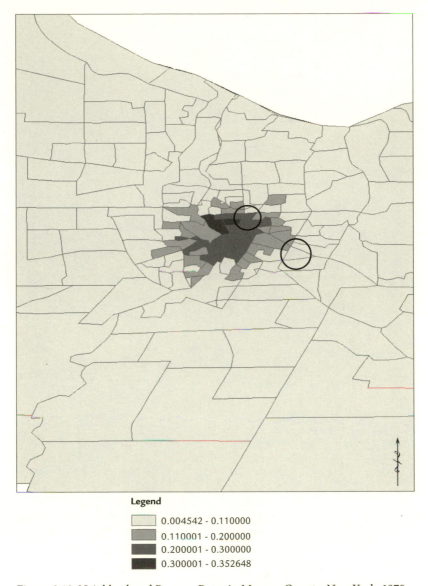

Legend

▢ 0.004542 - 0.110000
▨ 0.110001 - 0.200000
▨ 0.200001 - 0.300000
▰ 0.300001 - 0.352648

Figure 2.13. Neighborhood Poverty Rates in Monroe County, New York, 1970

Source: Urban Institute, and GeoLytics, *Neighborhood Change Database*, CensusCD neighborhood change database (NCDB) [electronic resource]: 1970–2000 tract data: selected variables for US Census tracts for 1970, 1980, 1990, 2000.

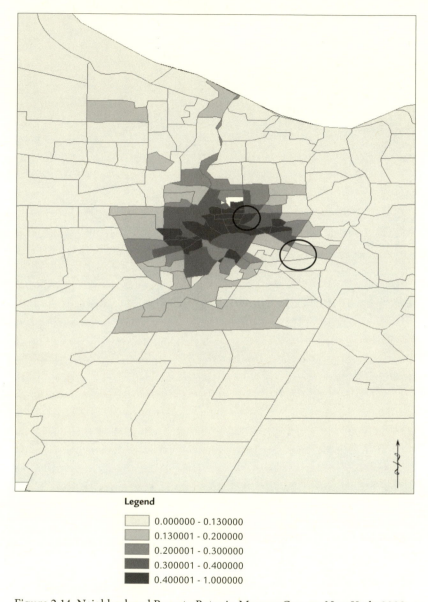

Legend

☐	0.000000 - 0.130000
☐	0.130001 - 0.200000
☐	0.200001 - 0.300000
☐	0.300001 - 0.400000
■	0.400001 - 1.000000

Figure 2.14. Neighborhood Poverty Rates in Monroe County, New York, 2000

Source: Urban Institute, and GeoLytics, *Neighborhood Change Database*, CensusCD neighborhood change database (NCDB) [electronic resource]: 1970–2000 tract data: selected variables for US Census tracts for 1970, 1980, 1990, 2000.

prosperous University neighborhood is in the southeast. This crescent-shaped swath of poverty emerges over time and is most clear in Figure 2.14, with the dark band of high-poverty neighborhoods creating a defined boundary between the poor in the northeast and northwest and nonpoor neighborhoods to the south, southwest, and southeast. The selected case-study impoverished Crescent neighborhood and the case-study prosperous University neighborhood are circled in Figures 2.13 and 2.14.

Figures 2.15 and 2.16 show that the residential pattern for African Americans is similar to the pattern of neighborhood poverty rates from 1970 and 2000, and also reveal a large black population in the southwest, as has historically been the case. Significantly, while there are greater concentrations of African Americans in the north and southwest, there are high numbers of blacks throughout the city and county, and the number of Hispanics in the Crescent is quite high, at 33 percent in 2000 (Table 2.4). Thus, when comparing Figures 2.14 and 2.16, it is clear that race and poverty are related in Rochester but that racial residential patterns do not directly overlap with economic residential patterns, indicating that racial and economic segregation are at least in some way distinct in Rochester.

These changes have resulted in concentrated poverty in the Crescent, bringing with it a decline in familial, social, and economic well-being, indicated by the number of female-headed households, high unemployment and residential mobility, low average wages and salaries, and low educational attainment (see Table 2.4).[107] Across town the University neighborhood has experienced rising incomes; high educational attainment, with 64 percent of the population holding a bachelor's, graduate, or professional degree in 2000; low unemployment; and low numbers of female-headed households. As has been demonstrated in the earlier examples of Atlanta, Kansas City, and Milwaukee, the effects of clustering people together in this way does more to the civic environments of these neighborhoods than scholars have appreciated, and later chapters will detail key ways that economic segregation affects the civic environments of communities and subsequent civic engagement by their citizens.

Conclusion

The history of these neighborhoods makes it clear that a number of factors reshaped urban America over the course of the last sixty years, including

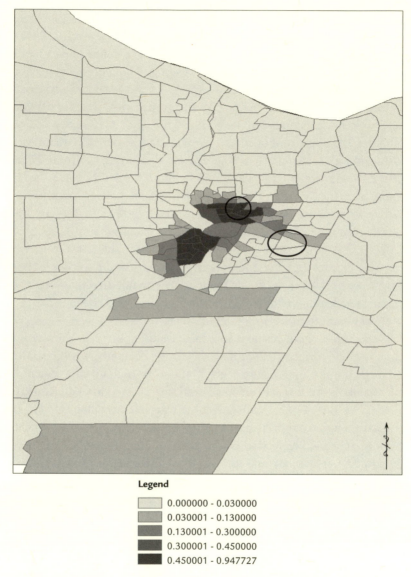

Legend

☐	0.000000 - 0.030000
☐	0.030001 - 0.130000
☐	0.130001 - 0.300000
☐	0.300001 - 0.450000
☐	0.450001 - 0.947727

Figure 2.15. Neighborhood Percentages of African American Residents in Monroe County, New York, 1970

Source: Urban Institute, and GeoLytics, *Neighborhood Change Database*, CensusCD neighborhood change database (NCDB) [electronic resource]: 1970–2000 tract data: selected variables for US Census tracts for 1970, 1980, 1990, 2000.

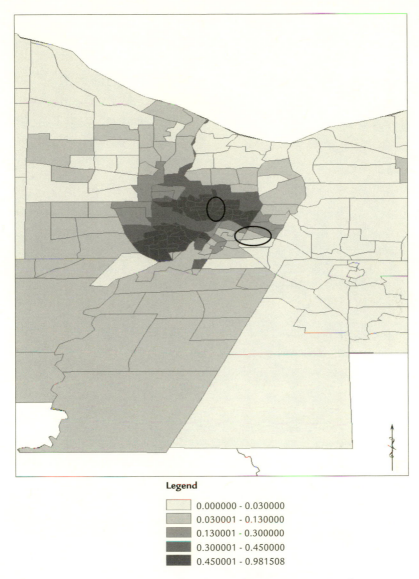

Legend

▢	0.000000 - 0.030000
▨	0.030001 - 0.130000
▨	0.130001 - 0.300000
▨	0.300001 - 0.450000
▆	0.450001 - 0.981508

Figure 2.16. Neighborhood Percentages of African American Residents in Monroe County, New York, 2000

Source: Urban Institute, and GeoLytics, *Neighborhood Change Database*, CensusCD neighborhood change database (NCDB) [electronic resource]: 1970–2000 tract data: selected variables for US Census tracts for 1970, 1980, 1990, 2000.

Table 2.4. Economic, Housing, Demographic, Educational, and Unemployment Trends: The Crescent and University Neighborhoods, Rochester, Monroe County, New York

Category	The Crescent				University			
	1970	1980	1990	2000	1970	1980	1990	2000
Total Population, Census Tract	3,492	2,116	1,645	1,560	3,078	2,618	2,537	2,217
% Below Poverty Line	21	38	57	62	7	4	8	8
% In High Poverty*	27	50	85	71	0	0	0	0
Average Wages and Salaries	$7,092	$12,641	$19,137	$40,465	$10,606	$19,631	$47,627	$57,561
Neighborhood Percentile	30	15	10	55	75	65	90	85
% Age 16+ Without High School Diploma	72	59	57	50	23	14	8	4
% With Bachelors/Graduate/ Professional Degree	1	0	1	5	28	40	57	64
% African American Population	49	63	72	66	2	2	4	3
% Latino Population	N/A	25	26	33	N/A	1	2	3
% In Different House from Five Years Ago	25	33	38	39	29	36	36	41**
Number of Renter-Occupied Units	672	466	477	403	785	1076	1059	952**
% Female-Headed Households	31	60	84	72	8	25	17	19
% Age 16+ Unemployed	32	45	58	45	35	34	27	22

Source: Urban Institute, and GeoLytics, *Neighborhood Change Database*, CensusCD neighborhood change database (NCDB) [electronic resource]: 1970–2000 tract data: selected variables for US Census tracts for 1970, 1980, 1990, 2000.

* High poverty is determined by calculating those living below 74.99 percent of the poverty line.

** It is important to note that part of this high number and rise in rental units on the wealthier side of town is the result of high-end condominium and mansion-conversion developments, many of which are rental units.

private realty interests, legal restrictions, zoning laws, and migration patterns. Yet it is also clear that urban renewal and transportation and housing policies cemented and often exacerbated (or exaggerated) the effects of these various factors, which ultimately altered the spatial arrangement of citizens and their resources in each of the case-study cities and neighborhoods highlighted here. Further, this spatial arrangement of citizens along economic lines ultimately altered the civic environments of these neighborhoods. The initial evidence of this transformed civic environment can be seen by simply looking at the sociodemographic characteristics of the people who lived in them. By 2000 the impoverished neighborhoods were filled with people with low incomes and low educational levels, less stable families, and other indicators that are typically correlated with lack of political participation. Conversely, the wealthy neighborhoods were filled with well-educated people who make more money and lived in more stable communities.

But there is more to the story than indicators like income or education level. Voting is an individual act, but it is one that can be encouraged or discouraged in particular ways. The economic segregation caused by midcentury land use and urban policies had civic and political consequences because it made it more difficult (in the impoverished areas) for voluntary associations and politicians to mobilize the citizenry, while at the same time making it easier (in the wealthy areas) for such mobilizing to occur. The segregated environments in which citizens live not only shape their day-to-day lives, determining in part where they work, live, and send their children to school, for example, but also shape citizens' civic environments. It is in neighborhoods where citizens develop the social networks vital for political mobilization and participation, where civic organizations operate and reach out to citizens, where political battles become real and tangible to citizens, and where politicians meet and greet their constituents. As neighborhoods change, the possibility for the type of healthy civic environment necessary for active civic and political mobilization may also change. I aim to explore exactly how in the following two chapters. Indeed, different levels and quality of civic and political mobilization in segregated, impoverished and segregated, prosperous neighborhoods may help explain different rates of turnout in these communities, the resulting different policies affecting each group, and ultimately the class gap within the American electorate.

CHAPTER 3

Economic Segregation and the Mobilizing Capacity of Voluntary Associations

During his visit to the United States in the 1830s, Alexis de Tocqueville famously noted that a defining feature of the American character was an enthusiasm for joining together in groups, from town-hall meetings and procedures of direct democracy to church communities working to address social concerns. The freedom to assemble is protected alongside the freedom to speak and worship in the First Amendment to the Constitution, and even in a nation that rewards individual initiative and prizes personal liberty, the propensity to come together in a voluntary, civic, or religious organization remains a distinctly American trait. Americans are more likely than citizens of most other countries to belong to voluntary and civic organizations, and this act of joining with others is an important way that Americans connect with one another and mobilize for civic and political action. It is not a coincidence that the world's oldest ongoing experiment in self-government has been maintained by a citizenry who has continually practiced the behaviors of and nurtured the attitudes to promote civic republicanism by joining local organizations to address problems in their communities.[1]

There are a number of civic benefits that individuals and communities accrue as a result of active participation in voluntary associations, church congregations, and community groups. Participation in these kinds of associations allows individuals the opportunity to express their interests, grievances, and hopes to their community and their elected officials, thus allowing these individuals to feel civically and politically efficacious. Participation in voluntary associations also instills in members habits of cooperation and public-spiritedness, as well as the skills necessary to participate in civic life more broadly. In other words, citizens gain both a sense of personal efficacy and a sense of community responsibility—one changes how an individual feels internally and the other changes how an individual engages in his or her community and society more broadly—making voluntary associations a kind of school or laboratory for practicing democracy.[2]

Voluntary associations also provide opportunities to develop social capital and trust among individuals. Belonging to a voluntary association allows individuals to embed themselves within social networks and gives them a sense of reciprocity. The process of seeing their own desires and actions put into practice over time promotes trust and creates connections between people who live among one another. This, in other words, creates a sense of civic virtue within individuals and communities, a sense of belonging and connectivity that remains strong because of the dense network of reciprocal social relations. Social trust and norms of cooperation are practiced by members of voluntary associations, laying the groundwork for later political action. Even churches, which gather people together around nonpolitical beliefs concerning spirituality, play a very important role in this regard. The sense of belonging, reciprocity, and communal concern that occurs within a church congregation helps nurture feelings of connectedness and civic virtue, while the act of attending church services and church events helps prepare citizens for volunteering and participation in the polity.[3]

In this way the existence of voluntary associations, churches, and civic organizations in a community provides a crucial foundation for participation in civil society. Without the social trust and norms of cooperation that these associations cultivate, the type of shared political action necessary for citizens to advocate for and protect their interests would carry too high a cost. Citizens would first need to identify like-minded individuals, build group trust, and develop and employ strategies of organization and civic action. If social networks predicated on shared interest and trust already exist, however, then most civic and political mobilization efforts can be built on top of these networks and the work of advocacy is made much easier. Voluntary associations and civic organizations help develop individual political efficacy as well as norms of civic responsibility, which are both important for community governance.[4] Yet, the civic environment of a neighborhood can promote or hinder the maintenance of strong associations and is in turn nurtured and maintained by the activities of these organizations.

Recognizing the vital role that voluntary associations play in helping citizens develop the practices and attitudes that lead to political participation addresses, in part, a question that has confronted political scientists for decades: why do people vote at all? The classic understanding of voter behavior is based on a formal decision theory model, and basically holds that the likelihood that one vote will determine the outcome of an election is low and therefore the cost of voting almost always outweighs the benefit.[5] Based on this decision model, voters should stay home, and yet many do not. Why do people turn up at the polls when in the most literal sense their vote makes no difference in determining the outcome of an election? Even if voter turnout in America is far below 100 percent, it remains somewhat astonishing that anyone bothers to vote at all.

There are several answers to this question. One explanation is that political mobilization by voluntary associations, political parties, and candidates running for office reduces the cost of participation and convinces individual citizens that their voices are important and should be heard at the polls. In other words, people participate because they are asked to do so, because they are convinced by someone—a politician, a minister, a local leader—that their participation is wanted and necessary.[6] Moreover, mobilization by voluntary associations, political parties, and other activists is key to encouraging political participation by augmenting the cost-benefit equation with both information and social goods. Many citizens simply do not have the time to conduct the necessary research to make sense of the various policies and candidate positions they are presented with in any given election. Voluntary associations, political parties, and individual candidates are useful conduits of information for citizens, making their research load lighter.

Citizens are also persuaded to vote because voting is viewed positively by others in their community, and many proudly sport their "I Voted" stickers hours after departing from their polling place. Conversely, citizens often think *not* voting is frowned upon, causing them to want to vote to avoid a perceived social stigma (or at least say they voted, which is one reason survey results often reveal higher levels of turnout among the American electorate than actually occur).[7] It is important to note that this way of thinking about voting suggests that the decision to participate is not simply an individual decision on the part of the citizen: the act of voting and the reasons for doing so are communal; are actively encouraged by organizations, associations, and political parties, and candidates; and are valued by society.

But if voting, the ultimate act of political participation, occurs because people are asked and encouraged to participate, we must try to appreciate a crucial additional piece of this process. The context within which citizens live conditions whether or not they are asked at all to participate and conditions their receptivity to that request. The next chapter will explore how efforts by politicians and political parties to engage with voters have been affected by economic segregation in cities, but this chapter will demonstrate how economic segregation circumscribes the capacity of voluntary and civic organizations, including churches, to mobilize for civic engagement. Residential segregation along economic lines has worked to deteriorate the civic environment in impoverished areas—or in the case of wealthy neighborhoods enrich the civic environment—and an important consequence of this is the degree to which voluntary and civic organizations can operate within these contexts. Because involvement by these types of groups helps cultivate and maintain the attitudes and behaviors that later lead to political participation by making it easier or harder for these groups to thrive, economic segregation actually contributes to the likelihood that a citizen will or will not vote.

The possibility that economic segregation may directly affect the mobilizing capacity of voluntary and civic organizations or mobilization efforts by political operatives, which is discussed later, remains poorly understood by scholars, policy makers, and lay citizens. Although explanations for declining levels of mobilization, volunteerism, and voting have been explored, the current consensus tends to focus on the rise of professionalism within political parties and civic organizations, with many scholars finding that rising professionalism inhibits participation in organizations.[8] Increased professionalism has increased levels of "checkbook participation": parties and activist groups actively cultivate financial contributions from individuals, and as a result most people only give money rather than time to support candidates or causes.[9] The rise of checkbook participation is assumed to explain why voters have become more detached from the political process and, concurrently, have been turning out to volunteer or vote in lower numbers. But most scholars who attempt to explain declining participation stop at this point, failing to consider the context of mobilization and the challenges those contexts might pose to effective civic or political mobilization.

An explanation that focuses on increased professionalism within political parties and voluntary associations fails to account for the crucial role that local context plays in shaping the activities of these organizations and their subsequent ability to create within individuals the sense of civic virtue that makes them more receptive to later appeals to participate, while those that do talk about the role of organizations often fail to account for

context in their stories of mobilization and participation.[10] Before a politician asks a citizen for money or their vote, that citizen has already been
prepared or conditioned to respond in particular ways because of their day-
to-day experiences in their neighborhoods and their involvement with their
local churches, civic associations, and voluntary organizations. The civic environment and the types of institutions that help create the civic environment of a community are profoundly affected by economic segregation, which
alters the ability of these institutions to operate. This study shows that in Atlanta, Kansas City, Milwaukee, and Rochester residential segregation along
economic lines worked to concentrate neighborhood characteristics that
promoted or hindered effective mobilization by voluntary associations, which
in turn shaped civic engagement and political behavior within these case-
study communities.

This chapter highlights local voluntary associations and churches, and
explores how the characteristics of economically segregated neighborhoods
alter the cultivation of community-level resources that could later be leveraged for civic and political mobilization within the eight case-study neighborhoods. By 2000 the four impoverished case-study neighborhoods were
populated by citizens who moved more frequently and had weaker family
structures, which harmed the development of social networks and trust
among neighbors and weakened community assets that supported networks
within these neighborhoods. Moreover, low educational attainment in these
neighborhoods combined with limited economic opportunities to diminish
economic assets and the pool of citizens with skills that could translate beyond the workplace into civic and political action. Finally, the public spaces
within segregated, impoverished neighborhoods were often contested areas,
with violence predominating in some communities and a general sense of de-
feat and despair permeating the atmosphere. Higher crime rates made neighborhood environments in segregated, poor neighborhoods relatively unsafe
when compared with other neighborhoods and prohibited neighbor interaction and the development of social trust.

This is particularly important to appreciate because mobilizing institutions rely on networks and neighborhood stability to spread information,
contact and attract citizens, and invite participation in meetings and protest—
and later, to vote on Election Day.[11] Organizations cannot do the work of mobilizing alone; they need networks and relationships within communities to
effectively use their resources. Isolated neighborhoods with high numbers of

impoverished individuals, physically segregated from other neighborhoods, make the work of churches and voluntary associations much more difficult by depriving them of these preexisting networks and relationships. Much as a farmer has a more difficult time coaxing plants to grow in thin, rocky soil, the cultivation of civic virtue and a thriving civic environment by local churches and voluntary organizations is made more difficult by thin social networks and volatile environments created by pockets of segregated poverty within cities. At the same time, segregated wealth isolates and concentrates these same sets of tools and assets, making mobilization easier in segregated, prosperous neighborhoods and helping maintain thriving civic environments.

When we think about the universe of civic and religious organizations broadly, it includes a great deal of variety, which means that in theory at the local level citizens could have diverse opportunities to participate. For example, in the middle of the twentieth century labor unions and professional, fraternal, and community organizations, including organizations ranging from chapter-based groups like the Elks, the Masons, and the League of Women Voters to neighborhood watch groups and parent-teacher associations (PTAs), were key components of civic life. Nearly 35 percent of non-agricultural workers were union members in the mid-1950s, the result of a surge of unionization following the Great Depression and World War II, while membership in eight of the largest professional organizations in the country as well as fraternal organizations and community groups reached their peak in the late 1950s and 1960s. Indeed, in the 1950s and 1960s PTA organizations were among the most popular organizations to join, with nearly 400,000 families a year added to PTA membership rolls between 1935 and 1960. Even church membership and attendance reached its peak between 1950 and 1960.[12]

These trends did not hold, however, and by 2000 all of these organizations had experienced a decline in membership. Yet many community-based organizations, such as neighborhood watch groups, PTAs, churches, and even racial and ethnic organizations, remain a part of the constellation of associations that work to recruit and mobilize community residents. These associations remain relatively active even while others have faded from community life, most notably fraternal organizations, or have shifted to "associations without member," relying on the check- and letter-writing capability of members rather than grassroots efforts.[13]

Among the hardest hit by declining associationalism, though, have been labor unions, which have lost density, both in absolute terms and in terms of geographic presence and strength. Only 9 percent of all private-sector workers were union members in 2000, and this decline in union strength can be seen within specific communities. In my effort to map associational life in the segregated, prosperous and segregated, impoverished neighborhoods of interest here, unions did not emerge as particularly important, as told by those interviewed, and the data support this. Union membership was higher than the national average in 2000 in Milwaukee, with a 14.6 percent membership rate among private-sector workers, but in the other case-study cities union membership rates among private-sector workers were on par with or below the national average: Atlanta had a membership rate of just 4.4 percent, Kansas City had a membership rate of 9 percent, and Rochester had a membership rate of 5.6 percent. Because of the declining importance of unions, the data and the findings presented here focus instead on community- and neighborhood-based organizations and churches.[14]

Figure 3.1 shows the number of organizations existing in 2000, organized by type, across the four impoverished and the four prosperous case-study neighborhoods.[15] Impoverished communities had more instances of ethnic and racial clubs, but generally, in terms of sheer number, prosperous communities benefited from greater associational presence. Prosperous communities had more types of organizations than impoverished communities. In addition to the types of organizations the two communities had in common, prosperous neighborhoods also had professional organizations, advocacy groups, and veteran associations. Even health and social-service organizations in prosperous communities outnumbered those in the impoverished case-study counterparts, as did advocacy organizations, despite the fact that segregated impoverished communities and their residents are arguably in greater need of social services and advocacy.

The raw numbers of organizations in the prosperous and impoverished neighborhoods in 2000 make it clear that the wealthy neighborhoods had higher levels of associational activity. This chapter seeks to understand why this might be the case, arguing that segregated wealth creates conditions that make it easier for such associations to survive, while segregated poverty creates conditions that make it more difficult for them to do so. The urban-renewal, transportation, and housing policies enacted in Atlanta, Kansas City, Milwaukee, and Rochester during the 1960s and 1970s created neighborhoods segregated along economic lines, altering three important charac-

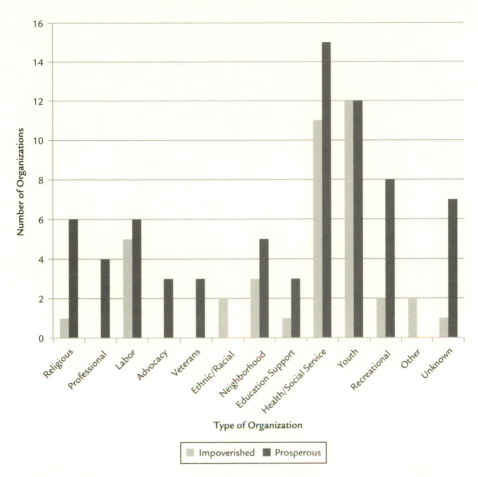

Figure 3.1. Organizations in All Eight Case-Study Neighborhoods by Type, 2000
Source: InfoUsa.com

teristics within these neighborhoods that created conditions that affected the organizing and mobilizing capacities of local associations, churches, and organizations.

If Joe Soss and Lawrence R. Jacobs are correct in suggesting that residential segregation determines to some degree the nature of the class gap in American electoral politics, it is possible that the effect of economic segregation on mobilizing institutions contributes to the phenomenon of the increasing gap in turnout and political power between economic classes.[16] This chapter draws on census data and, perhaps most important, qualitative evidence from structured, open-ended interviews with local leaders conducted in each of the eight case-study neighborhoods, although it should be noted that all names of organizational and church leaders have been changed to protect their confidentiality.[17] The evidence presented here paints a clear picture of similar neighborhood attributes developing across all four of the case-study cities, attributes that are necessary for promoting organizational capacity and mobilization, including stable families and communities, social and economic assets, and open and accessible public spaces.

Local civic, church, and community leaders in all of the case-study neighborhoods give specific examples of the ways in which residential segregation helped or hurt their efforts to organize and mobilize members of their communities during the 1980s, 1990s, and early 2000s. Their observations serve to reinforce the idea that voluntary associations are important for the development of social capital and civic mobilization but underscore the importance of context and local circumstance in determining their effectiveness at doing so. In this sense these findings build upon and advance our existing knowledge that voluntary associations are important for mobilization and civic engagement by demonstrating how the civic environment of the voluntary associations actually conditions the work that these organizations can do.

Voluntary Associations and Mobilization in Segregated Neighborhoods

The civic lives of many communities across the country are driven by the organizations that are housed in, that work in, and that care about these communities. The types of work and organizations within communities can vary greatly—from racial or ethnic clubs, to veterans groups, to social service and advocacy organizations, to neighborhood groups and PTAs, to churches and other religious associations. And the work that these various groups do might change from community to community based on need, even if they are a similar type of group. For example, one community organization I visited in the Silver Spring neighborhood of Milwaukee focused on after-school programming for its youth and on drawing in families of children through educational programming, while a community organization in Rochester's Crescent neighborhood focused on broader social-service provision and support, helping area residents navigate enrolling in benefits they were eligible for or providing community forums to address neighborhood concerns. In fact, the focus on providing a safe space for educational opportunities in Milwaukee and providing a welcoming and informative staff to help neighborhood residents in Rochester shows the important role these organizations play in simply providing open and accessible space, even while addressing different community needs.

As the data show, different types of organizations, and in some cases a more diverse array of organizations, existed in segregated, wealthier neighborhoods, in part because the social and the economic assets of these communities provide the base to support other efforts. There were more churches and religious organizations in the segregated, prosperous communities, and more organizations in general willing to participate in this study. The reticence to participate in this study exhibited by organizations in the segregated, impoverished communities hinted at a key problem that was ultimately revealed in the investigation here and that is a profound problem facing these communities: the trust required to maintain a robust civic environment within these types of communities is weak or nonexistent, making communication with outsiders seen as suspect and communication within the neighborhood difficult to sustain in order to develop strong social networks.

The data and interviews presented here indicate that in all four of the case-study cities, three specific neighborhood-level resources highlighted in this brief consideration of associational life were necessary to allow voluntary associations to flourish and mobilize neighborhood residents, creating the conditions for a healthy civic environment. First, stable families and stable communities, including the number of long-term residents, strong family units, and deeply rooted social networks, provide organizations access to existing networks of citizens. Low-income communities are often plagued with rental housing, absentee landlords, and poor code enforcement, producing high residential turnover and decreasing residential stability. This instability makes the work of mobilizing institutions much harder to accomplish.

Second, social and economic assets, reflected by the demographic compositions of neighborhoods, including levels of employment and educational attainment, help promote familial and residential stability while also providing neighborhoods with key resources necessary for participation, specifically time, money, and skills.[18] If the residents of a community have more time or money, or both (as the result of employment and education), the cost of joining, volunteering for, or donating to an organization goes down, while the skills learned through formal schooling and employment can be used in the civic arena. Wealthier, better-educated people have more time, money, and skills to contribute than poorer, less-educated people, and thus voluntary organizations in wealthy neighborhoods are able to solicit higher levels of participation from members of their communities.

Third, open and accessible public spaces are important components of civic environments. It is crucial that public spaces exist for community members to congregate, socialize, and ultimately meet to express and address grievances. Voluntary associations are important as a mobilizing tool, but they operate within physical neighborhoods; the relative safety of those neighborhoods helps dictate how people behave within them. Without neighborhood safety the likelihood of neighborhood residents accessing these organizations and engaging in civic life declines.

All three of these factors that constitute civic environments combine dynamically to create the conditions within which voluntary associations can work to nurture the civic environment of and foster civic engagement within communities. Improving any single feature on its own does not necessarily provide a significant boost to the overall environment. For example, a neighborhood could have long-term family residents but a crime rate so high no one leaves their home. Even if the housing component of a neighborhood would seem to make it inviting for voluntary associations to operate, the lack of safe public spaces would mitigate any advantage gained by residential stability. A neighborhood needs to be stable and safe, and have at least some social and economic assets among its members in order for local associations and groups to survive and thrive. As demonstrated in Chapter 2, the segregated conditions in each of the four case-study cities and eight case-study neighborhoods were created in specific ways based on local conditions, but the experience of local organizers in all four cities were remarkably similar, revealing that these three factors are crucial if the civic environment is going to thrive.

Stable Families and Stable Communities

In the 1960s the Thomasville Heights neighborhood of Atlanta was established as a low-income and working-class neighborhood with eighty-one homes, populated by residents displaced by downtown urban-renewal projects. Thomasville Heights began as a community with few services, minimal landscaping in public areas or even around homes, and only a handful of street signs. And yet the neighborhood was safe and the families were stable and optimistic, excited about owning their new homes. These families worked together to beautify the area and to organize the Thomasville Heights Civic Club; and they lobbied to secure mail service, a satellite library branch, and a recreation center for families and children in the neighborhood. Residents were active in civic organizations, maintained strong social networks, successfully advocated for increased services and facilities, and even successfully protected their neighborhood against expressway encroachment; in the 1960s the city wanted to build a six-lane highway through the area, but the residents organized so that the route of the expressway was moved, the number of lanes reduced to four, and a retaining wall built to protect against noise.[19]

The neighborhood began to change in the 1970s as public officials in Atlanta continued to struggle with how to address blight in the urban core and chose to develop low-income housing in this area for other city residents displaced by more recent blight clearance and other renewal projects. This meant that large numbers of poor people were relocated to the neighborhood and surrounding area, and the housing stock was ill-equipped to handle the new arrivals. As part of the relocation process the city constructed more apartment buildings, replacing some of the single-family homes that had previously existed. The new residents tended to be younger, with fewer family ties and less in common with the family-dominated community that had thrived in the 1960s.[20] Speaking about the evolution of his neighborhood over time, Leroy Perkins, former longtime president of the Thomasville Heights Civic Club and still active member, said, "[Of] course you know, the kind of houses we got now [we] haven't always had, you know, because the city's just packing us in."[21]

As the original homeowners from the 1960s aged and moved out throughout the 1980s and 1990s, their owner-occupied homes were often converted into rental properties.[22] The number of rental units in this neighborhood increased by 78 percent between 1970 and 2000, while owner-occupied units declined by 40 percent over this same period, a trend made possible because of zoning laws that permitted this type of rental housing in some parts of the city and forbade it in others. The Thomasville Heights neighborhood also saw a dramatic increase in the proportion of female-headed families with children under the age of eighteen, growing from 9 percent in 1970 to 72 percent in 2000, contributing to instability in this community. Indeed,

Perkins lamented that the young women in the neighborhood were "nothing but bab[ies] trying to raise a baby."[23] Moreover, in the year 2000, 32 percent of residents in this neighborhood had changed residences in the last five years, further demonstrating the lack of stability in the community. This changing demographic composition and housing in the neighborhood increased the number of low-income residents and decreased the number of stable families.

These demographic changes in Thomasville Heights as a result of broad economic shifts and relocation projects over the last several decades worked to erode the familial and social networks that once had thrived, making it difficult for organizations like the Thomasville Heights Civic Club to tap into existing, strong relationships. According to Perkins, by the turn of the century the Civic Club had fewer members, fewer funds, fewer volunteers, and therefore less political clout to advocate on behalf of the neighborhood.[24]

Likewise, the demographic makeup in 2000 in the impoverished case-study neighborhood in Kansas City, the Ivanhoe neighborhood, reveals a similar level of family and community instability. In Ivanhoe this is illustrated by the number of female-headed families with young children, which was 24 percent in 2000, and in the number of rentals in the community, in part determined by city land-use policy. Gloria Miller, the head of the Ivanhoe Community Organization, explained that "we need to increase our home ownership. We have 45 percent home ownership and 55 percent renters and we have been told that you need have to about 70 percent [home ownership] in order to really stabilize a neighborhood."[25] The concern among neighborhood leaders in high-rental communities is that the more rental properties a low-income neighborhood has, the more likely their residents will be transient because of the difficulty many have meeting monthly financial obligations, such as rent and utility bills, which makes it very difficult for organizations to recruit and maintain active membership and participation.[26] Despite Miller's knowledge and efforts, by 2009 the Ivanhoe neighborhood was estimated to have 72 percent rentals among occupied housing units, a figure that seems likely to continue to remain high or, worse, climb.[27]

While in the Thomasville Heights neighborhood in Atlanta the obstacle of age came as a result of increasingly younger heads of households dominating the neighborhood family units, one of the problems in the impoverished Silver Spring neighborhood in Milwaukee has been the increasing numbers of elderly residents raising their grandchildren. Eric Bryant, the director of the Northwest Neighborhood Network in Silver Spring explained that "parent involvement pieces [in educational programs] are kind of hard," as "a number [of residents] are caring for their grandchildren."[28] The challenges facing grandparents raising children are different from those facing young parents. Many grandparents are retired and have even fewer financial resources and less energy and ability to care for a child than younger parents, particularly when the child is young. Voluntary associations in this community have yet to figure out the best way to encourage participation among an overburdened elderly population, let alone successful strategies for mobilizing the resident population around civic or political issues.[29]

In addition to an increase in the aging population raising young children, Silver Spring has also undergone a dramatic increase in the number of female-headed families with children under the age of eighteen, up from 13 percent in 1970 to 70 percent in 2000, and in residential mobility, with 60 percent of Silver Spring residents having moved (at least once) within the last five years in 2000, up from 40 percent in 1970. As a result, one pastor of a church that serves the impoverished Silver Spring neighborhood faced similar challenges in getting people involved in his church because residential mobility was so high in the community. While he had been pastor of Union Baptist for only nine years, he noted the difficulty for the church to maintain a close connection with residents in the neighborhood because the rate of residential mobility and turnover was so high. Explaining the consequence of this, Pastor Benjamin Paisley said "the relationship we have within our community is not as good as it could be" because he cannot sustain long-term relationships with neighborhood residents and therefore few neighborhood residents are longtime congregants.[30]

Indeed, many of Union Baptist's members now come from other, wealthier parts of the city and suburbs. The church is still predominantly black, as it has been throughout its history, but it now draws a middle- and upper-middle-class black population that drives in from the suburbs or from other, more upscale parts of Milwaukee. This is not the relationship that Pastor Paisley wants with his community. He appreciates having congregants, and the disposable income of some of his church members allows them to support the church in ways that many local residents cannot. But this is a variant on the problem of "checkbook participation," and this does not help Pastor Paisley connect with the transient and economically disadvantaged people who live in the immediate vicinity of his church. The residential instability and general community decline has made recruitment difficult and outreach and mobilization nearly impossible.

Weakened families, the changing composition of households, and residential mobility also affected who participates in neighborhood civic life and the ability for organizations to maintain contact and mobilize residents in the impoverished community of Rochester. When asked about who participates in her organization, Tamara Thompson, president of the Crescent Tenants Association, responded with "mostly women," explaining "we don't have any mens who live here. It's mostly single-family housing, apartments with women, not too many men. We have, maybe, two or three or four maybe that's got a mother and father, but most of the household contains mothers."[31] The data bear this out; in 1970, 28 percent of households were female-headed households with children under the age of eighteen. This statistic peaked in 1990 at an astonishing 80 percent and then dropped to 58 percent in 2000, which is still quite high.

Thompson connected the presence of single-parent households to residential stability by saying that these women and their families "come and go" in Crescent Housing, which she says plays a part in their lack of interest in the organization: "Some have never heard of the tenants' association, so they don't know what it's all about. We try to keep them updated, like when somebody move in we try to introduce ourselves to the tenants and stuff . . . but we don't get to know the parents as good because they flip over so much." To encourage participation in the association's meetings, the group offers food and babysitting, "but they still don't come." Indeed, the number of single-parent households and the difficulty of raising kids as a single parent make it hard for Thompson to attract any interest in the tenants' organization at all. Thompson sounded weary as she continued: "Yeah, we try everything we can to get them to come out, but they just don't seem to show no interest in it."[32] Despite the fact that civic leaders in this impoverished neighborhood believe that their organizations contribute to neighborhood stability, the problem of transiency makes it difficult for these associations to contact and mobilize the residents in their community because the population is in constant flux.[33] As one head of a neighborhood organization put it, "If I register a hundred people in this community, a month from now at least fifty of those people will no longer be at the address."[34] This high residential turnover, in part shaped by the type of housing built in the Crescent as a result of city housing and land-use policy, makes organizing and mobilizing for civic or political activity extremely difficult.

Another way residential mobility hurts mobilizing capacity is by weakening social trust and social capital in impoverished neighborhoods. The demographic shifts and residential mobility in the Crescent neighborhood of Rochester make it difficult for residents to form the types of social networks that build social capital, which can aid in group mobilization and translate into civic and political engagement. When Thompson spoke about the children in the development and whether residents of Crescent Housing felt comfortable talking to one another about their children, or whether residents would feel comfortable talking to the children directly, she said, "There'd be a lot of fights around here if you did that." Drawing on the phrase made popular by Hillary Clinton, "it takes a village," Thompson went on to say that "one village can raise a child, that thing . . . that don't work around here."[35] The high residential mobility of residents in this neighborhood diminishes the likelihood of talking to one another or developing strong social networks. This hinders the ability of social networks and friendships to form, which in turn affects the possibility for organizations to draw in new participants and maintain effective civic mobilization.

As in Milwaukee, another challenge in this neighborhood is that many elderly are raising children. This makes it hard to attract a large number of older residents to participate, those who traditionally have the time to do so, because they are busy raising kids. Harriet Taylor, president of the Crescent Neighborhood Association, explained that she has raised four grandchildren: "They all are grown now but one. It's a job to raise grandchildrens after you done raised yours." While Taylor has remained active in her community despite extra parenting duties, her comments indicate that this is not common, making it nearly impossible to promote participation and organize for civic or political activity. Indeed, when asked about how often her group meets, Taylor said, "We ain't had no meetings lately because there ain't enough of us to have a meeting." The demographic and household shifts that have occurred in this neighborhood over time have dramatically altered the stability of families and the larger community, and therefore have decreased the ability of organizations to hold regular meetings, let alone more sophisticated civic or political action around issues facing the community.[36]

Across all four of the impoverished case-study neighborhoods, local organizers sounded a similar refrain: there has been an increase in numbers of rental properties, female-headed (or grandparent-headed) households, and younger residents that has occurred as a result of urban-renewal, housing, and transportation policies, and the displacement and dislocation that followed have made it increasingly difficult for local associations to function.

The work that civic associations, churches, and other organizations might be able to do to improve the lives of people in their community is made more difficult by the effects of residential economic segregation and isolated poverty. However, the effects of residential economic segregation and isolated wealth produce precisely the opposite result. Organizers in the four wealthy case-study neighborhoods enjoy circumstances that are markedly different from their colleagues in these poor neighborhoods.

For instance, in contrast to Leroy Perkins in Thomasville Heights in Atlanta, on the other side of town, Shirley Jackson, president of the West Manor Civic Association, told a different story. There are some similarities between the origins of the two neighborhoods, but the trajectory and the long-term success of Jackson's neighborhood and its organizations have been very different. In the 1960s West Manor was originally home to ambitious young African Americans who were "educators or, if they weren't educators, they worked for the post office" or held some other government position. Like Thomasville Heights, the West Manor area was filled with single-family homes, and local residents were organized and active. West Manor residents initially came together in their Civic Association "to be able to know things that was happening in the city" and also for the purpose of neighborhood beautification. As with Perkins, Jackson noted that the physical appearance of the neighborhood was very important, and the Civic Association worked "to keep the environment [the] way it still is, because it's always been kept up very pretty."[37]

Crucially, the urban redevelopment projects that prompted low-income residents to move to Thomasville Heights did not direct a similar flow into West Manor, in part because of neighborhood activism in the area.[38] On the contrary West Manor became more and more entrenched as a wealthy black enclave during the latter decades of the twentieth century. In 2000 this neighborhood was still composed of moderate to large single-family homes that were 88 percent owner occupied; there were no apartments and very few rental homes. Those that did exist were single-family homes that had been vacated by aging parents and converted to rentals by their children.[39] Moreover, the majority of the households were occupied by strong family units; as of 2000 West Manor contained half the number of female-headed households with young children than in Thomasville Heights, and only 15 percent in West Manor had changed residence within the last five years (see Table 2.1). Because many of these residents have lived in the neighborhood for many years, and the new families moving in were stable and intent on staying in the neighborhood, the community sustained strong social relationships among neighbors.[40] The presence of stable families in the neighborhood created an easily accessed network of family and friends, a supply of skilled organizational leaders and volunteers, and money for dues and other activities. These neighborhood features have allowed the West Manor Civic Association and other organizations to continue working to maintain stable social networks, robust community assets, and safe public spaces, creating an environment that was both aesthetically pleasing and civically robust.

Meanwhile, in Kansas City, although the prosperous neighborhood of Union Hill actually had a relatively high rental rate of 66 percent in 2000, the trend was toward more homeownership. Christopher Ingram from the Union Hill Neighborhood Association explained that the neighborhood had experienced a great deal of development during the 1990s and 2000s so that by the early 2000s the neighborhood ownership rates were up and rental rates were trending down. In fact, the estimates from the 2005 to 2009 American Community Survey conducted by the U.S. Census bear this out: by 2009 it was estimated that 55 percent of households in the Union Hill neighborhood were owner occupied, while 45 percent were rentals, an important residential shift driven in part by Kansas City's housing and land-use priorities and permitted by the city's zoning laws. The Union Hill Neighborhood Association did whatever they could to encourage and accelerate this change by recruiting active members and strengthening the capacity of their organization.[41]

By the early 2000s they had a core group of fifty residents who were active and "show[ed] up to the meetings all the time" and who were willing to pay dues and volunteer time.[42] This group was double the reported size of the crosstown Ivanhoe Community Organization. Community change in Union Hill spurred cohesiveness and organizational strength because of new home-ownership opportunities, which increased stability. Housing development in this community strengthened the organization and increased the necessary conditions to support mobilization of neighborhood residents, while housing policies had the opposite effect in highly segregated, impoverished communities.

The importance of both stable families and communities for creating a healthy civic environment within neighborhoods is clear when talking to civic leaders and when looking at the data in Milwaukee. Danielle Hines, the president of a PTA in a school serving the prosperous east-side neighborhood of Murray Hill, explained that the city and her neighborhood have changed a lot: "Pockets of the city have really improved. Some of that is spreading. . . . There's a lot of neighborhoods that used to have big lake housing, like this [one]. . . . A lot of those homes are being bought and rebuilt by, you know, upper-middle-class young people." She explained that it has not been hard for her to get parents, including new, young parents, involved. She simply sends an e-mail to all parents and has never had trouble finding volunteers or getting parents to a meeting. This is not surprising given that in 2000 female-headed households with young children, which tend to be more resource strapped, were just 2 percent of households in the neighborhood, and only 15 percent had moved in the last five years (see Table 2.3). The key to encouraging participation by parents, according to Hines, is that "you have to be open to what they want to be involved in doing. . . . Part of it is just being flexible."[43] It seems that this flexibility, though, is only possible because of the luxury of stable families and the stable community surrounding the school.

Presidents of neighborhood associations, PTAs, and churches in the Murray Hill community repeatedly commented on the ability to recruit and mobilize their members around community issues. Indeed, Reverend Christopher Williamson of Christ Church commented on how demographic changes to his and his church's neighborhood have translated into increased resources and increased community power, which is quite the opposite from the sentiments expressed by Pastor Paisley in the impoverished Silver Spring community. One of the changes the Murray Hill neighborhood experienced was that the families moving in were younger and upper-middle class, resulting in families purchasing homes with the intent to stay, supporting the point made by Hines, who also lives in the neighborhood. As a result, both Reverend Williamson and Hines have found increased motivation to participate in their organizations and to push their organizations to become more actively engaged in the wider community.[44]

Reverend Williamson found his growing congregation to be actively engaged, with a greater movement away from "pocketbook justice, where there was a focus on what we give in money, to a more effective engagement in issues."[45] Therefore, not only did membership increase in this congregation as a result of growing residential population, stability, and vitality, but the ways in which congregants participate changed as well. Christ Church is predominantly a neighborhood church and Williamson is able, willing, and driven to organize and mobilize his congregation around community and political issues. While he noted the racial and class differences between his church and others in the city—89 percent white, with 65 percent holding advanced degrees—the tone of optimism was notable when compared with Pastor Paisley's across town.

The prosperous community in Rochester mirrors many of these same trends, with active and engaged residents. However, because of the distinct, historic nature of the neighborhood, the types of housing and dominant concerns in this neighborhood were different from the other cases. Patrick Logan, president of the University Neighborhood Action Network, explained that the community is actually relatively diverse with regard to housing type, with high-end single-family homes, moderate- to high-end condominiums (often in the old mansions that dot the neighborhood), and rentals occupied by young, upwardly mobile, trendy twenty-somethings. Indeed, the data bear this out: in 2000, 67 percent of housing in this neighborhood comprised occupied rentals. Interestingly, this does not suggest economic diversity, as the mix of rental and owner-occupied housing often does; in 2000 the median income was over $68,000.[46] However, Logan did note that property owners were more likely to participate regularly in his organization, with anywhere from twenty-five to fifty members in attendance at any given meeting. Moreover, these residents tend to be motivated by issues of historic preservation, zoning, and maintaining the vibrant, unique culture of the community. When issues pertaining to these concerns arise—for example, when Wegmans wanted to build a grocery store in the neighborhood—meeting attendance was regularly well over a hundred.[47] It should be noted that civic leaders in this community seemed to recognize the importance of their work, not just for the neighborhood but for the residents as well; Pastor Jeanette Keane noted that community work, speaking particularly of the work her church does for the impoverished residents of Rochester, establishes in "the hearts and minds of young people" the importance of civic and voluntary engagement.[48]

The effects of these local conditions have been almost entirely overlooked by previous studies of local associationalism. Yet it seems that segregated, impoverished neighborhoods have increasingly found themselves populated by very young and much older residents overburdened by financial and familial obligations, while the population of segregated, prosperous neighborhoods seems generally to be a combination of older, married couples and new, younger stable families. If segregation of impoverished communities has made it harder to mobilize residents and promote civic and political activity because of the concentration of unstable and weak family units and unstable communities, organizations in prosperous neighborhoods have found a stable base of mobilization in their older, married residents and newer, younger families because they have the resources to be civically engaged—those resources that are freed up as a family moves toward greater stability, namely, time, money, and skills. This allows neighborhood residents to get to know their neighbors, and as a result these residents are more easily mobilized for civic and political activity.

Social and Economic Assets

In addition to stable families and communities economic segregation has affected the social and economic assets in both impoverished and prosperous neighborhoods. Social assets include the inclination and opportunities for neighbors to socialize, while economic assets mean more than just income; this refers to all features of a community that generate economic benefits, including educational attainment and employment-unemployment rates. It might not seem obvious at first how educational attainment and low unemployment help foster a healthy civic environment, especially since employed residents may spend many hours a day at jobs physically removed from their communities. But the skills one gains with higher levels of education and employment are skills that transfer to the civic arena; indeed, inequalities in civic engagement "derive not only from differences in motivations but also from differences in access to the resources of time, money, and *skills that facilitate activity.*"[49] The accumulation, or amelioration, of these kinds of skills in neighborhoods helps create civic environments in which these assets combine to promote stable, well-resourced, and robust networks and organizations within neighborhoods, which are important for civic engagement.[50]

The nature of community life in the prosperous West Manor neighborhood in Atlanta was and is more social than the crosstown impoverished Thomasville Heights, with residents coming together for different types of social gatherings, ranging from summer barbecues to Christmas parties to Easter dinners. The presidents of the West Manor Civic Club and the West Manor Block Club both said that the social gatherings coordinated by their associations are vital for the civic and political work of each organization.[51] Social events allow neighbors and their families to get to know one another, which makes the type of grassroots mobilizing that small organizations engage in, including spreading information through the use of phone trees or door knocking, more successful because neighbors are more likely to take time on the phone or open the door if they know the person calling or knocking. In West Manor this kind of familiarity exists; as the president of the West Manor Community Organization commented, "We all went to school together, and now we all live together."[52]

Moreover, as of 2000, 42 percent of residents in West Manor had a bachelor's degree or higher, and another 26 percent had some college experience, including having earned an associate's degree, with just 2 percent not having finished high school. It makes sense then that the median family income in West Manor was $69,219, a level of prosperity that helps promote stability and investment in the community.[53] Further, residents in West Manor are older, with 65 percent of the population over the age of twenty-five and more than half of that group falling between the ages of thirty-five and fifty-four. Research has shown that this age group is more likely to participate, especially if they possess greater resources, which we know they do, so that when a pastor from a "prominent church" near the West Manor neighborhood that draws primarily from the surrounding communities "call[s] it from the pulpit, then we're on it."[54] Taken together, many of the residents of West Manor have known each other for quite some time and socialize together, and many go to church together. These dense social networks are important assets of the West Manor neighborhood and make mobilization easier for community organizations and churches.

Similar types of socializing occurred in the Union Hill neighborhood of Kansas City, though these activities reflected the interests and inclinations of the neighborhood residents; events in this community ranged from garden and home shows to block yard sales and cookouts.[55] While the median family income of Union Hill in Kansas City is not extravagant, at $51,875, 57 percent of the population had a college degree or higher in 2000.[56] While there was no similar account of a call to arms by Ingram of the Union Hill Neighborhood Association, as in Atlanta, the type of work these neighbors do together, coupled with the regular and regularly attended formal meetings, provide for a tight social network that can be tapped for civic and political causes. When these types of social assets are coupled with the economic assets embedded within these communities, the civic and political clout of these neighborhoods increases.

Comparable educational and economic features exist in the prosperous neighborhoods in the other case-study cities. Murray Hill, in Milwaukee, was teeming with college graduates in 2000; 77 percent of residents had a college degree, professional degree, or graduate degree. There were no teenage dropouts, and just 1 percent of the adult population was without a high school diploma. And these residents were thriving: the median family income in Murray Hill was $101,826. In Rochester the University neighborhood enjoyed a median family income of $68,068, a 78 percent employment rate, and 64 percent of adults had a bachelor's degree or higher.

But if segregation helped cluster together individuals with social networks and assets that make organizing easier in the prosperous areas, the effects in the impoverished areas were devastating. The Civic Club in Thomasville Heights, in Atlanta, occasionally tries to use social events to reach out to members of the community, but interest is generally low.[57] This is likely due in part to the fact that 52 percent of the residents in this neighborhood were under the age of twenty-five in 2000, and a full 71 percent of that population was under the age of fifteen. Young people are much less likely to participate in civic life, and so when half of your neighborhood population is under the age of twenty-five, and the vast majority of that group is younger than fifteen, it is not surprising that engagement is low.[58] Moreover, educational attainment in Thomasville Heights is very low, with only 4 percent of residents in the neighborhood holding a bachelor's degree or higher in 2000 and 41 percent holding no high school diploma. Finally, the unemployment rate was quite high in 2000, at 44 percent.[59] Perhaps unsurprisingly then, the median family income in Thomasville Heights in 2000 was $14,703, well below the poverty line, which was $17,463 for a family of four at the time.[60]

Deindustrialization and economic segregation also damaged economic ties in Atlanta. While there was once a thriving General Motors plant in southeastern Atlanta, it is now a vacant building that has been empty for twenty years. According to Councilwoman Carla Smith, the city council representative for the district that encompasses Thomasville Heights, when the plant was operational, it employed many from the neighborhood, creating the opportunity for dense economic and social networks to form—the types of networks that organizations could tap into for civic and political mobilization. When the plant closed and new populations moved into the neighborhood as a result of cheap housing in the area, the collapsed economic base combined with the changing demographics to weaken the once strong economic and social ties among residents in Thomasville Heights.[61] This is just one example of how a confluence of factors—the closing of a factory and policy decisions to build housing and relocate people to a particular area—can combine and over time dramatically alter the civic environment of a neighborhood.

Part of this is the result of decreased shared economic experiences. While this is not obviously important to the associational and civic life of neighborhoods, George Lawson of Holy Trinity Ministries in the Crescent neighborhood of Rochester revealed why this might matter and how economic segregation has altered this aspect of the environment in many impoverished neighborhoods. When talking about the Crescent neighborhood in Rochester, he said, "These neighborhoods were Kodak people. They worked that way [pointing], and they worked that way [pointing], but it was only three miles either way. The commute was shift work and as Kodak dried up, so have the jobs."[62] Sharing shifts with people in the neighborhood at a common place of employment allowed neighbors in this one-time working-class community to meet each other, share rides, share child-care responsibilities, share free time, and maybe even belong to a union together. Kodak, along with Delphi, "were big manufacturing plants that used to employ thousands of people, and that doesn't happen anymore. So as these organizations [corporations] have lost their vitality, so have these neighborhoods lost some of their vitality."[63] As a result, in addition to the economic resources lost because of plant closings, the sense of bonding in these impoverished neighborhoods also declined because shifting employment opportunities have weakened the economic and social ties that came about because of these shared work experiences.[64]

Similar patterns of depleted economic and social assets occurred in the segregated, impoverished communities of Kansas City and Milwaukee. In 2000, 43 percent of sixteen- to nineteen-year-olds were neither enrolled in nor had graduated high school in the impoverished Ivanhoe community in Kansas City, while 28 percent of the adults, those twenty-five and over, also had no high school diploma and no residents had a bachelor's degree or higher. It is not surprising then that 43 percent of those sixteen and older were unemployed and that the median family income was just $12,500 in that same year. In Milwaukee the numbers are similarly grim: in 2000, 17 percent of sixteen- to nineteen-year-olds had not graduated high school, and 43 percent of the adult population had not either; just 2 percent of residents in the Silver

Spring neighborhood had a college degree or higher. Milwaukee also demonstrates a striking disparity of income levels between the wealthy and prosperous neighborhoods: the median family income in the wealthy Murray Hill neighborhood was $101,826, five times that of the median family income in the Silver Spring community.[65]

Consistent with an emergent issue facing the other impoverished communities in this study is the fact that both impoverished communities of Kansas City and Milwaukee also have many young residents. Indeed, in these communities residents under the age of twenty-five far outnumber older residents; 43 percent of the population in the Ivanhoe neighborhood in Kansas City is under twenty-five, with more five- to nine-year-olds than any other group. This number goes up to 59 percent in the Silver Spring neighborhood of Milwaukee.[66] The presence of large numbers of young children in communities that are also struggling with weak family units, unstable neighborhoods, and poor economic prospects produces a situation in which many of these youth are left to fend for themselves, which in turn affects the nature of the public space in these neighborhoods.[67]

These same problems of depleted social and economic assets exist in the Crescent community of Rochester as well, where in 2000 half of the residents were under the age of twenty-five and nearly half of this population ranged in ages from five to fourteen. Moreover, the median family income in the Crescent was just $14,432 in 2000, 45 percent of the residents were unemployed, and 55 percent of adults had no high school diploma. Compounded by the residential instability of the largely female-headed households in this neighborhood, general interest in organizational participation is quite low. Tamara Thompson said that she struggles with recruiting participants and volunteers to help with social events, such as an annual barbecue, explaining that usually just she and her vice-president put events together, when events happens at all. When a picnic does happen, tenants are so uninterested in meeting their neighbors that parents often "just send their kids out to get food and go back into the house."[68] Social and other organizational events are hard to have in Crescent Housing, in part because the youth living in the development scare the adult residents and, as we know, there are many of them but very few checks on their behavior. This issue will be explored in depth in the following section about open and accessible public space, but it is important to see how it bears directly on the development of social networks by preventing social interactions from occurring in the first place.[69]

These data and stories tell us that as households in impoverished neighborhoods became fractured and neighborhoods less stable, the social networks necessary for civic and political mobilization have also frayed, and the economic assets that could be leveraged to support civic action and engagement have deteriorated. This has occurred while the social networks in prosperous neighborhoods are stronger and easier to tap into, particularly because of the larger number of older residents and stable families and because the economic assets in these neighborhoods are more abundant and easier to deploy in the civic arena. This supports and strengthens voluntary associations in segregated, prosperous communities and weakens voluntary associations in segregated, impoverished ones. As a result, the ability of mobilizing institutions to promote civic engagement among segregated, impoverished residents has declined. This is not the case in prosperous neighborhoods, where economic segregation has increased the concentration of these assets, which strengthen the mobilizing capacities of voluntary associations there.

Open and Accessible Public Space

If stable families and communities and social and economic assets are to promote healthy civic environments and civic engagement, there must be space for these neighborhood features to coalesce and converge in public. In other words, there needs to be open, accessible, and safe public spaces where neighborhood residents can come together—to socialize, to talk, to air grievances, and to develop action plans to address those grievances. This space can come in many forms, from buildings that house civic organizations and churches to sidewalks and street corners, parks and playgrounds, and other aspects of the physical neighborhood environment. Accessible, open, and above all safe public spaces are crucial if organizations and associations are able to develop, grow, and thrive.

Indeed, while the presence of organizations is important in promoting an active civic environment, the physical environment itself is also crucial. The streets must be safe enough so residents actually go to or engage with neighborhood organizations. Of course, as Jane Jacobs said, "A city sidewalk by itself is nothing. It is an abstraction. It means something only in conjunction with the buildings and other uses that border it."[70] And yet, as Jacobs also notes, city sidewalks are the primary landscape of spontaneous urban interaction, including nefarious or at least threatening acts. The task of creating safe city or safe neighborhood sidewalks and other public spaces falls to community police, individual neighborhood residents, and in some neighborhoods neighborhood watch groups.

Because of the nature of urban living and the spontaneous interaction that occurs on city streets, a safe neighborhood environment is a key aspect of civic environments identified by residents of the case-study communities as necessary for promoting and maintaining civic engagement. The importance of safe neighborhoods for strong civic environments and voluntary associations may seem obvious at first. However, it is important to examine how safety is understood by residents of neighborhoods and what it means for voluntary associations, particularly in segregated, impoverished areas, as neighborhood safety is generally not a concern among those organizing in the prosperous communities. The role that economic segregation and public policy play in promoting safe neighborhoods makes the story even more complicated.

In the case of Thomasville Heights in Atlanta, for instance, the 1980s was a particularly bad decade for the neighborhood: "What really give the community a hard time was drugs in the community." The "drugs, dope dealers coming and going," all of this "really took its toll. . . . That's when it got out of control and it was, ooh, it got rough."[71] After that, many residents in the neighborhood grew afraid to even leave their homes. When residents are fearful to leave their homes and they do not feel as though the city is responding to their concerns, it is difficult to socialize or organize for civic or political action.

When discussing neighborhood safety, Gloria Miller, executive director of the Ivanhoe Community Organization, made the connection between policy and safety; she pointed out that transportation policy in Kansas City dictated property acquisition and land clearance for the South Midtown Freeway–Bruce R. Watkins Drive, which began in the 1960s. However, because of legal battles construction on the expressway in her community did not begin until the 1990s, which meant that the Ivanhoe neighborhood had a large swath of vacant land running through the middle of it for many years before construction began. The effect of this on the community was significant, not just because the vacant lot sat undeveloped for so long but because of the public-safety issues that emerged as a result. The land "became a broken window for this neighborhood. . . . It became an area where people who wanted to do criminal activity would gather, and from that, that decay, disorder, fear, everything, kind of, in my mind emanated from that."[72] Another community organizer stated the problem for the Ivanhoe neighborhood most clearly: "In fact, I would say safety and education are the primary factors we lack."[73]

As a result, the Ivanhoe Community Organization, which was organized in opposition to expressway development, had to shift focus to begin addressing issues in the neighborhood that emerged as a result of land clearance for an expressway that took thirty years to build; chief among those concerns was neighborhood safety. When asked about organizational participation as a result of changes to the neighborhood in the 1970s and 1980s, Miller said, "There just wasn't much, and because of all the crime and other symptoms of helplessness, people were not coming out of their houses. They were afraid."[74] Miller spoke primarily about the deleterious effect of drugs on the community—drug houses, drug trade, and the violence that accompanies this enterprise—stating that by 2000 her neighborhood had the highest crime rate in the city.[75]

Crime was an overriding feature in the Silver Spring neighborhood of Milwaukee by the late 1990s and early 2000s as well. Two different community leaders warned of violent crime in this neighborhood, explaining that the criminals in the community were quite "sophisticated," setting up lookout and warning systems if police approached and preventing "snitching" through violent and coercive tactics. As a result, waiting on a street corner to meet someone or just walking around was deemed too risky by these neighborhood insiders, even in broad daylight.[76] If crime and criminal activity prevent "the trust of a city street," which "is formed over time from many, many little public sidewalk contacts," then "the sum of such casual public contact at the local level . . . a feeling for the public identity of people, a web of public respect and trust" can never form.[77] Consequently, neighborhood safety not only affects the ability to mobilize neighborhood residents; it affects the development of social capital as well.

Tamara Thompson of Crescent Housing Tenants Association in Rochester tries to organize a social event every year for residents of the housing development. However, a challenge she has faced in recent years is the fact that "there's a lot of kids" in the development. When asked why this would present an obstacle, she explained, "There's some bad kids living in these projects," and this has gotten worse over time. Thompson has lived in Crescent Housing for twenty years and said that the children are more violent than when she first moved to Crescent Housing.[78] Pastor Martin Jefferson of Second Baptist Church, also in the Crescent, agreed that the neighborhood has "changed tremendously," explaining that when he was growing up "we had, first of all you had a fear for your parents because you knew if you disobeyed you knew what was going to happen. So now, that seems to have gone out the window. . . . If there's no obedience in the home, there will be no obedience in the church and the streets."[79] These characterizations of the neighborhood together paint a picture of large numbers of fearless youth deterring adults from leaving their homes in this impoverished community in Rochester, which is supported by the fact that 50 percent of the residents are under twenty-five, with 48 percent of those between the ages of five and fourteen. As a result, community leaders are unwilling or unable to organize the types of events that foster the development of social capital and trust, and, when they do, residents are often unwilling to attend.[80] This diminishes the likelihood that social trust among neighbors will form, which is essential for developing the types of relationships necessary for mobilizing citizens around civic and political issues.

Owing to the upscale nature of segregated, prosperous neighborhoods, the residents of these communities only speak about crime to note that it is not a problem. Patrick Logan, a community leader in the University neighborhood of Rochester, made clear that his neighborhood "has never been a neighborhood where there was high crime. Traffic has been an issue. New businesses come in," bringing "their issues," or "if somebody was going to be doing something to their home, or one of the big apartment buildings was going to be making some changes and they weren't complying with preservation guidelines," then the organization would get involved. Traffic, congestion associated with new businesses, and historic preservation topped the list of problems for this community.[81] William Howard, the head of the West Manor Neighborhood Council in Atlanta, mirrored this sentiment; while there was the occasional petty crime in his neighborhood, he said that West Manor was generally a safe neighborhood that received a great deal of assistance from the police when anything did occur.[82] This allowed his community to be proactive and focus on advancing its needs and desires. So, while a lack of security can diminish organizational infrastructure, social capital, and skew issue saliency toward quality-of-life concerns in impoverished communities, increased safety and security in prosperous neighborhoods allows for the community to advocate for resources and can even increase attention on "postmaterial" concerns, such as traffic and historic preservation.[83]

Conclusion

Taken together, we can see that economic segregation deeply affects the ability of voluntary associations and churches to recruit and mobilize neighborhood residents around civic and political activity. Data and interviews with community leaders living in segregated, prosperous and segregated, impoverished neighborhoods in Atlanta, Kansas City, Milwaukee, and Rochester reveal the dynamics of this relationship and how changes to neighborhood civic environments alter civic mobilization. The findings presented here provide one part of the explanation for why the class gap in participation has increased in American politics, as well as why civic and political engagement may be so low among low-income citizens and so high among prosperous ones. As income inequality has risen dramatically since the 1970s, and the wealthy have been able to increasingly isolate themselves in segregated communities, the prosperous seem also to be benefiting civically: economic segregation isolates and concentrates resources derived from high levels of education, employment, and stability, promoting vibrant civic environments and organizations that can magnify the voice of the wealthy. A similar, negative cycle emerges in impoverished communities, with economic segregation isolating and concentrating formally uneducated, low-skill and unemployed, and low-income populations, thereby weakening civic organizations and muting the voice of the impoverished.[84]

Key sources of this transformation were urban-renewal policies, including local housing, economic revitalization, zoning, and land-use policies, which changed the landscapes and environments of inner-city neighborhoods, especially in impoverished communities. Three specific features of neighborhoods are particularly important in understanding how economic segregation shapes civic environments, active civic engagement, and ultimately political behavior. In other words, in addition to individual resources, an analysis of these neighborhoods shows that the presence of voluntary associations alone may not be enough to mobilize neighborhood residents to participate in civic and political affairs, as other scholars have suggested.[85] Instead, the evidence presented here indicates that specific neighborhood attributes are necessary to support and maintain the organizational and mobilizing capacity of voluntary associations within neighborhoods.

First, as capable and willing as the young and the aged may be, nontraditional families often lack the economic and social resources that promote *stable families and communities*, while residential mobility in impoverished communities destabilized entire neighborhoods. Demographic changes and deindustrialization have undermined *social and economic assets* within segregated, impoverished communities, and these changes further undermine stable families, social networks, and strong economic ties, which are vital for maintaining a vibrant civic environment and active organizational mobilization. Finally, *safe neighborhood spaces* are important for fostering feelings of security, so that neighborhood residents are willing to attend neighborhood meetings or social events, and feelings of social trust, so neighbors are not afraid to talk with one another.

Without some combination of all three elements civic environments that foster the social capital and trust necessary for promoting the associationalism required for civic engagement cannot develop. Put another way, while research shows that associationalism promotes the creation of social trust and social capital, some level of stability and trust must exist within communities for associations to grow and thrive in the first place, and this is affected by residential economic segregation. The three conditions identified here create a neighborhood's civic environment and support (or hinder) strong voluntary associations and promote (or suppress) mobilization.

As the evidence suggests, however, economic segregation weakens these neighborhood attributes in impoverished communities and strengthens them in prosperous neighborhoods, which in turn seems to translate into increased neighborhood political power and policy response from the city. This exacerbates already low levels of participation among low-income residents by virtue of living in segregated, impoverished communities, while promoting increased participation among the already participatory residents in segregated, wealthy communities. Thus, economic segregation alters the structure of civic environments, thereby weakening organizational capacity and mobilization efforts in segregated, impoverished communities while simultaneously strengthening the resources and civic environments of and mobilization efforts in segregated, prosperous neighborhoods. This civically alienates already economically and socially alienated populations in highly segregated, impoverished neighborhoods.

The next chapter explores the political implications of these trends by examining how candidates and other political operatives mobilize residents and voter turnout in economically segregated communities. The problem of declining civic mobilization within segregated, impoverished communities has effects beyond supporting vibrant civic organizations; it also shapes whose voices candidates hear in the political and electoral arenas, thereby contributing to the ever-widening gap between the rich and the poor in the United States.

CHAPTER 4

Economic Segregation, Political Parties, and Political Mobilization

Citizens learn and practice some of the important building blocks for political participation by way of their involvement with voluntary associations, and residential segregation along economic lines diminishes the ability of community organizations to recruit and mobilize neighborhood residents in impoverished communities, while in prosperous communities these same types of organizations thrive and often flourish. But while organizations are vital for promoting civic engagement, levels of political participation are also more directly influenced by political parties, political operatives, and candidates. In a democratic republic, where citizens choose delegates to serve as their representatives, the relationship between elected officials and the public is crucial. Elected public servants must listen to and understand the needs and desires of the people they represent, while those represented must articulate their wishes and monitor how well their representative is performing. This reciprocal relationship is affected by residential economic segregation in much the same way as the efficacy of voluntary associations: politicians and political operatives are better able to mobilize and respond to the desires of individuals living in prosperous enclaves, while such mobilization and communication is much more difficult in impoverished areas.

Traditionally, political scientists have studied the effects of political mobilization on voting behavior by examining this relationship through an institutional lens, focusing on political parties in particular. This argument is based on analyzing the role that parties have played and continue to play in mobilizing and admitting citizens into the electoral process. This is a historical process that has changed over time, as parties have grown and adapted to different circumstances and performed this function in different ways.[1] In the early twentieth century parties engaged in a number of tactics to win elections, only one of which was getting voters to the polls and which often involved voters voting multiple times. Generally speaking, political corruption in the late nineteenth and early twentieth centuries prompted a series of reforms grounded in ideas of "good government," first taking hold at the city and state levels and gradually resulting in constitutional amendments like the direct election of senators and women's suffrage. Electoral rigging, ballot-box stuffing, and other suspect practices that political parties engaged in during the Gilded Age were addressed during the Progressive Era through reforms like off-cycle elections, primary elections, voter registration, the secret ballot, and discouragement of patronage by clarifying the professional qualifications for holding jobs in the public bureaucracy. Over time the parties adapted to these changes and have continued to play a large role in the political process, but most scholars accept that a certain amount of "dealignment," or declining partisan identification, among the American electorate has occurred as a result, producing a political system that is decidedly more candidate centered than it once was.[2]

In this reconfigured political landscape candidates more than parties have become the focus of campaigns.[3] This is true at the national level, where large numbers of voters are registered as Independent, and at the state and local levels, where elections for many offices are explicitly nonpartisan. Even in local elections where party affiliation is identified, politicians articulate specific policy preferences and discuss certain issues in order to create a personal political philosophy designed to resonate with the local electorate. The positions they take, the blame they assign, and the credit they claim are all designed to actively court constituents and seek out supporters.[4] As such, political candidates and campaign workers speaking for them on the campaign trail play a very important role in mobilizing the citizenry; their appeals to, or indifference to, individual voters or groups of voters helps cultivate, or alienate, the sense of civic connection felt by these citizens. A striking example of this can be seen in the downward trajectory of voter turnout and mobilization efforts; as political mobilization has decreased during the past few decades, so too have voter-turnout levels dropped.[5]

Yet as political campaigns and political parties have become more adept at using computers and other forms of technology, they have been able to target with increasing accuracy the message of the candidate(s) to different constituency groups. Shopping habits, cultural consumption of radio and

television programming, church affiliation, and other such social characteristics can combine to predict with startling accuracy the kinds of political
appeals that will work for certain voters.[6] However, even the most sophisticated microtargeting, which occurs mostly in national elections by candidates
with sufficient resources, still requires candidates to undertake the most important kind of mobilization effort: face-to-face contact and an ask for a
vote. Other efforts, too, like placing signage, advertising locally, distributing
literature, and otherwise creating awareness of and connection to a particular candidate, have to take place within the physical environment of a neighborhood. This is especially true for local-level elections, like for city council
or mayor, where the candidate-centered framework is crucial for understanding how people get elected to these offices. Mobilization at the neighborhood level occurs, if and when it does, by candidates and campaign
operatives, not by political parties, and it is important to consider how local
mobilization strategies work within specific contexts.

Assessing the likelihood, efficacy, and consequences of political mobilization by political operatives within segregated, impoverished and prosperous neighborhoods is logistically challenging. The eight segregated case-study
neighborhoods in Atlanta, Kansas City, Milwaukee, and Rochester were chosen by analyzing data on segregated poverty and wealth, but to appreciate
how political mobilization occurs within these specific neighborhoods, more
qualitative methods are necessary. Open-ended interviews with elected officials, city representatives and staff, and neighborhood leaders begin to tell
the story, and archival records and newspaper accounts of campaigns, elections, and other important political moments over the past half-century help
provide further details and context.[7]

One key finding that becomes clear from considering these sources is
that not much political mobilization occurs within highly segregated, low-
income neighborhoods. This seems to be an important factor in the decline
in political participation among low-income citizens. Economic segregation
has created a situation where significant resources gaps have emerged across
different types of neighborhoods, with fewer resources and assets in segregated, impoverished communities and more resources and assets in segregated, prosperous ones. This allows candidates and elected officials to
alter the political calculations they use when determining whom to mobilize because the resources that compose a neighborhood's civic environment are strengthened or weakened by economic segregation, especially, as
discussed in the previous chapter, the neighborhood associations that are

key assets within communities and that often serve as megaphones for neighborhood concerns and interests.

As neighborhood context and civic environments alter the capacity of voluntary associations within economically segregated neighborhoods, the ability for campaigns and politicians to mobilize residents through traditional civic channels within these communities changes as well. This further confounds the ways in which different interests or groups of people participate in the political system and the coalitions that drive local politics because political mobilization and participation vary as a result of different economic contexts.[8] Ultimately, this sets up a cycle of weakened civic environments, diminished civic capacity, and lower political participation that further promotes weak civic environments in segregated, impoverished communities and cycles of strong civic environments and high levels of participation in segregated, prosperous ones.

This chapter discusses the consequences of residential economic segregation for the political life of segregated neighborhoods by focusing on two specific factors. First, it is important to appreciate how economic segregation shapes the calculations political candidates and elected officials use to determine whom to mobilize. Politicians are always compelled to make efficient use of their limited time and resources, and patterns of segregation change the way candidates think about how to spend their money and effort. This leads to a second important factor: the degree to which this kind of decision making alters which ideas and interests are represented in urban politics. As politicians focus their efforts in certain areas, a virtuous cycle develops in prosperous areas: citizens get accustomed to having their needs addressed, which demonstrates clearly the benefits of continued engagement and participation. Conversely, in impoverished areas citizens get accustomed to neglect from elected officials, which obscures the possible benefits of engagement and depresses participation further. As a result, a virtuous cycle (in the prosperous case-study neighborhoods) and a vicious cycle (in the impoverished case-study neighborhoods) can be clearly observed in the voter-turnout results in Atlanta, Kansas City, Milwaukee, and Rochester.

Elected officials are rational seekers of reelection, which requires them to focus resources on key constituents who will put them in office. By recognizing the patterns of economic segregation within a city, political operatives are able to ignore not just individuals with fewer resources but entire neighborhoods. This has two repercussions: it allows for the alienation of entire communities by not representing their needs and therefore not delivering much-needed city services, and, because contact by elected officials promotes civic learning and civic engagement, diminished contact as a result of this segregation actually diminishes civic learning opportunities among a population that is arguably most in need of a political voice. In this way economic segregation not only residentially isolates impoverished citizens but politically alienates them as well, suggesting that economic segregation is a key contributor to the growing class gap in participation and representation in American politics.[9]

Political Mobilization in Segregated Neighborhoods

Although a great deal of research demonstrates that mobilization is important for encouraging political participation, the relationship remains poorly understood. Most significantly, while studies of Get Out the Vote and on-the-ground mobilization efforts exist, the specific actions that help increase voter turnout need to be further examined.[10] How exactly, for example, do parties and candidates relate to constituents? What are the mechanisms of mobilization? And, crucially, for the purposes of this study, how is this relationship shaped by the context in which the citizen lives? This last question is most important because much of the research about party and candidate mobilization focuses on congressional or state-level campaigns, and uses only public-opinion polls or National Election Study surveys to examine their claims. This approach obviously obscures how parties and candidates actually relate to and mobilize constituents on the ground and at the local level, thereby missing key parts of civic learning and contact within neighborhoods and civic environments, as well as glossing over how residential patterns matter for understanding party and candidate mobilization. If, as the saying goes, all politics is local, it seems important for scholars interested in political mobilization to try and understand how this occurs locally.

Political Calculation and Mobilization in Context

Discussions with elected officials and community leaders suggest that an important part of why political participation may be declining, especially among the least advantaged citizens, is because economic segregation prompts candidates and elected officials to alter the political calculations they use when determining whom to mobilize. Put simply, elected officials or their representatives and community leaders in all four of the impoverished case-study neighborhoods said that they believe segregated poverty diminishes the returns on mobilization efforts and therefore diminishes the likelihood of mobilization. As noted earlier, this creates a vicious cycle of indifference on the part of both officials and their constituents: as officials ignore groups of impoverished citizens, those citizens quickly (and correctly) come to assume that their representatives are uninterested in their concerns or in providing assistance, which further alienates the citizens and makes them more suspicious of government and politicians. It is important to note that this cycle begins when pockets of segregated poverty are created. The creation of these types of neighborhoods weakens the civic associations, churches, and other organizations that serve as crucial links between the citizenry and politicians, as politicians typically rely on these organizations as an entry point into neighborhood organizing and mobilization. Once a politician concludes that it is not worth his or her time and effort to try to make connections within these communities, the cycle of alienation and indifference is continued.

The role that neighborhood associations play in this dynamic is important to emphasize. Chapter 3 discussed the role that these associations played in helping citizens learn and practice the building blocks of civic engagement, but these organizations also play a direct role in political mobilization. On the ground, neighborhood associations often serve as points of contact between campaign operatives, elected officials, and neighborhood residents; such associations can hold events to facilitate constituent contact or help advocate on behalf of the neighborhood. As neighborhood context and civic environments alter the capacity of voluntary associations within economically segregated neighborhoods, the ability for campaigns and politicians to mobilize residents within these communities changes as well. The entire process of developing the disposition that leads to political participation as well as developing the on-the-ground network of contacts that are available to politicians is maintained by civic organizations and local associations, and as these are weakened by the economic segregation of poverty, so too does the political life of segregated, impoverished communities begin to wither. This in turn affects which ideas and interests are represented in political debates and policy and whose voices are heard in shaping political and policy outcomes.

To be sure, politicians are in some respects acting logically and rationally, if not necessarily civic-mindedly, when they choose to focus on areas with active citizens and organizations. With a limited amount of time and money to spend and a seemingly endless cycle of reelection campaigns to run, politicians have to make strategic decisions. The problem is that many citizens and groups in segregated, impoverished communities are inactive not because they do not have grievances or interests they would like addressed but because they simply do not have the assets, including economic assets and social networks, to participate. But their disengagement is thought to be a choice freely made, not a symptom of living circumstances that are often circumscribed by factors well beyond their control. As a result mobilization efforts are not targeted in these communities, even though, ironically, these would seem to be the communities most in need of attention by local officials. Rightly or wrongly, politicians consciously make the decision to undertake different levels of mobilization depending on economic context, as can be seen when examining the relationships between city council members, mayors and staff, and constituents in the case-study neighborhoods in Atlanta, Kansas City, Milwaukee, and Rochester.

Councilman C. T. Martin, who in 2007 was representing District 10 in Atlanta, which includes the segregated, prosperous West Manor neighborhood, and who has been active in local Atlanta politics since he was a teenager, offered his interpretation of low civic engagement among impoverished city residents: "There's a feeling out there that local government don't care about them, so the less they'll care about you, i.e., they don't vote."[11] While Councilman Martin was speaking about current levels of voter apathy, this statement is as applicable to the late 1970s and 1980s as it is today. As Leroy Perkins of the Thomasville Heights Civic League said, the 1980s were the roughest decade in the neighborhood in terms of crime and general disorder, and fear in the community kept many citizens indoors and decreased their belief that government could, or would, help them.[12]

Indeed, in Thomasville Heights economic revitalization and urban-renewal policies have continued to exacerbate segregated and concentrated poverty in the twenty-first century. The northern neighborhoods in Council District 1, which encompasses Thomasville Heights in the southern portion of the district, have been undergoing dramatic revitalization in the past ten years, with newer and more expensive homes having been built in the northernmost portion of this district. This revitalization has displaced some residents, pushing them farther south. As a result the southern portion of

District 1 in southeastern Atlanta has continued to experience increasing economic segregation of its low-income neighborhoods, even as those in the northern part of the district have experienced renewed vitality.

This segregation and concentration of poverty in the southern portion of District 1 has resulted in an increasingly distant relationship between constituents in that area and their councilwoman, who comes from the northern part of the district. With redevelopment communities in the northern portion of District 1 stabilized, and the types of networks and organizations needed for political mobilization flourished, all while these types of social networks have become nearly nonexistent in neighborhoods to the south. Because neighborhood leaders coordinate meetings and events, provide access to numerous constituents for politicians, and provide access to elected officials for neighborhood residents, the relationship that forms between neighborhood leaders and elected officials or candidates is very important and can be tapped by both sides: the neighborhood leaders can call the representative with concerns, issues, or demands from their community, while the representative can call the leaders if he or she needs a venue at which to speak, volunteers, or a push to get out the vote; it can be a mutually beneficial relationship.[13]

This is not always the case, however. Councilwoman Carla Smith, the representative from District 1, was guarded when discussing her relationship with her constituents in the southern portion of her district, while the civic leaders in these southeastern neighborhoods who were interviewed were at best ambivalent about their relationship with their council member when compared with their counterparts across town. Smith had close ties to residents living in the northern neighborhoods of District 1, where much of the revitalization has occurred recently and where she lives, but she seemed reluctant to work with leadership in the southern portion of her district who she perceived as weak or inefficient. The councilwoman explained that the organizations she tended to work with more were "the more active ones [that] figured out how the process works," and so "they contact me less." These organizations are "smart enough to realize I'm actually a legislator. . . . They kind of realize 'oh, she doesn't have as much power,' you know?"[14] Further, she said that leaders who "have to whine about everything" make it hard to accomplish goals for her district. Operationally, these may be valid points of concern—elected officials are more successful and efficient when their constituents are more successful and efficient—and yet, perhaps these less knowledgeable organizations are the very organizations and citizens most in need of assistance.

Indeed, leaders of two organizations in the highly segregated, impoverished Thomasville Heights neighborhood in the southern portion of District 1 say their neighborhood is facing some serious issues: high crime, dilapidated housing, and skyrocketing unemployment. Leroy Perkins and Harold Painter, head of the Thomasville Heights Neighborhood Association, indicated some hope that the new revitalization to their north could spread to their neighborhood, bringing much-needed new housing and jobs.[15] But the organizational efficacy of Perkins's and Painter's groups has declined so dramatically that the type of advocacy work needed to address these issues is much harder to mobilize than it used to be.[16] This loss in efficacy has created the type of group that Councilwoman Smith admitted to working with less. As a result, Smith's meeting attendance in Perkins's neighborhoods also seemed less frequent than it did across town, with Smith explaining that she can't "go every time, because I can't. I can't go to every single meeting. I mean, that's all I'd do." This rejoinder is not heard by Councilman Martin, who represents the segregated, prosperous West Manor neighborhood.[17]

Martin has been in office for fifteen years and continues to be successful at raising funds and representing his district in city hall, making the candidate-constituent relationship mutually beneficial. This reciprocal relationship has allowed Martin to develop a base of economic and financial support, which in turn gives him the opportunity to engage in high levels of mobilization during his campaigns, including handing out lawn signs, attending meetings, and even providing shuttle transportation to the polls for those who need it on Election Day.[18] In return district residents continue to turn out for Martin—both for community advocacy events and at the polls. When I asked one neighborhood leader if Martin ever called on the presidents of associations to mobilize their neighborhoods' residents, Shirley Jackson of the West Manor Civic Association said, "Oh, yeah, he calls." She explained that if Councilman Martin says, "'Come on, let's go, we have a meeting,' we go," while another neighborhood leader talked of calls for campaign volunteers and yard sign placement.[19]

Some scholars of elite mobilization would argue that this is a rational calculation by the council member—he contacts and mobilizes citizens who actually vote for him—but the high opinions and level of responsiveness by the residents of his district suggest that they too are benefiting from having an attentive council member. Moreover, because his neighborhoods are concentrated with citizens with higher economic resources and educational attainment, the quality of the contact is different: the cost of contacting is low because these citizens have higher levels of educational attainment and skill and are embedded in strong social networks, making the contact and mobilization worthwhile. As such the political calculation of candidates in highly segregated, wealthy areas is augmented by the ease with which they can tap into the dense social networks and the stable social and economic assets in these neighborhoods.

These two districts in Atlanta highlight yet another way in which high levels of economic segregation change the political calculation of elected representatives and candidates. It does not just alter who is targeted for mobilization around election time or a specific issue. Rather, highly segregated poverty creates a web of community problems that may be so entangled and so difficult to solve that the few resources local elected representatives have at their disposal may be better spent elsewhere, as they simply would not accomplish much in the most impoverished communities. In other words elected officials and candidates may in fact want to invest time and work in the neediest of communities, which could help promote a more virtuous cycle of political responsiveness and citizen political engagement, but this may not be possible given the few resources they have. And then, when political actors make the decision to disengage from these communities, citizens may perceive that as a political slight, when in fact the decision may have been dictated solely by the economic resources and political power of the official or candidate, perpetuating the perception that politicians do not care about those living in segregated poverty. Thus, even the types of casework and issues representatives take on are affected by the economic segregation of low-income citizens.

The problems connected to deficient public goods and resources, from weak organizations to low levels of education and other resources, in segregated, impoverished communities were mentioned by representatives and political operatives working in all the segregated, impoverished case-study communities. Unlike Councilman Martin, Councilwoman Smith in Atlanta was relatively new to public office at the time this study was being conducted. As a result, her support network and financial resources were fewer. Coupled with the impoverished nature of the southern portion of her district, this resource deficiency made it hard to mobilize and organize residents in the most impoverished neighborhoods; Smith did not have a lot of time or money to focus on these neighborhoods, and the impoverished neighborhoods in her district did not have a lot of resources to offer Smith. Moreover, Smith could not advocate for increased funds for her district because many neighborhoods in her district contribute fewer tax dollars to the city than others. Therefore, the type of targeted work and campaigning practiced by Smith may have been the result of a simple cost-benefit analysis, since she was operating with fewer resources and ran in a resource-deficient district. Put another way, some neighborhoods have so many needs and so few assets that the limited resources held by the councilwoman may seem better spent elsewhere, while other neighborhoods in her district are generating resources that give her incentives to address their needs. It seems reasonable that she might choose to focus efforts on the latter since these are likely where her work would be most appreciated and most likely to benefit her in the future. However, this is precisely how the cycle of demobilization is perpetuated.

We see another manifestation of the problems associated with resource deficiency in Kansas City. Troy Nash, the at-large representative from the Third District, representing the Ivanhoe neighborhood in Kansas City, acknowledged that his constituents "don't really care about government per se because for a lot of people, government represents a large-scale intimidating institution," explaining that his constituents do not have experience with complicated bureaucracies or institutions—like universities—and so many "find it intimidating." Nash, who seems to be more involved in his impoverished community than Smith in Atlanta, has found some ways to draw people to events, one of which is to feed them: "Literally, offer food. . . . You treat people with dignity and respect; you show them that you care about them." He does, however, offer the caveat that "we have a machine too—I'm not naïve to the fact of how the political process works."[20] And herein lies the problem.

On the one hand, Nash, not surprisingly, represented himself as a friend to and leader of his constituents. On the other hand, both constituents and city hall staff painted a different picture, one of Third District representation that lacked substance. This suggests that he may have provided food at meetings because he recognized that feeding constituents draws them to events but that he may not have leveraged his power and relationships to follow through on community concerns or even to mobilize his constituents on Election Day. While he criticized those who have won election to city council by "appeal[ing] to a narrow, vested interest," Nash himself relied almost solely on civic leaders to garner support—courting their vote specifically—rather than appealing to a broader group of neighborhood constituents through these leaders. When asked if he thinks about encouraging civic involvement on a regular basis, Nash did not directly answer the question but rather responded by explaining that many of his supporters are community leaders who "are personal friends, come over to my house for dinner . . . so yeah, they may be neighborhood presidents or neighborhood leaders, but they're also just people who live in the community."[21] It seems that even within the context of segregated poverty, those with more resources are peeled off and mobilized in a way that the average resident is not, in part because constituents with fewer resources require so much more support and local politicians simply do not have resources to offer that kind of support, creating further class and political divisions, even *within* this impoverished community.

What Nash's account suggests is that the quality and context of the political contacting may matter in ways not previously recognized. Contact from a candidate may occur—say, an invitation to attend a campaign event that is free and provides free food—but it may not be the type of attention communities need or be sufficient to motivate most residents in segregated, impoverished communities to get to the polls, while more sophisticated strategies of targeting and mobilization are used on fewer, better-resourced residents within the neighborhood. From this we can deduce that contact alone is not enough. Rather, contact that specifically promotes engagement—for example, substantive conversations between friends or over a meal—must occur within a sufficiently resourced community to promote mass, or at least increased, civic engagement among the majority of residents.[22] In this way segregated and concentrated poverty skews the political calculations of representatives running for (re)election in these segregated, impoverished neighborhoods as it distorts their perception of how to relate to and contact constituents in their district, the quality of which affects subsequent political behavior.[23]

While resource deficiency skews political calculations of candidates, another complicating factor in matters of mobilization is that many neighborhood associations are Internal Revenue Service–designated 501(c)3s, which cannot legally promote a political agenda and thus are often wary of wading into electoral politics directly.[24] Indeed, Gloria Miller of the Ivanhoe Community Organization in Kansas City said, "We are a 501(c)3, so we can't support any particular candidate, but we think it's important that we share information." She paused to correct herself: "Not share, but get information and the facts upon which to base a voting decision."[25] Miller had to be careful explaining her organization's political activity because of laws governing 501(c)3s, though it is clear she still tries to disseminate information. This care was handled more cavalierly by Councilwoman Smith's organization in

Atlanta. When talking about her run for office, she explained that she "didn't rely on [her] neighborhood association itself because we're a 501(c)3, and most of them are. So what they do, if they have a debate or something, they'll go and do a little bit of business and then say 'we're really here for the debate,' so they'll close the meeting and then say 'okay, the meeting is closed, now we're going to have a debate.'"[26] This suggests that every organization handles the legal guidelines for 501(c)3s differently, and therefore it is difficult to consistently rely on them as agents of mobilization for particular candidates. However, more highly functioning organizations may be better than others at manipulating the rules governing 501(c)3s to achieve political ends, as the comparison between Miller's and Smith's groups highlights.

As was the case in Atlanta, the political calculations of candidates in segregated, wealthy communities in Kansas City are also skewed as a result of the wealth in their district. The distortion, however, rests on a different arrangement of community characteristics. Kansas City's Union Hill neighborhood is in the Fourth District, which is "very actively involved. . . . There's more educated, higher educated people in the Fourth District. Their incomes are higher." These differences shape how citizens and candidates relate to each other and in turn how these constituents are represented.[27] For example, Judie Callahan, an assistant to the then at-large councilman and who was once the in-district councilwoman for the Fourth District herself, explained that "you do contact individuals to help you campaign. You have them sign up, usually when you have your fundraiser and things, and you ask them 'do you want a yard sign,' 'do you want to be a volunteer,' 'do you want to phone bank,' 'do you want to do this or that?'"[28] Not only can Fourth District constituents afford to attend fundraisers, but these types of events are fertile ground for cultivating volunteers and other campaign activists. This is a strategy that would not work in a neighborhood with a different arrangement of resources. This also highlights a difference between campaigns in the two different types of districts: Councilman Nash does not use his events to get the names and contact information of his constituents to promote participation at a later date, while representatives in other, wealthier districts in Kansas City do. This suggests that it is not just that low-income citizens do not volunteer; rather it seems that they are not asked to volunteer in the same way as residents of prosperous communities. Representatives view these constituents differently and therefore mobilize them differently in accordance with those views.

Similarly, Alderman Michael D'Amato described the Murray Hill neighborhood he represented in Milwaukee as "educated, definitely the most educated. It's the most wealthy. . . . I have a lot of intelligent, progressive people who insist on their alderman being involved in larger issues."[29] As a result the volume of contact between segregated, wealthy residents and D'Amato has had political and educational benefits for his constituents. Reminiscent of Smith's attitude in Atlanta, Alderman D'Amato explained that "as people become more savvy about what local government can do . . . I think that you will see a lot more constituency groups, grassroots groups go to local level of government," but he cautioned that government should "teach a man to fish" so "we don't have to feed him fish every day." He explained that "there are some other districts around here in which there is a mentality that 'I called my alderman, he better damn well take care of this problem for me every single time I call.' My constituents . . . they call with the problem that they will say how [can] I solve this next time myself."[30]

Comparing D'Amato's district to the crosstown segregated, impoverished neighborhood of Silver Spring, Rebecca Jones, an assistant to Mayor Mark "Tom" Barrett of Milwaukee, explained the effect of residential sorting and economic segregation on local politics by saying, "It's that horrible circle of poverty, which unfortunately may have been created by race and now it's economics." Jones described a situation wherein there are people in segregated and concentrated poverty "that are requiring many more resources from the city," creating political problems for the mayor because there are a lot of working- and middle-class families who "are saying, you know, we struggle to pay the bills . . . yet we pay so much in taxes and none of this goes to benefit us." This presents a challenge for those trying to balance governing with mobilization efforts: the mayor tries to "give attention to [the areas not receiving as many benefits] in other ways that he can, by going and showing his face in those areas." Most pointedly, when discussing the effect of residential segregation and resource distribution across the city on campaign politics, Jones said that one of the biggest political challenges facing politicians in the city is that "most of the city resources above and beyond just general city services go to the inner-city. . . . Yet even though an elected official may designate so many resources to that area, that doesn't mean they are going to get the vote, which means that at some point you have to say what vote am I going to get, one vote, and devote your time to those areas."[31]

In creating pockets of poverty throughout Milwaukee, residential economic segregation has also created pockets of middle-class neighborhoods on the south and west sides and very wealthy neighborhoods on the east side. This residential segregation along economic lines produced tensions among neighborhoods—who gets what, when, and how—which in turn generated political pressure on Mayor Barrett and others to compensate for perceived unfairness in the distribution of resources. Moreover, when considering these neighborhood tensions, the mayor and other elected officials think carefully about who is actually going to vote. So, although the mayor and other elected officials provide many resources to low-income neighborhoods, the perception throughout the city is that residents of these neighborhoods do not vote and so mobilization efforts in these communities have been curtailed in favor of campaigning in more politically lucrative communities because residents there may feel slighted by receiving fewer city resources. This occurs despite the fact that throughout the 1970s residents in the low-income northwestern neighborhoods actually voted at rates similar to or higher than the residents in the crosstown comparatively wealthy neighborhood.

Many of these same problems are visible in Rochester. In order to mobilize people during elections Ben Douglas, the council member who represented the northeastern Crescent neighborhood from 1992 to 2007, when he left the city council to work in Mayor Robert "Bob" Duffy's administration, said there was little he could do because the best way to mobilize citizens is through organizations, and there are simply many fewer capable organizations in segregated, impoverished communities. Discussing neighborhood organizations and resource deficiency, Douglas explained that in many cases organizations "were born because the neighborhood was still strong enough to complain. It's like the patient who is complaining about the aches and pains and conditions. The ones who are in serious trouble are the ones who don't complain anymore because they're near death." Connecting this simile to neighborhood organizations, he went on to say that "neighborhoods can get that way. Nobody complains anymore, nobody comes down and storms city hall. Nobody marches or advocates for anything because the positive, healthy part of that community has disappeared." This makes it difficult to mobilize residents through these types of organizations, though Douglas claimed to have attended a number of meetings and block parties in the segregated, impoverished Crescent community in order to develop the type of relationship you need to get people to the polls on Election Day.[32]

Councilman Douglas's claims of active participation in community events were contradicted by statements made by residents in his district. When discussing the relationship between the community and then Councilman Douglas, Frances Coleman of Northwest Neighborhoods for Action, said that this community did not have a "council person working with us and for us. And we worked our butt off in this area, but [energetic representation] was not there. . . . The help that you needed from your council person was not there." She lamented, "Why were you elected if you are not going to work for your people?"[33]

This mismatched perception of the relationship between elected official and constituency has emerged in the other impoverished case-study neighborhoods as well, in both Atlanta and Kansas City. One devastating result of this cycle of demobilization and detachment between representatives and constituents is that the expectations and perceived political rights in segregated, impoverished neighborhoods also appear to decline; much like a dying patient, citizens in the Crescent in Rochester no longer actively advocate on their own behalf or expect their representative to be present at all meetings, whereas citizens in the prosperous southeastern University neighborhood frequently organize meetings and events around community issues and expect to see their elected representative at every one of their meetings.

While it is true that neighborhood organizations cannot work solely with one candidate or endorse specific candidates, they can conduct candidate forums and Get Out the Vote drives, for example. And there are certainly ways that the leaders of neighborhood organizations can, through informal conversations and implicit understandings, urge their members to vote for a particular candidate. According to Councilwoman Lois Geiss, this certainly occurs in the crosstown, comparatively prosperous University neighborhood in Rochester.[34] Such activities enable the neighborhood organization to engage in political mobilization without explicitly endorsing any one candidate and violating any laws governing incorporated nonprofit organizations. In this way the politically savvy neighborhood groups in more prosperous neighborhoods engage in political mobilization in ways generally not used by less savvy groups in impoverished communities. During campaigns candidates do not appear to tap into these groups as mobilization networks in segregated, impoverished communities, while they do in segregated, prosperous ones.[35]

It seems clear that economic segregation changes the political calculations of candidates and other political operatives when determining whom to mobilize for civic action. In economically segregated, impoverished communities the public goods and resources that compose strong civic environments simply do not exist, including strong social networks, voluntary associations, and knowledgeable citizens with time and money to pool toward civic efforts.

Consequently, politicians and other political operatives fail to organize and mobilize within these communities because the voluntary associations that often serve as channels of contact are weak, and other resources important to campaigns are not available in these communities (e.g., social networks, volunteers, and donors). This is not the case in segregated, prosperous communities, where public goods and resources support a robust civic environment, and therefore these residents enjoy more active mobilization.

Interest Representation in Urban Politics

Because residential segregation along economic lines changes the way that politicians relate to particular areas of a city, skewed mobilization produces urban political systems that only hear from the best organized and mobilized interests and constituencies. Thus, political mobilization affects not only citizen civic engagement but also the kinds of messages candidates, elected officials, and other governing elites hear from city residents around political and policy decisions. This is particularly important given how economic segregation came about, which was largely the result of urban-renewal policies involving housing, transportation, and relocation of citizens. In other words urban-renewal policies created an urban landscape increasingly defined by economic segregation, which helped create a situation whereby politicians and other operatives could effectively ignore some interests and privilege others. And then as new political or policy issues emerged, the most isolated and impoverished neighborhoods have had a harder time rallying around their concerns, which resulted in policies that further alienated these communities. This feedback loop created active participation in some neighborhoods and inactivity in others, fundamentally altering the interests represented by and groups active in the governing coalitions of American cities. We can see this process by examining each of the four case-study cities discussed here. It seems that even in local politics the "chorus sings with a strong upper-class accent."[36]

In 1974 Atlanta's city council established the Neighborhood Planning Unit (NPU) system. This created twenty-four units throughout the city, each composed of neighborhoods and their associations that were clustered into groups. The NPU system was created at the request of Maynard Jackson, Atlanta's first black mayor, who had been elected the previous year, and the twenty-four-unit system was designed to increase citizen participation in the new city charter and in the city's then Comprehensive Development Plan, now called Atlanta's Strategic Action Plan.[37] To support the NPU system Mayor Jackson set up a city-level Division of Neighborhood Planning in order to assist neighborhoods in prioritizing development goals and in communicating with planners and elected officials.[38] As had been the case in other cities, concerns over housing and urban-renewal policies spurred Atlanta's neighborhood movement during the previous decade, and fights over proposed urban-renewal plans fortified neighborhood advocacy efforts. This occurred while the governing institutions of Atlanta were restructured, allowing for more input by neighborhood organizations and increasing the number of interests considered by the coalition driving urban growth in Atlanta during this time, composed largely of business and political elites.[39] Active neighborhood involvement in city government was brought about in part by Jackson himself and the new political era he ushered in. The NPU system remains in place today, with twenty-five NPUs identified in the year 2000 throughout the city to serve as vehicles of resident and community participation.

Yet, according to one official in the city planning office, how the city works with NPUs and whether it listens to citizen input depends on who the mayor is and who is involved in his or her administration. Some administrations really listen, while others "don't have much interest in citizen input, in, say, the Comprehensive Development Plan."[40] This difference among mayors and their administrations has been noticeable since the inception of the NPU system: Mayor Jackson was interested in working with grassroots neighborhood organizations and the NPU system, while Andrew Young, who followed Jackson and took office in 1982, actively sought to decrease neighborhood strength in city politics and decreased the NPU office staff to one person.[41]

The implementation of the NPU system also coincided with a change to the political status quo.[42] In focusing on grassroots organizations, citizen input, and increasing economic participation by minority businesses, Mayor Jackson angered the business community dominated by white business elites. Harold Brockey, the chairman of Central Atlanta Progress, which was an organization composed mainly of downtown business leaders, sent a letter to Mayor Jackson in which he outlined concerns about the "lack of easy access to the mayor and the breakdown of close government-business cooperation," as well as articulating the perception that Jackson was "antiwhite."[43] National newspapers got hold of the story, and in response Jackson and local business elites came together to reach an agreement between city hall and local business leaders and to establish the Atlanta Economic Development

Corporation to oversee and prioritize Atlanta's economic development projects.[44] This relationship grew stronger throughout Young's term and continued when Jackson returned to office for a third term after Young's eight years
in office, extending through the tenures of the two subsequent mayors, all
while the role of neighborhood input on issues of governance declined.

The bond between business and city hall, the creation of Atlanta's Economic Development Corporation, and the decline of citizen input through
grassroots mechanisms coincided with rising economic segregation within
the city of Atlanta. This ultimately translated into lower levels of input from
residents, particularly those in segregated, impoverished communities
because residents in segregated, prosperous communities remained connected to the governing coalition through other means: their voluntary associations remained strong, their elected leaders communicated well with
them, and many residents of prosperous areas were likely to be part of the
business elite of the city. Councilman C. T. Martin has worked in Atlanta
politics most of his life, and, despite representing the segregated prosperous
West Manor neighborhood in Atlanta, his experience in the city has made
him acutely aware of the dynamic of interest representation there. He explained that "it's the standard trend—poor area is less voting, less contact,
fewer organizations. . . . There's no community bond"; but in the prosperous
neighborhoods in his district the residents "go to church together, they went
to college together, they work together. Their kids came up together."[45] The
connectedness allows for stronger interest advocacy, organization, and mobilization.

Indeed, the social networks that flourish in Councilman Martin's prosperous district make the type of one-to-one mobilizing Martin believes in
easier to conduct. According to residents of his district and to the councilman himself, Martin is a regular fixture at neighborhood meetings, NPU
meetings, PTA meetings, and church gatherings, with an explicit mission
to "educate people on how to penetrate the system and get it to work [for
them]."[46] However, the fact that his constituents are educated, are economically successful, and are embedded within strong social networks provides
a base upon which Martin can mobilize around community issues and elections, and suggests that his residents are starting with more knowledge
about the system than the residents of Thomasville Heights across town.[47]
This knowledge and access is important if neighborhoods are to hold their
own in the governing coalition of Atlanta. Further, this type of knowledge
and access accrues over time, while the dearth of information and lack of

access to the governing coalition grows more dire as segregated poverty is allowed to remain.

Kansas City, much like Atlanta, experienced significant demographic, economic, and residential changes during the last half of the twentieth century. The most significant result of these changes was to alter the residential and spatial arrangement of citizens in the city, with the majority of low-income residents living on the east side of Troost Avenue and wealthy residents living west of Troost. This pattern of residential segregation and concentration of resources emerged as a result of urban-renewal policies, as discussed in Chapter 2, and in this way residential patterns are political in origin. This is an important point to remember because the effects of these residential patterns have consequences that are political as well. Indeed, zoning laws in Kansas City were crucial for creating and perpetuating the pattern of residential segregation and, as one elected official suggested, might be the key to its undoing.[48]

Arguably one of the most successful urban developers in America, and one of the most committed to restrictive covenants and the promotion of segregated neighborhoods, was J. C. Nichols. Nichols developed wealthy neighborhoods throughout Kansas City, Kansas, and Kansas City, Missouri, during the beginning of the twentieth century, and is probably most famous for developing the Country Club Plaza in Kansas City, Missouri. He is also famous, or perhaps infamous, for his racially restrictive covenants that dictated who could and could not live in his neighborhoods and for his requirement of homeowners in his planned communities to form associations to enforce these covenants, recognizing that the "success of racially restrictive covenants in keeping blacks out of white neighborhoods depended on neighborhood solidarity."[49] Thus, Kansas City's segregation is racial in origin by design. Yet, while racial segregation determined much of residential living before the 1960s, in the decades that followed legal barriers to racially integrated housing were struck down, and as some blacks moved into the middle and upper classes, residential segregation based on income emerged.[50]

Zoning laws determine the type of housing and economic development that can occur within neighborhoods, and city councils and mayors are responsible for legislating and passing zoning laws, often under great pressure from coalitions of powerful interests. In the case of Kansas City, real-estate interests and local land-use politics played vital roles in shaping the post–World War II residential landscape in the city.[51] Therefore, elected officials can have a direct effect on the spatial arrangement of citizens. But citizens vote for these elected officials and can organize to have a voice in the governing coalition of the city, as evidenced by the neighborhood movement that emerged in response to expressway development, though ultimately unsuccessful, in the Ivanhoe neighborhood.

The ways in which emergent economic segregation in Kansas City has shaped political mobilization and participation was clearly articulated by members of Kansas City's mayoral staff during a discussion in 2007.[52] The two staff members confirmed the story of a growing divide, primarily throughout the 1970s and 1980s, between the poor and wealthy that is physically manifested by Troost Avenue, and also explained that this divide "started out racial" but over time has become predominantly a dividing line between the low-income and wealthy residents in the city.[53] The political consequences of this have been devastating for the segregated, impoverished community, as "some of the [city council district] boundaries lie on Troost, which . . . is unfortunate, but that's the way it is."[54] So, in addition to a clear class division running through the middle of the city, there is also a strong perception of a political divide between the haves and the have-nots. And in many ways this perception is accurate: "The leadership out of the Third District—it's the most impoverished—and, you know, it's a difficult community to provide good leadership from," commented one of the mayor's aides.[55] So as the impoverished Ivanhoe neighborhood in Kansas City has become increasingly segregated and impoverished over time, the quality of representation of this district has declined. Civic leaders in the Third District shared similar opinions, with one explaining that their at-large representative "started out being [helpful], but he, you know, he just talks a lot and no follow-up action."[56]

A similar story unfolds in Milwaukee. By 1950 "as the urban fringe, both city and suburban, looked newer and newer, the heart of Milwaukee looked more and more decrepit." Indeed, in 1951 the *Saturday Evening Post* ran a story stating that "Milwaukee, though more than a century old, has a look of being half-finished. Parking lots and filling stations make ugly gaps, like missing teeth, in the downtown business district. Block on block of run-down frame houses blights the center of the city."[57] In response, the city launched a series of economic revitalization and housing-renewal efforts. To accommodate anticipated growth expressways were also built to facilitate the movement of people and goods into and throughout the city, connecting those living in the expanding suburbs to an anxiously anticipated new and thriving urban center.

As part of this renewal blighted housing and empty businesses that composed the majority of inner-city blocks were torn down to make way for new businesses, new housing, and expressways. This created thousands of displaced low-income residents who needed to be relocated as a result of these economic, housing, and transportation renewal policies. The path of low-income displacement and relocation in Milwaukee extended from the center city to the far northwest, which created many problems associated with segregated and concentrated poverty in the Silver Spring neighborhood. These problems continue to shift and grow in the far northwest as a result of new housing development in Milwaukee that favors high-end condos, in large part driven by the composition of the coalition that emerged around downtown development. Interestingly, in Milwaukee more than in the other case-study cities, private interests have emerged as most powerful in coalitional politics, not just because they have money, property, and access to politicians but because private interests have actively formed their own civic organizations.

The Greater Milwaukee Committee (GMC), a "private sector civic organization" composed of representatives from business, labor, education, philanthropy, and the nonprofit communities in Milwaukee, was formed in the late 1940s. "Much of the GMC's work until 1980 focused on 'brick and mortar' projects," but "by the mid-1980s, the GMC began taking on more complex social issues."[58] In the early years analysts dubbed Milwaukee a "regime-less city," using the language of urban political theory, in part because of Milwaukee's progressive (and socialist) Mayor Zeidler who was able to keep elite governing coalitions at bay. But "by the 1980s, the leaders of industry and government saw two emerging issues: the signs of deindustrialization and the emergence of the 1960s generation of politicians in the city."[59] And without a progressive check on this elite power in the city, in the early 1980s the "movers and shakers" in the city were "aging, white, and male," and "overwhelming made up of corporate leaders connected to the Greater Milwaukee Committee."[60]

This rise in power of moneyed elite translates to the neighborhood level as well. In the segregated, impoverished Silver Spring neighborhood landlords have formed their own civic organization, though the primary goal is to advance the economic interests of landlords and not to build or promote the civic environment of the community.[61] And in the prosperous Murray Hill community Alderman D'Amato was clearly enthusiastic about his very active constituents because they "pushed him to address not just issues in their own community, but broader needs of the world and the city as well," including antiwar positions and affordable housing issues.[62] Yet this highlights a fundamental problem with the democratic process in the United States, namely, that the most visible needs and preferences presented to politicians are advanced by citizens who do not represent those who are inactive in the political process. The most active citizens may hold positions similar to those held by less active citizens—for example, support of affordable housing—but "they differ in their personal circumstances and dependence upon government benefits, in their priorities for government action, and in what they say when they get involved."[63] This suggests that even if the issues advocated in this wealthier community benefit others in the city, residents living in segregated, prosperous neighborhoods are still unrepresentative of the experience and preferences of those living in segregated poverty and thus increase the gap in representation between economic classes in local politics and policy.[64]

The result has been to produce feelings of cynicism and helplessness among churches and neighborhood organizations in the segregated Silver Spring neighborhood. Pastor Benjamin Paisley said that the GMC holds all the power in Milwaukee but "that the powers that be are not elected officials, just people with money, and power, and prestige." He went on to say "if any frustration is felt by the people in our city, it's that they don't have enough money to be able to voice like the people that have money." This has produced not just feelings of inefficacy among the segregated poor, mostly black residents of Milwaukee but a real sense that they are not meaningful participants in city life, with Paisley explaining that downtown "isn't really set up" for the disaffected in the community.[65] This has had direct consequences in Silver Spring, as residents in the neighborhood do not feel like the city is being redeveloped for them, and so their participation in civic life feels pointless.[66]

As with the other cities, Rochester has experienced a great deal of change over the last century, but in contrast to Kansas City and Milwaukee the major changes in Rochester have occurred since 1970. Ben Douglas, the council member who represented the northeastern Crescent neighborhood until March 2007, knew the history of the city and experienced the changes that occurred in the northeast firsthand as a community organizer in the 1970s. When asked how the city and his former district have changed, he replied, "It has changed significantly over the years," explaining that "for several generations [it was] a blue-collar working class neighborhood primarily. And they thrived in times when the clothing factory was going full strength here, when jobs were plentiful." The industrial base of Rochester was vital for the early success of neighborhoods in this part of town: "Things worked out well as long as there were jobs. As long as there were people prepared to walk into those jobs. . . . But as times changed, the city changed." One of the biggest changes was that white residents in the northeast "moved out for a variety of reasons . . . and left a lot of vacant properties. And the city's still struggling with that."[67]

In order to address this problem of vacant housing and to use the federal funds that were coming into cities through various federal urban-renewal programs, the city began developing primarily low-income and Section 8 housing in and near the already impoverished Crescent neighborhood, which has not changed much. This is in part because cities fall into cycles of securing federal funds for urban renewal and housing, but, when forced to spend it, they follow the path of least resistance and build more low-income housing in already impoverished areas. "So eventually what happens is when you take a step back from that, you have created a city with a good many of its neighborhoods that has no wealth in it. The property tax levy goes down because the assessed evaluation goes down. The service needs go up because now that you've packed families in like that, that have a lot of social issues that goes along with poverty," creating "a downward spiral following what was good intentions." Essentially, urban renewal in Rochester and the other cities has "institutionalized the ghetto; you have made it so that it can never be anything other than what it is," because cities are stuck with huge swaths of land with low-value housing and low-resourced communities, with high social-service needs.[68]

Electoral politics has been affected by this segregation and concentration of the most impoverished. When asked how these trends map onto election cycles and political mobilization, Douglas responded, "In no way that's productive." Asked to elaborate, he explained that candidates in their efforts to get elected "don't want to say anything out there that's going to leave something for your opponent to pick up and beat you over the head with. So they all do this dance that sounds good, but . . . when they get into office, they've found that it's tough. It's very tough. The amount of latitude and resources you have to make certain things happen, it is not great."[69] This sentiment echoes Councilwoman Smith's in Atlanta who said one of the biggest challenges with working in segregated, impoverished areas is that the resources held by individual city representatives are pretty low, which means that in the cases of segregated, impoverished neighborhoods, where community resources are also low, the representative cannot do much to address the intractable problems related to segregated poverty.[70] When representatives campaign in neighborhoods and mobilize residents, often all they have is empty rhetoric, leaving residents in these communities without effective interest representation.

In sum, the residential segregation along economic lines, created by housing, transportation, and urban redevelopment policies, set in motion a chain reaction of developments that have harmed the civic environment in poor neighborhoods while nurturing the civic environment in rich ones. First, by concentrating people of similar economic backgrounds, segregation made it more difficult for local civic associations and other organizations like churches to maintain social networks within poor communities. Participating in these social networks is a key step in developing the behaviors and attitudes that underlie civic engagement, and weakening these institutions results in a citizenry that is less informed and practiced when it comes to political participation. Moreover, because politicians and campaigns look to these types of organizations to gain a foothold for political mobilization, economic segregation makes it all the more difficult for political candidates to connect with the poorest and neediest citizens. This leads politicians to spend more of their time and effort in places where it is easier to mobilize, such as in segregated, wealthy neighborhoods, and the thriving civic life in prosperous areas gives politicians incentives to listen and respond to the needs and wants of those citizens while continuing to ignore the poorer ones. The final step in this grim cycle can be seen at the ballot box, in the voter-turnout numbers for the eight case-study neighborhoods. Unsurprisingly, turnout has declined in segregated, impoverished areas, while it has held steady and even increased in segregated, prosperous neighborhoods.

Consequences for Voter Turnout

The voter-turnout trends presented earlier in Chapter 1 (especially in Figures 1.4, 1.5, and 1.6) indicated that the difference between voter-turnout rates in segregated, prosperous and segregated, impoverished neighborhoods has increased in all types of elections between 1970 and 2000, so that prosperous residents voted at rates 28 points higher in presidential elections, 24 points higher in congressional and state elections in nonpresidential years, and

27.5 points higher in mayoral elections by the end of the twentieth century. The differences were particularly pronounced for the years between 1980 and the mid-1990s, the period during which economic segregation increased the most. In fact, between 1970 and 1980 the difference in voter turnout between impoverished and prosperous neighborhoods was largely nonexistent, reflecting a broader trend toward economic and civic equality in American society that had begun in the 1950s, likely the result of vibrant neighborhood movements and perhaps remnants of the civil rights, student, and feminist movements.[71] These movements may have generated an impetus to participate, driving up trends in voter participation among the civically disaffected, causing minimal or decreasing difference in voter behavior between impoverished and prosperous neighborhoods, and even some elections in which impoverished citizens voted at higher rates.

Beginning in the late 1970s and early 1980s, however, economic segregation began to grow, and the following graphs indicate that political inequality simultaneously grew during this period as well.[72] Key sources of this trend were declining voter-turnout rates in segregated, poor neighborhoods and rebounding or increased turnout in segregated, wealthy communities. Looking at voter-turnout results across all four case-study cities illustrates a larger point about voter participation and economic segregation in urban America. The case-study cities and neighborhoods within those cities are in different regions of the country, have different racial and ethnic compositions, and have their own history of civic life and participation. That all of the case studies demonstrate a similar trend in voter participation seems to suggest strongly that economic segregation is an important factor that can help explain the emergent class gap in American politics, ultimately creating a political landscape in these cities in which political power is dramatically skewed toward prosperous neighborhoods.

Figure 4.1 shows voter turnout in the case-study impoverished and prosperous neighborhoods in Atlanta in presidential elections.[73] In the year 2000 there is a 21-point difference in voter-turnout rates between the prosperous and the impoverished neighborhoods, up from a 16-point difference in 1984. Before 1984 the difference in turnout was higher, up to 26 percentage points in 1980. The low percentage point difference in 1984 reflects a trend of general declining difference between wealthy and low-income neighborhoods throughout the 1970s, which is followed by a resurgent difference in the 1980s and 1990s. While the current rate of difference is lower than the peak in 1992, there is a small but notable divergent trend between voter-turnout rates in

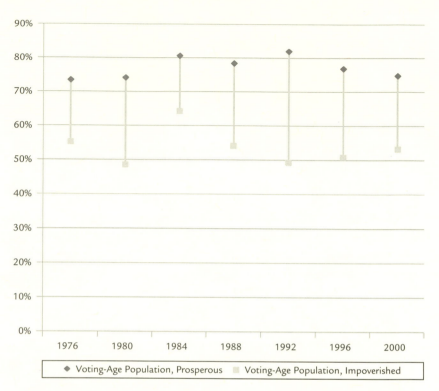

Figure 4.1. Voter Turnout in Presidential Elections, 1976–2000: Atlanta, Georgia

Source: Author tabulations based on election return records from Fulton County Registration and Elections, Elections Division, Fulton County, Georgia.

segregated, prosperous and segregated, impoverished neighborhoods in presidential elections.

A difference of 21 percentage points in voter turnout between prosperous and impoverished neighborhoods for the presidential election of 2000 is important to note, but the increase over time is small. More remarkable is that the difference and increase is greater in congressional elections in nonpresidential years and local elections. Figures 4.2 and 4.3 show voter-turnout trends in the case-study neighborhoods for congressional and mayoral elections, respectively. Owing to missing data Figure 4.2 only tracks congressional elections between 1982 and 2000, and yet over this period the difference between voter turnout in the prosperous and impoverished neighborhoods increased from 12 percentage points in 1982 to 29 points in 2000.

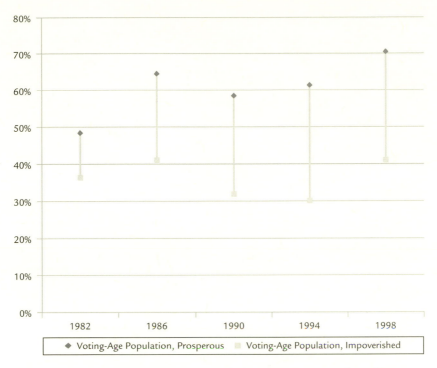

Figure 4.2. Voter Turnout in Congressional Elections in Nonpresidential Years, 1982–2000, Atlanta, Georgia

Source: Author tabulations based on election return records from Fulton County Registration and Elections, Elections Division, Fulton County, Georgia.

This 17-point increase is caused in part by declining participation through the 1980s and early 1990s in the impoverished Thomasville Heights neighborhood, but more important, it is caused by a dramatic increase, 22 percent, in voter turnout by residents of the prosperous West Manor neighborhood.

This trend of increasing difference in voter-turnout rates between the two case-study neighborhoods holds in mayoral elections as well. In 1973, when Atlanta elected its first black mayor, voter turnout in the all-black, low-income neighborhood was 47 percent compared with 61 percent in an all-black, wealthy comparative neighborhood—a difference of 14 percentage points. Despite the increasing political clout of neighborhood organizations through the 1970s in Atlanta, voter turnout among low-income citizens steadily declined.[74]

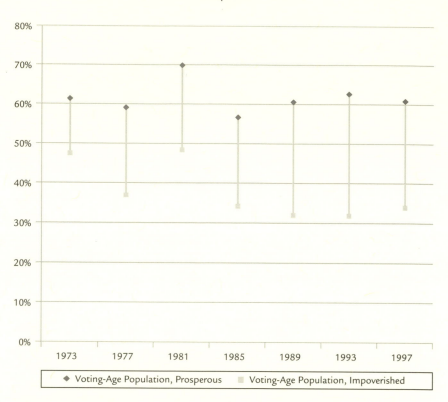

Figure 4.3. Voter Turnout in Mayoral Elections, 1973–1997: Atlanta, Georgia

Source: Author tabulations based on election return records from Fulton County Registration and Elections, Elections Division, Fulton County, Georgia.

It is worth restating that each of the case-study neighborhoods in At-lanta has been overwhelmingly black over the time frame studied here and that these trends occurred despite the election of black mayors since 1973. During this time voter turnout in mayoral elections among citizens in the impoverished neighborhood declined, reaching a low point in the 1993 con-gressional election, at 32 percent, and has remained low. Voter turnout in the segregated, prosperous neighborhoods has fluctuated but has also increased since its low in 1985 at 57 percent, with 61 percent of the voting-age residents in the prosperous neighborhood voting in 1997. The difference dropped a bit in 1997 to 27 percentage points, but there was a net increase of 13 percentage points in voter-turnout difference between these two types of neighborhoods from 1973 to 1997.

These two features of this particular Atlanta case study—two all-black neighborhoods and black elected mayors—helps "control for" or remove race as a factor when considering turnout among residents of these neighborhoods, particularly the impoverished community, at least to some degree. Because of the nature of this case study we can reasonably conclude that the economic segregation of poverty promoted a process whereby resources and assets dried up, voluntary associations withered, and political mobilization declined, producing lower voter turnout in the impoverished Thomasville Heights, while segregated wealth strengthened resources and assets, voluntary associations, and mobilization efforts in West Manor and therefore voter turnout over time. This is not to suggest that race is not a factor in elections but to observe that when race can be more or less removed from the situation, economic differences produce dramatically different civic environments and lead to clearly divergent voting patterns.

A similar cycle emerges in Kansas City: as economic segregation increased, the level and quality of contact between voluntary associations and political candidates, their staff and low-income citizens living in the segregated, impoverished case study community declined. As a result of this segregation candidates have been able to alter the political calculation necessary to earn and maintain support among the electorate, only contacting the neighborhoods with the greatest number of potential voters and effectively dismissing constituent demands when they are seen as politically unimportant. This has soured attitudes held by the least advantaged toward elected officials and government as a whole and may help explain the diminished likelihood of participation by these citizens in the electoral process.

Figures 4.4, 4.5, and 4.6 show turnout and difference trends in presidential, congressional, and mayoral elections, respectively, in Kansas City from 1970 to 2000. Throughout the 1970s the difference in voter turnout in national elections between the impoverished and prosperous neighborhoods was small or nonexistent: in the 1972 presidential election there was a 1-point difference in turnout, indicating that residents in the prosperous community were voting at higher rates than those in the impoverished community, but not by much. In 1980, however, residents in the impoverished community were voting at a rate of 3.5 points higher than their prosperous counterparts; but by 1984 voters in the prosperous neighborhood were voting at a much higher rate, and this trend continued to 2000 (Figure 4.4). Voter turnout in presidential elections has increased in the impoverished community, just not at a pace that brings its level anywhere near voter-turnout rates in the

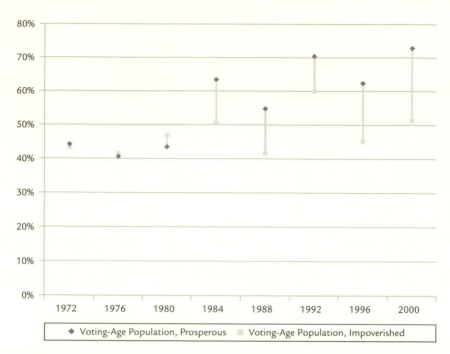

Figure 4.4. Voter Turnout in Presidential Elections, 1972–2000: Kansas City, Missouri

Source: Author tabulations based on election return records from the Kansas City Board of Elections, Kansas City, Missouri, and the Kansas City Public Library, Kansas City, Missouri.

wealthier Union Hill neighborhood or that helps close the difference between the turnout rates in the two neighborhoods.

In the 1974 congressional election (Figure 4.5) voters in the impoverished neighborhood voted at a rate 3 points higher than the residents in the prosperous neighborhood, perhaps driven by the active neighborhood movement in the city.[75] Yet there was a sporadic but notable increase in difference between the two neighborhoods so that by 1998 the prosperous community voted at a significantly higher rate, more than 22 points higher, than the impoverished neighborhood. The same trend holds in the Kansas City mayoral elections from 1971 to 1999. As Figure 4.6 shows, residents in the impoverished neighborhood voted at a much higher rate than residents of the prosperous neighborhood in the mayoral election of 1971, with an 18-point difference in turnout. This graph is particularly interesting because it reveals the volatility of voter turnout among residents in the impoverished neigh-

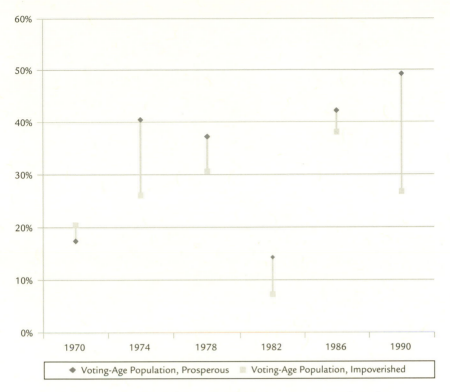

Figure 4.5. Voter Turnout in Congressional Elections in Nonpresidential Years, 1974–2000: Kansas City, Missouri

Source: Author tabulations based on election return records from the Kansas City Board of Elections, Kansas City, Missouri, and the Kansas City Public Library, Kansas City, Missouri.

borhood and contrasts it with the near constant increase of voter turnout among residents in the prosperous neighborhood, culminating in a difference of nearly 16 points in the mayoral election of 1999.

These trends make sense when placed in the proper economic and political context. Throughout the 1980s and 1990s county-level neighborhood poverty and residential patterns began to shift. Between 1970 and 2000 the impoverished Ivanhoe community—and Jackson County, Missouri, as a whole—experienced a great deal of change: the poverty rate of the low-income case-study neighborhood increased from 11 percent to 52 percent while the county's segregation grew. These economic and residential changes coincided with an increase in voter turnout among the residents of the segregated, wealthy neighborhood and increasingly volatile political behavior among

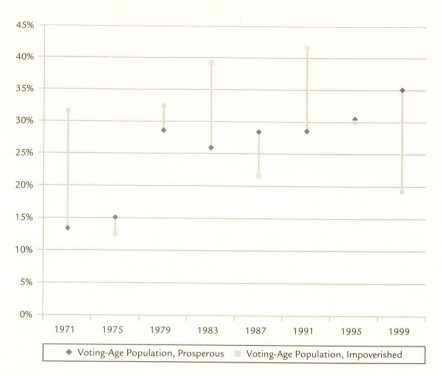

Figure 4.6. Voter Turnout in Mayoral Elections, 1971–1999: Kansas City, Missouri

Source: Author tabulations based on election return records from the Kansas City Board of Elections, Kansas City, Missouri, and the Kansas City Public Library, Kansas City, Missouri.

residents in the impoverished counterpart, ultimately producing a difference in voter turnout between the prosperous and impoverished neighborhoods of Kansas City of 22 points in the presidential election of 2000, 26 points in the congressional election of 1998, and 16 points in the mayoral election of 1999. This is a striking shift given the equal voter-turnout rates or turnout rates in favor of the low-income community in the early 1970s.

Another important feature of turnout in the impoverished community is its relatively volatile nature, particularly in congressional and mayoral elections. Throughout the 1950s and 1960s, like many cities, Kansas City had to negotiate battles among various constituent groups over the placement of expressways and which neighborhoods would bear the burden of necessary population relocation. Like most cities, the burden of this development fell disproportionately on low-income communities. Unlike other cities, however, Kansas City took several decades to complete construction of its expressway. According to civic leaders interviewed for this study, the city cleared homes and relocated families, and as a result crime surged in vacant lots slated for expressway construction. Yet the city made no progress on the project for thirty years, which may have contributed to variable mobilization and demobilization in this low-income neighborhood and variable voter turnout.[76] Despite this, the broad trend seems clear and indicates that economic segregation has negatively affected active political participation in the segregated, impoverished neighborhood while positively shaping political behavior among residents in the segregated, wealthier neighborhood.

Milwaukee presents another very different case of community and political culture, and yet voter-turnout trends between segregated, impoverished and segregated, prosperous neighborhoods are largely the same as in Atlanta and Kansas City. Settled in 1830 and incorporated in 1846, Milwaukee had its first civic and cultural club by 1853. Between the city's founding and the turn of the century, increased immigration by peoples of German, Polish, British, Irish, Scandinavian, and Russian descent created an ethnically diverse city divided into ethnic and cultural enclaves. These various ethnic and cultural groups help account for the many organizations that also emerged during this time: each immigrant group began its own organization, making Milwaukee a civically and culturally vibrant city at the turn of the twentieth century.[77]

In addition to having a long history of active and organized community and voluntary associations, Milwaukee is also one of few cities in the United States to have a long-standing socialist tradition. Between 1910 and 1960 city hall was predominantly occupied by socialist mayors with the explicit agenda of advancing the causes of the working-class citizens of Milwaukee. While the 1960s through the 1990s ushered in an era dominated by the traditional urban politics of class, race, and urban renewal, these two trends— high levels of participation in community and civic organizations and socialist leadership promoting policies aimed to support workers—could have promoted a political culture fostering broad citywide participation in national and local elections. Figures 4.7, 4.8 and 4.9 reveal the voter-turnout trends in the impoverished and prosperous case study communities in Milwaukee for presidential, gubernatorial, and mayoral elections.

In both national and state elections (Figures 4.7 and 4.8) the difference between voter turnout in the case-study prosperous and impoverished neighborhoods fell until the presidential election of 1980, when 60 percent

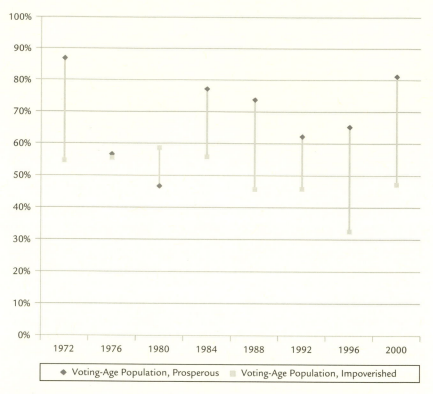

Figure 4.7. Voter Turnout in Presidential Elections, 1972–2000: Milwaukee, Wisconsin

Source: Author tabulations based on the Board of Election Commissioners, City of Milwaukee, Biennial Reports, 1970–2001.

of residents in the low-income neighborhood voted and only 47 percent of the residents within the wealthy neighborhood turned out to vote, a difference of 13 points in favor of the impoverished neighborhood. Residents in this neighborhood also voted at higher rates than residents in the prosperous neighborhood in the gubernatorial election of 1978, 35 percent to 32 percent, respectively.[78] As in Kansas City, this difference between turnout rates in favor of the impoverished community is as much the result of relatively high turnout in the impoverished community as it is of lower turnout in the prosperous neighborhood in 1980. Between 1980 and 2000, however, the difference between turnout rates in presidential and gubernatorial elections increased to 34 points and 19 points, respectively.

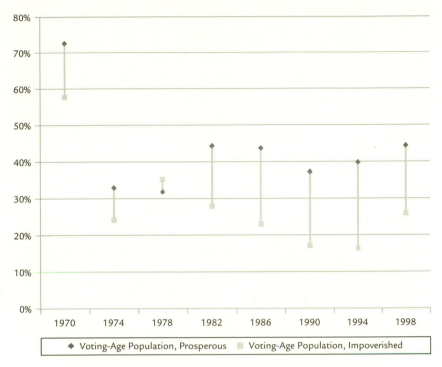

Figure 4.8. Voter Turnout in Gubernatorial Elections in Nonpresidential Years, 1970–1998: Milwaukee, Wisconsin

Source: Author tabulations based on the Board of Election Commissioners, City of Milwaukee, Biennial Reports, 1970–2001.

Turnout in the impoverished neighborhood for mayoral elections experienced a similar trend as in national and state elections (Figure 4.9). There was higher voter turnout in 1972 in both types of neighborhoods, and the difference in voter turnout between these impoverished and prosperous neighborhoods declined through the 1980 election because wealthier residents were voting less. Following 1980, however, residents within the increasingly impoverished and segregated Silver Spring neighborhood began voting less. Unlike the prosperous neighborhoods in Atlanta and Kansas City, the residents in the prosperous Murray Hill neighborhood did not begin voting at higher rates after 1980. And yet, by the year 2000 the difference in turnout between the wealthy and low-income neighborhoods was nearly 14 percentage points, up from 6 percentage points in 1980. This is because less than 10 percent of the voting-age residents in the segregated, low-income

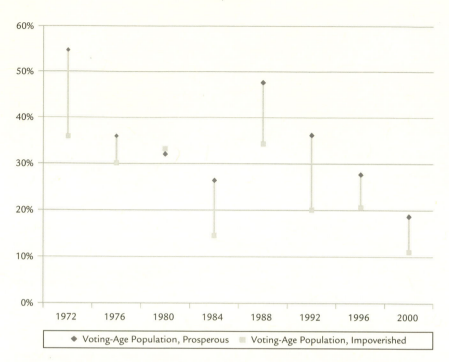

Figure 4.9. Voter Turnout in Mayoral Elections, 1972–2000: Milwaukee, Wisconsin

Source: Author tabulations based on the Board of Election Commissioners, City of Milwaukee, Biennial Reports, 1970–2001.

neighborhood voted for the mayor, making the 23 percent turnout in the prosperous counterpart seem high. While there is some variation in the trends for mayoral elections, notably that the difference peaked in 1992, this may actually support the claims here, given that we also know segregation peaked in the early 1990s. Thus, it seems that increased segregation in Milwaukee may have played some role in shaping citizen participation at the polls in economically segregated neighborhoods.

In the final case study Rochester's political system emerged from party machine and patronage politics in the early part of the twentieth century into a new political landscape in the middle of the twentieth century, and experienced a strong neighborhood movement in the 1960s and 1970s.[79] Yet, while some organizations still operate in the northern and near north-eastern neighborhoods surrounding the city, where the impoverished case-study Crescent neighborhood is located, voter mobilization efforts

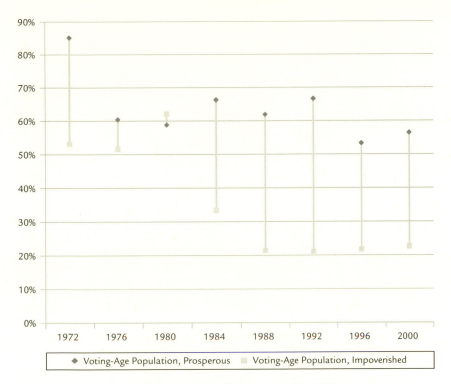

Figure 4.10. Voter Turnout in Presidential Elections, 1972–2000: Rochester, New York

Source: Author tabulations based on the Official Canvas of Monroe County, 1972, 1974, 1976, 1978, 1980, 1982, 1984, 1986, 1988, 1990, 1992, 1994, 1996, and 1997.

appear to have been severely hampered as a result of increased economic segregation.

Voter turnout in presidential elections follows a similar pattern in Rochester as in the other three cities. The presidential election of 1972 sparked a great deal of interest and came at a time when the neighborhood movement was strong across all four cities. Despite this, the difference in voter turnout in 1972 between the impoverished and prosperous neighborhoods in Rochester was quite high, at 31 points (Figure 4.10). This difference declined in 1976, perhaps as a result of the strengthening neighborhood movement, and was negative by 3 percentage points in the presidential election of 1980, indicating higher turnout in the impoverished Crescent neighborhood in that election year. However, by the year 2000 only 23 percent of the residents

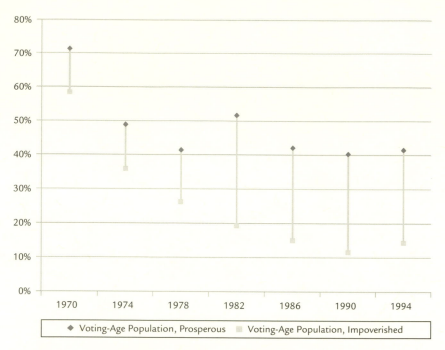

Figure 4.11. Voter Turnout in Congressional Elections in Nonpresidential Years, 1970–1994: Rochester, New York

Source: Author tabulations based on the Official Canvas of Monroe County, 1972, 1974, 1976, 1978, 1980, 1982, 1984, 1986, 1988, 1990, 1992, 1994, 1996, and 1997.

in the impoverished case-study neighborhood voted, while 56 percent of the residents voted in the prosperous University neighborhood across town, a difference of 33 percentage points, higher than in 1972.

In congressional elections voter-turnout trends in Rochester are slightly different from the other cities because there was no decline in difference through the 1970s. Rather, difference in voter turnout between the prosperous and impoverished neighborhoods remained relatively constant between 1970 and 1978, at 13 percentage points (Figure 4.11). The difference grew from 13 points in 1978 to 27 percentage points in 1994, peaking at 32 percent in 1982, a net increase of 14 percentage points over the entire period.[80] The difference of 36 points in presidential elections since 1980 and 14 points in congressional elections since 1973 suggests a diminished political voice among residents in the impoverished neighborhood in national elections.

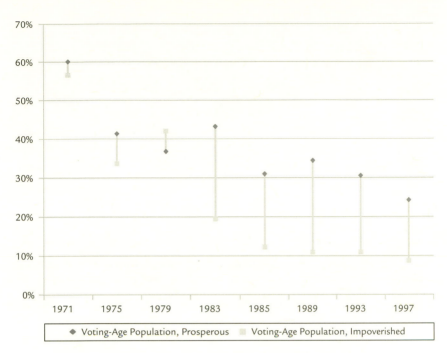

Figure 4.12. Voter Turnout in City Council/Mayoral Elections, 1971–1997:
Rochester, New York

Source: Author tabulations based on the Official Canvas of Monroe County, 1972, 1974, 1976, 1978, 1980, 1982, 1984, 1986, 1988, 1990, 1992, 1994, 1996, and 1997.

Figure 4.12 reveals trends in mayoral elections between 1971 and 1997. Owing to Progressive Era reforms enacted in 1925, Rochester had a council-manager city government for nearly sixty years. Consequently, until 1985 the measure for voter turnout in Rochester's mayoral election used here is turnout in city council elections, as it was the city council that elected the city manager. While no grassroots organization emerged around the strong-mayor issue, it was particularly salient throughout the 1970s, and by 1985 the citizens could once again elect their mayor.[81]

Voter turnout in the 1971 city council elections was extremely high in both neighborhoods: 57 percent in the impoverished neighborhood versus 60 percent in the prosperous neighborhoods. Throughout the decade, however, voter turnout fell, and by the 1979 city council election only 37 percent of residents voted in the prosperous neighborhood while 42 percent voted in the impoverished neighborhood, slightly higher than their wealthier counterpart.

Voter turnout continued to fall throughout the 1980s and 1990s in both neighborhoods, and yet the decline was much more dramatic in the impoverished community, with only 9 percent of voting-age residents voting in the mayoral election of 1997, a difference of 16 percentage points from turnout in the prosperous University community. This difference in voter turnout between the two neighborhoods has increased by 21 percentage points since 1979. Thus, as residents in the impoverished case-study neighborhood found themselves increasingly impoverished and isolated from the rest of the city, their level of participation in city governance declined, diminishing their opportunity for and likelihood of representation in city hall.

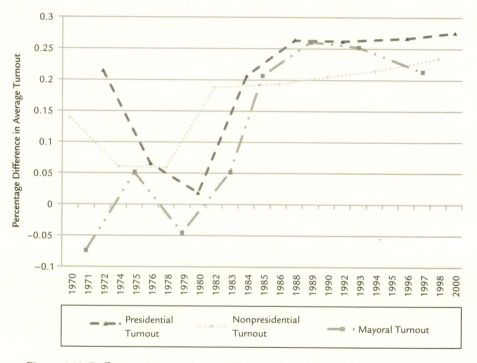

Figure 4.13. Difference Between Average Turnout Rates in Presidential, Congressional-Gubernatorial, and Mayoral Elections, 1970–2000, in Impoverished and Prosperous Neighborhoods

Source: Author tabulations based on election return records from: Fulton County Registration and Elections, Elections Division, Fulton County, Georgia; Kansas City Board of Elections, Kansas City, Missouri; Kansas City Public Library, Kansas City, Missouri; Board of Election Commissioners, City of Milwaukee, Biennial Reports, 1970–2001; and, the Official Canvas of Monroe County, 1972, 1974, 1976, 1978, 1980, 1982, 1984, 1986, 1988, 1990, 1992, 1994, 1996, and 1997.

What is important in these twelve graphs is not the actual level of voter turnout in each type of neighborhood, or even the volatility that exits in turnout rates, but rather the difference in voter-turnout rates between the two types of neighborhoods. When we note this difference, we see that it was often high in the early 1970s; decreased during the 1970s, an era of activism in local politics; but resurged in the 1980s and 1990s, as residential economic segregation took its hold on urban landscapes. When we look at the trend line of the difference between average voter-turnout rates across all four cities by elections, this trend becomes clearer (Figure 4.13). The difference between turnout in prosperous and impoverished communities declined in the 1970s but increased between 1980 and 2000 across all elections, though this trend is most striking in presidential and mayoral elections, with the 1980s and early 1990s exhibiting the greatest increase in difference, precisely when economic segregation grew the fastest and became more pronounced.

Conclusion

The evidence presented in this chapter complicates the traditional understanding of on-the-ground political mobilization. The economic segregation of wealth has made it easier and less costly to target neighborhoods with stronger civic environments—specifically, robust social networks, active voluntary associations, and higher levels of education and income. This has altered the composition of and interest representation by the dominant governing regime, effectively organizing out the voices and interests of low-income citizens who live in less vibrant civic neighborhoods. The relationship this produces between representatives and constituents suggests, at least for wealthy citizens, an example of "homestyle" politics in local jurisdictions and elections; there is a clear, positive reciprocal relationship between residents living in segregated prosperity and their representatives, while a much weaker, less positive relationship exists between residents living in segregated poverty and their representatives.[82] These augmented political calculations, governing coalitions, and the reciprocal relationship between elected representatives and constituents produces demonstrable political consequences in the form of lower voter turnout in segregated, impoverished communities and higher voter turnout in segregated, prosperous ones, which directly translates into more responsive elected officials and therefore more representation in the halls of government. In this way urban-renewal policies that created these patterns of economic segregation have perpetuated a vicious cycle of political quiescence in communities of segregated poverty and a virtuous cycle of civic engagement in segregated, prosperous ones.

These case studies present examples that seem to add an additional layer of complexity to the common understanding of who votes and why. The standard theory of political participation promotes the idea that individual motivation and resources drive civic and political engagement, but a key flaw in this position is that it does not take into account the civic environments in which civic and political mobilization and engagement occur and how these vary depending on the economic context in which one lives.[83] Proponents of the mobilization theory of political participation regularly argue that citizens participate in politics when they are asked to do so.[84] If political engagement is incited by contact and context, the evidence offered here suggests that political disengagement among low-income citizens has been brought about by a lack of civic and political mobilization caused by neighborhood context and weakened civic environments. Put simply, there are certain neighborhood conditions necessary to promote associationalism and civic mobilization, which in turn affect political mobilization and ultimately voter turnout. This has produced an urban political landscape heavily skewed toward representing the interests of the prosperous over the impoverished.

Conclusion: The Dynamics and Implications of Economic Segregation, Civic Engagement, and Public Policy

The findings offered in this book suggest that the commonly accepted notion that low-income citizens do not vote because of their individual economic status misses a significant point: low-income citizens are increasingly finding themselves living with other low-income citizens, which diminishes the neighborhood's civic tools vital for civic and political mobilization. Conversely, wealthier citizens have been able to segregate and isolate themselves in prosperous communities with robust civic environments. The result is an urban landscape increasingly defined by enclaves of not just economic wealth and poverty but also civic wealth and poverty. This in turn promotes certain levels of voter engagement; voter turnout has declined across all types of elections—national and local—in segregated, impoverished communities but has remained steady or increased in segregated, prosperous ones.[1] These trends occur across different segregated, impoverished and segregated, prosperous communities regardless of racial composition: impoverished citizens in one city behaved in ways similar to impoverished citizens in other cities, as did prosperous residents. This indicates that rather than race or ethnicity alone the economic context of neighborhoods is crucial for understanding political behavior.

These findings are particularly important given the almost unrelenting focus on individual explanations of political behavior pursued by most political scientists. This has prompted some recent calls for greater focus on context and for the examination of structured political behavior, or the analysis of political behavior within the various political-policy and community structures that shape civic engagement and political behavior.[2] A contextual approach to political behavior is particularly important given the rising trends in income inequality and the geographic, physical manifestation of this inequality in economic segregation. The analysis offered here heeds this call and provides a clear picture of *how* economic segregation promotes political quiescence among the least economically advantaged in the American polity and "a growing participatory tilt toward the economically advantaged."[3]

These findings are also important for understanding the feedback effects of a gap in participation and representation between economic classes, or what we have been calling the "class gap," in American politics. Recently, Jacob Hacker and Paul Pierson took on the issue of "winner-take-all politics" in an era of rising income inequality and, not surprisingly, found that the very wealthy in America have benefited a great deal from economic and labor policies that favor this economic class. One reason we may have missed this trend over the last few decades is, once again, the focus on individual-level political behavior and on the median voter. By focusing on what the median voter does or might do in a context of income inequality, Hacker and Pierson argue that we cannot see what other types of voters are doing.[4] And the consequences of the class gap are stunning; Martin Gilens finds that when the preferences between the wealthy and poor differ, resulting government policy reflects the interests of the wealthy and has little to do with the degree of support or opposition to the policy by the poor. In essence there is a "complete lack of government responsiveness to the preferences of the poor," a finding supported by Larry Bartels who has examined taxation and minimum-wage policies and by the evidence presented here.[5]

This understudied cycle of increased economic segregation, decreased civic and political mobilization and participation, and subsequent policy output is a prime example of a policy feedback loop. Public policies are not just outputs of a legislative process; they are inputs as well.[6] Throughout the interwar era cities failed to create comprehensive housing and urban-renewal plans, which led to a crisis in the inner core of many American cities following World War II. To respond city governments put into place a web of urban-renewal policies that promoted economic segregation. Each new policy created a new arrangement of resources and incentives for governing elites, organizations, and the general public to organize and promote their own policy agenda. This altered the political landscape in which voluntary associations, churches, political parties and candidates, and citizens operated, all while making it harder for those living in segregated, impoverished neighborhoods to access the new institutional and political arrangements. As the political landscape continued to shift, the individual incentives or disincentives for voting due to economic status were enhanced by context (incentives for a prosperous neighborhood or disincentives for an impoverished neighborhood), by the changing nature of civic resources, by the organizational-institutional arrangements within each neighborhood, and by the social interactions with similarly empowered or disempowered citizens.

Kansas City serves as a prime example of this process at the local level; as a staff member in the city's Neighborhoods and Community Services Department stated, "Housing was heavily driven by the electoral body."[7] In order to influence housing policy citizens must have effective representation in city hall. As housing in Kansas City became increasingly economically segregated, impoverished communities came to dominate the east side, where the Ivanhoe neighborhood community is located, which in turn produced poor representation on the city council from this district.[8] The ability for citizens from these neighborhoods to advocate for better housing policy declined. As a result, since "housing in the city was based on someone coming to the table with the deal of the day," those with the best representation were able to shape housing-policy decisions, including policy design and implementation, in Kansas City, while those on the losing end of these deals could not.[9] This further promoted the segregation of the poor, making it harder for low-income citizens to get a seat at the table during the next round of policy discussions.

This dynamic is important because, as Theda Skocpol states, "Experiences with governmental institutions and political processes profoundly affect the way people understand and evaluate alternative policy possibilities."[10] In other words policies shape civic environments and affect political mobilization and contact by voluntary associations as well as by political parties and candidates. This contact changes how residents of these different neighborhoods understand the potential political and policy possibilities for accomplishing community goals. As this understanding of possibility and feelings of civic efficacy are heightened or lowered based on the prosperous or impoverished nature of a citizen's neighborhood context and civic environment, the inclination to act on behalf of those policy possibilities and goals increases or decreases based on context as well. Indeed, ideas and notions of what government can do help transform politics by opening avenues of advocacy and policy possibilities, but the ability of citizens to influence policy depends on how political institutions organize interests and political competition.[11] Because organizational and institutional avenues of interest representation and political competition are more available to citizens in segregated, prosperous neighborhoods, residents in these neighborhoods have more vibrant civic environments and participate more at the polls than residents in impoverished neighborhoods. This has occurred because organizational mobilization and individual efficacy have been encouraged in the former and discouraged in the latter by political and policy decisions over time.

A final note about the policy feedback cycle is that it simultaneously affects the political well-being of the neighborhood as well as the individuals within the neighborhood. While increased segregation has altered the civic environments of communities, including the organizational and mobilizing capacity and willingness of voluntary associations and political candidates to mobilize residents, this cycle also reminds us that policies teach lessons about what certain citizens are "worth" in the polity, what they deserve from the government, and what is expected of them as citizens.[12] Indeed, Councilman C. T. Martin, representing the segregated, prosperous West Manor neighborhood in Atlanta, said that one of the biggest obstacles to getting impoverished communities to participate in local and national governance is that "there's a feeling out there that local government don't care about them."[13] If an impoverished neighborhood in which an individual lives is politically alienated through residential segregation, civic and political demobilization, and declining representation, and if this individual internalizes his or her day-to-day experiences within this impoverished community—with the police, the benefit offices, and city services, for example—it is little wonder that turnout has declined as severely as it has in these communities.

An important contribution of this study is to show how public policy helped create these trends, which suggests that it is possible that public policy can help reverse them as well. One way of doing this may be through the promotion of mixed-income communities and housing development. Indeed, since the mid-1990s mixed-income development has become more popular as a vehicle to promote both economic and racial integration.[14] While there is no commonly accepted definition of mixed-income housing, one way to think about it is a development that provides a mix of housing units that are affordable to households at different income levels—those with above-average incomes for their area, with average incomes for their area, and with well-below-average incomes or incomes below the poverty line.[15] There are two ways that mixed-income housing developments are thought to benefit cities. First, they are a way to engage both public policy and market forces to address decades of economic segregation. Second, mixed-income housing is viewed as a way to bring together disparate groups of people and different political constituencies by capitalizing on the availability of and increasing desirability of housing in center cities, which would in turn generate the financing required to redevelop inner-city areas.[16]

The theory behind mixed-income housing as a possible solution to persistent urban poverty is that by desegregating and deconcentrating poverty the problems associated with it are also diffused, including weak social networks, unsafe neighborhoods, transiency, low educational attainment, poor health, and unemployment, to name a few attendant consequences. The majority of research examining the detrimental effects of living in poverty and the benefits of mixed-income housing has typically focused on adolescents—educational attainment, crime, and employment, for example—and concludes that movement out of segregated and concentrated poverty has profound benefits.[17] If moving from concentrated poverty into mixed-income communities can improve the health, educational attainment, and employment opportunities for individuals and families, perhaps it can improve civic and political opportunities as well.[18]

Another way of thinking about mixed-income housing, though, is to see it as an opportunity to develop social capital and tools of civic engagement among both the impoverished and the prosperous. Robert Putnam distinguishes between *bridging* (or inclusive) and *bonding* (or exclusive) social capital, with the former focused on creating relationships across different groups of people and the latter focused on creating relationships among similar groups of people. Cross-class fraternal organizations are good examples of organizations that help build bridging social capital, while church groups are good examples of organizations that promote bonding social capital. While bonding social capital is good for "getting by," bridging social capital is crucial for "getting ahead."[19]

Mixed-income housing may promote bridging social capital in two ways. First and most obvious, an economically integrated neighborhood would cut down on the cost of organizing diverse groups of people. The proximity of these different income groups could allow for shared experiences and the development of a shared fate and common, community-focused goals. Second, mixed-income housing could promote the creation of "weak ties" by encouraging relationships among people who normally operate in very different economic and social circles. This would most obviously help lower-income residents who may have previously lived in isolated impoverished communities with no weak or strong ties. However, this would also help residents of prosperous communities by expanding their networks and communities to be more inclusive of citizens who, if given the chance, could be creative and industrious participants in neighborhood, social, economic and civic life.

Another effect mixed-income communities may have is on the bonding social capital of low-income citizens. As this study shows, social trust is very low in segregated, impoverished communities. This is largely due to the fact that neighborhood resources and infrastructure in segregated, poor communities have been decimated by years of urban-renewal policies and displacement, which has also caused social networks to deteriorate in these neighborhoods. Moreover, the lack of safe spaces and high residential mobility diminish the opportunity for long-term relationships to develop. The chance to reestablish relationships in a stable neighborhood setting could promote increased social cohesion among low-income citizens and foster the creation of "strong ties" in this community.

There are several types of policy tools that promote mixed-income communities. One policy development that has occurred over the last fifteen years is the U.S. Department of Housing and Urban Development's (HUD) HOPE VI program. According to HUD, the aim of the HOPE VI program is to revitalize severely distressed public housing by investing in physical improvements of public housing facilities, improving management of these facilities, and bringing social and community services to address residents' needs.[20] One of the primary ways that HUD has attempted to accomplish these goals is through promoting the development of mixed-income housing projects, either by providing funding for redeveloping public housing to include units at different price points or by providing funding for the development of affordable housing in what HUD calls "Main Street revitalization efforts." To date, however, mixed-income housing promoted through the HOPE VI program has been only moderately successful in achieving its stated goals. There have been dozens of developments built under the HOPE VI program, but these developments have faced several challenges, primarily attracting higher-income residents, offering the services that low-income residents need to achieve stability beyond housing, and providing access to economic opportunities.[21]

An alternative to accomplishing mixed-income housing may be to continue to pursue more inclusive zoning laws and reform those exclusionary zoning laws that allow some neighborhoods to "zone out" certain types of housing. Inclusionary zoning is a land-use policy intended to make it possible for lower- and moderate-income households to live in middle- and upper-income communities, by either mandating or encouraging housing developers to set aside a certain number or percentage of units to be rented or sold at below-market prices.[22] The idea is that this type of zoning promotes access to low-poverty neighborhoods for low- and moderate-income families, and therefore also promotes the creation of mixed-income neighborhoods over time. In other words, rather than attempting to create mixed-income communities in blighted areas, which may have available land and zoning laws that allow for this type of development but not much success at attracting market-rate renters and buyers, an alternative route to socioeconomic integration could be to pass more robust inclusionary zoning laws so that previously exclusive communities become more inclusive over time.

One charge against this approach may be that proponents of inclusionary zoning laws are using them to socially engineer a desired residential outcome. Yet, as we have seen, throughout the twentieth century zoning laws in cities and suburbs have long been used to engineer desired outcomes, first by making some neighborhoods inaccessible to African Americans to more contemporary efforts that make some neighborhoods inaccessible to low-income populations.[23] Moreover, recent findings suggest that homes in inclusionary jurisdictions serve low-income people well, as low-priced and moderately priced homes in jurisdictions with inclusionary zoning tend to be spread out throughout the jurisdiction, which translates into low- and moderate-income households being assigned to better-performing schools.[24]

A final way that communities have pursued more comprehensive and inclusive redevelopment is through a reimagining of the Empowerment Zone and Enterprise Community Initiative, which Congress passed as part of the Omnibus Budget Reconciliation Act of 1993 and appropriated funds for implementation in 1994, and which President Barack Obama extended through December 31, 2013 as part of the American Taxpayer Relief Act of 2012.[25] Empowerment zones use not just tax incentives to revitalize distressed communities; instead the designation requires that enterprise zones also develop community-based partnerships and sustainable community development plans in order to promote a more holistic approach to community revival and renewal.[26] Though much was made of this more holistic approach, especially following the deep social cuts of the Reagan and George H. W. Bush administrations that represented almost a decade of national neglect of central cities, more recent assessments of the enterprise zone program do not suggest a great deal of success. Deirdre Oakley and Hui-Shien Tsao's analysis of enterprise zones across several cities indicates that the community building and participation components received the least amount of funding and that the more traditional economic development programs did not translate into meaningful improvements across a variety of socioeconomic indicators.[27]

It would seem then that despite decades of rhetorical commitment to crafting policy that addresses the problems of distressed communities and that promotes mixed-income communities, these policies have generally not met with a great deal of success. Examining the barriers to successful mixed-income housing implementation may shed light on ways to improve the provision of housing in economically integrated neighborhoods. However, and more important for the purposes of the research presented here, there must be a clearer sense of the goal of mixed-income housing.

One implication of the findings offered here is that decreasing economic segregation, or promoting economic integration, may increase civic engagement and political participation by underrepresented constituents. If this occurs, public policies may become more representative of all citizens, thereby promoting balanced and integrated neighborhoods and communities through increased political equality. Given this, one potentially fruitful line of research would be to assess if and how mixed-income housing promotes increased civic and political engagement within these types of communities. Mixed-income communities might foster the bridging and bonding social capital necessary for strong civic environments within communities.

One could hypothesize that as these neighborhoods likely would not have experienced the dramatic alteration in their arrangement of resources due to the concentration of extreme wealth or poverty, it is possible that the voluntary associations would have remained active and these communities would be ideal targets for any campaign. Thus, civic and political mobilization should be high. As a result, political participation at the polls among all economic strata should also be high. To be sure, finding such a case study may be difficult, but the implications of this for future housing policies would be clear; if mixed-income communities provide all (or even most) of the benefits theorized above—social capital development and the exercise of civic and political strength—then it would behoove policy advocates and policy makers to redouble efforts to craft and implement mixed-income housing policies that work, if for no other reason than to strengthen the health of our democracy, which is predicated on equal access by all citizens to the democratic process.

Since America's founding, its citizens have struggled to broaden the rights of individuals, access to democratic institutions, and promote active and equal participation in civil society and the governance of our cities, states, and nation. However, "the scourge of overt discrimination against African Americans and women has been replaced by a more subtle but potent threat—the growing concentration of the country's wealth, income, and political influence in the hands of the few."[28] The findings presented here expand upon this understanding of political inequality by revealing important mechanisms through which political inequality becomes manifest; specifically, that it may be due less to diminished individual resources and more to increasing political power within segregated, prosperous communities, which are occupied, protected, and perpetuated by the "haves" in American society. This leaves entire communities of "have-nots" to struggle in silence with ever-diminishing social, economic, civic, and political resources. Thus, through public policy and the political activism of wealthy communities, residents in low-income communities have been systematically organized out of the civic and political process.

If the phenomenon of overt discrimination against African Americans and others has been overcome, it is time to turn attention toward the discrimination against the poor that remains. This can only be done by expanding our efforts beyond the individual and addressing the development of persistent problems within segregated, impoverished neighborhoods and communities. Without strengthening the civic environments within which the poorest among us live and learn how to be good citizens, the health of American democracy will decline and the legitimacy of our democratic outcomes will seem dubious at best.

Vote Counting Decisions in Atlanta, Kansas City, Milwaukee, and Rochester

Atlanta

1972–1982:	CT 71 =	ED 12P, ED 12R
	CT 79 =	ED 10L, ED 10M
1982–2000:	CT 71 =	ED 1P, ED 1R
	CT 79 =	ED 10L, ED 10M
2000:	CT 71 =	ED 1P, ED 1R
	CT 79 =	ED 10L

Kansas City

1974–1982:	CT 44 =	½ ED 107
	CT 35.02 =	¾ ED 1507
1982–1991:	CT 44 =	½ ED 403, ¼ ED 107
	CT 35.02 =	½ ED 1412, ½ ED 1510
1992–2000:	CT 44 =	¼ ED 106, ½ ED 107
	CT 35.02 =	½ ED 1411, ½ ED 1412

Milwaukee

1966–1969:	CT 74 =	AD 3, ½ ED 1, ½ ED 3, ½ ED 4
	CT 12 =	AD 9, ED 9, ¹⁄₁₀ ED 10
1970–1981:	CT 74 =	AD 3, ½ ED 1, ⅓ ED 4, ⅕ ED 5
	CT 12 =	AD 9, ½ ED 8, ½ ED 13, ¹⁄₁₀ ED 14
1982–1991:	CT 74 =	AD 3, ED 40, ED 41
	CT 12 =	AD 9, ⅔ ED 172, ⁹⁄₁₀ ED 173

| 1992–2000 | CT 74 = | AD 3, ¾ ED 42, ED 43 |
| | CT 12 = | AD 9, ⅔ ED 166, ⁹⁄₁₀ ED 167 |

Rochester

1971–1981:	CT 78.01 =	ED 1, ED 2, ED 10
	CT 15 =	ED 3, ED 4
1982–1984:	CT 15 =	⅓ ED 9, ⅔ ED10
1985–1990:	CT 15 =	⅓ ED 9, ⅔ ED 10
1981–1990:	CT 78.01 =	ED 1, ED 2, ED 10[a]
1991–2000:	CT 78.01 =	ED 1, ED 2 in LD 21, and ED 10 in LD 23[b]
	CT 15 =	ED 9, ED 10

Key
AD = aldermanic district
CT = census tract
ED = election district
LD = legislative district

[a] There was a typo under the vote totals for the president and vice president in ED 1 and ED 2: the presidential turnout column listed 513 votes cast, but all other total columns in other races for that election district listed 512. I use 512 votes cast for analysis here.

[b] There was a typo under the vote totals for the president and vice president in LD 23 and ED 10: the presidential turnout column listed 509 votes cast, but all other total columns in other races for that legislative-election district listed 504. I use 504 votes cast for analysis here.

Interview Protocol and Schedule for Neighborhood Associations, Parent-Teacher Associations, and Churches

In order to investigate how economic segregation may alter associational life and mobilization efforts of voluntary associations and churches, I examined census and organizational data and interviewed forty-four civic and religious leaders across all four selected case-study neighborhoods. All community organizations within the case-study neighborhoods were identified using city directories of organizations and churches, and include block or neighborhood associations, tenant associations, merchant associations, parent-teacher associations or organizations (PTAs), and churches. Each interview conducted was a standardized, open-ended interview.

It should be noted that this qualitative methodology has some drawbacks. For example, I have only two interviews from members of the Thomasville Heights community in Atlanta. I made repeated attempts to contact other neighborhood organizations, churches, and PTAs on the southeast side of Atlanta and in the Thomasville Heights neighborhood specifically, but to no avail. One thing I encountered again and again in my interviews in the impoverished communities I visited was a high level of suspicion of me and my motives, at one point being asked who sent me, why, and who was paying me. I suspect that this suspicion kept many in the impoverished communities from returning my calls or responding to my letters. I did not encounter this in the prosperous neighborhoods.

All interviews took place between March 2006 and May 2007 in a variety of locations, including private residences, community centers, schools, and churches, and ranged from forty-five minutes to more than two hours. In some cases these interviews yielded recommendations for other neighborhood leaders and activists I should contact and interview; taking advantage of this "snowball method," I interviewed these additional individuals and triangulated multiple sources of data, such as newspaper articles and official city records as well as other interview data, to ensure the validity of my findings when possible.

As the interview schedule indicates below, some of my questions are rather specific and some are fairly open-ended. But the questions are generally broken down into four categories: the first set of questions focuses primarily on the history of the respondent's association; the second set of questions is about the respondent's neighborhood and community; the third and largest set of questions is about the members of the respondent's organization and the relationships among the organization, the organizational leadership, and members; and the last set of questions ask about the future of the respondent's neighborhood, community, and city.

To protect confidentiality all respondent names have been changed, as has the name of the respondent's organization or church. If the neighborhood has a name that is commonly used, I use it here; if not, I created one for ease of comparison. Therefore, the reader may be able to identify which part of the city the respondent is from but not the specific organization or respondent.

Interview Schedule

Organizational

1. How long has the association/organization/church been in existence?
   a. Have there been any breaks in its operation?
2. How did it get started?
3. How did you come to be involved with this association/organization/church?
4. How long have you been working for the association/organization/church?
5. What is the mission or purpose of the association/organization/church?
   a. How do you work to achieve this/these goal(s)—programs, events, etc.?

6. Who do you work with primarily—church membership, neighborhood residents, parents, school officials, city/county officials?
    a. Do you rely a lot on local, citizen leadership?
    b. If so, how?
7. Are there multiple groups of people that matter—i.e., the city, the county—to the organization?
    a. As an organization, how do you prioritize the interests of multiple groups and address different priorities?
    b. Is building a relationship with your neighborhood an organizational goal, or are you more focused on accomplishing your goals through a wider network, such as by developing a relationship with the city?
8. Do you have paid staff?
    a. If so, how many?
9. Do you rely on volunteers to accomplish much of your work?
10. Do you have a budget and where does your funding come from?

Community

11. How would you define your community (i.e., the neighborhood/school population, members, city, etc.)?
12. Are their different groups of people within your community?
    a. If so, how would you define these groups and do they have different interests?
13. What community issues does your association/organization/church deal with mostly?
14. Are there some issues that are more pressing than others?
    a. Has this changed over time?
15. Have there been any changes to your immediate neighborhood—more/fewer residents, changes to median or average income, appearance, etc.?
16. Has this community change resulted in a change of issues that your association/organization/church addresses?
17. Have these changes changed or affected the association/organization/church in any other way?
    a. If so, how?

18. Does your association/organization/church have a relationship with all residents/parents, or are some more active than others?
    a. Why some and not others?
    b. What is the association/organization/church's relationship with its neighborhood—volunteers, programs, residents on board, leadership programs, etc.?
    c. How do you think its presence affects the lives of people here/parents?
19. Has this changed over time—the type of people who are more active—because of changes in your community?
20. How do you encourage participation in your association/organization/church (i.e., recruit)?
21. What types of participation do you encourage—membership, volunteering, sitting on a committee or board?
22. Have you seen an increase or a decrease in participation, challenges to raising money, ability to achieve goals, or have your association/organization/church's goals changed as a result of changes to your community?
23. Is it challenging or relatively easy to find local volunteers and leaders?
    a. Why or why not?
    b. Has this changed at all over time?
24. Do you think that changes in the community have affected your ability to get volunteers?
    a. If so, how?
25. Do you have leadership positions for members?
    a. If so, what are they?
26. Do you think that changes in your community have affected your ability to find local leaders?
    a. If so, how?

Public Participation

27. Does your association/organization/church encourage its members and/or neighborhood residents to participate in other areas of public life?
    a. If so, how do you encourage this participation?
    b. If so, what types of participation do you encourage?

28. Do your members and/or neighborhood residents actually participate?
29. Is it challenging or relatively easy to encourage this participation?
    a. Why or why not?
    b. Has this changed over time?
30. How does your association/organization/church interact, or what is your organization's relationship with, local political leaders—program participation, funding from city or county offices, etc.?
31. Does your association/organization/church provide opportunities for political leaders to speak to neighborhood residents/parents/members, or do you organize other educative events?
32. One of the things I'm also interested in is voting. Does your association/organization/church encourage voter participation?
    a. If so, how?
    b. Is it primarily issue-based or more general?
33. Are neighborhood residents, or are you, involved in campaigns during elections?
    a. If so, how?
34. Do local politicians contact you, as president/pastor of your association/organization/church, during campaigns?
    a. If so, why—to speak, recruit volunteers, attend meetings, put up signs, etc.?
35. Do you think getting your members to the polls is easy or hard?
36. Are there any obstacles to getting people to vote?
    a. If so, what are they?
37. Do local politicians help members/residents/parents/volunteers get to the polls/overcome these obstacles, or is it the responsibility of the residents/parents/volunteers?
38. What about your association—does it do anything to help residents/parents get to the polls, or do you leave that up to the members/residents/parents/volunteers?
39. Is getting people to vote something you think about regularly as president of your association?
    a. If so, why?
    b. If not, what are your main goals as president?
40. When you think about the last election, did you or your association encourage voting?
    a. If so, how?

41. Did you find some strategies more effective?
    a. If so, what worked, what didn't?
    b. If you had to do it again, or when you do it again, what might you do differently?
42. Was it challenging or relatively easy to encourage people to vote?
    a. Why or why not?
    b. Do you think that it has become more or less difficult to encourage people to vote, and why?
43. Do you think that there are some people who are just more likely to vote than others?
    a. If so, why do you think some are more likely?
    b. Do you think this has changed at all or that who is more likely to vote has changed?
44. Do you think there are other forms of political participation that are more important or just as important as voting?
    a. If so, what are they?
45. Do you think that participating in this association has made you or your members more active in other areas of public life?
    a. If so, why?

Future

46. Over the next ten years, how do you think the community might change?
47. Why do you think these changes will occur—are there city-wide changes happening (i.e., new development, new populations, etc.)?
48. What do you think will be the most important issues facing your community over the next decade?
49. How do you think individuals, community groups, and politicians can best respond to these challenges and issues—what goals/issues/strategies should they be focusing on?
50. It seems that part of your mission is to empower your members to participate in their own communities and address some of the issues they face in their daily life.
    a. How would you define empowerment?

51. Do you think associations like yours can empower members and local residents to act in public life?
    a. If so, how?
    b. Do you think that they actually do?
    c. Do you think there are challenges to empowerment?
    d. If so, what are they?
52. Do you think that it has become easier or harder to empower your members and local residents, or how has this changed over time?

Interview Protocol and Schedule for Elected Officials and Public Officials

In order to investigate how economic segregation can alter political mobilization efforts among residents of segregated, prosperous and impoverished neighborhoods, I interviewed fourteen elected officials, city representatives, and staff members representing the four cities and eight case-study neighborhoods. All interviews took place between March 2006 and May 2007 in the offices of the representative or staff. In one case, Councilman Nash of Kansas City, the interview took place over the course of several hours while touring the city, but most interviews ranged from forty-five minutes to more than two hours. If the interview subjects were elected officials at the time of the interview, or had been and so were reflecting on their time as an elected official, their names have not been changed. If the interview subject was an unelected city staff member, his or her name has been changed to keep confidential all contributions to the study. When possible, I triangulated multiple sources of data, such as newspaper articles and official city records as well as other interview data, to ensure the validity of my findings.

As the interview schedule indicates, some of my questions are rather specific and some are fairly open-ended. But the questions are generally broken down into four categories: the first set of questions focuses primarily on the respondent's personal and professional history; the second set of questions is about the respondent's neighborhood and the community they represent or focus on; the third set of questions is about the respondent's relationship to constituents and their efforts to encourage civic engagement; and the final set of questions ask about the future of the neighborhood and community the respondent represents or thinks about.

Interview Schedule

Personal and Professional History

1. Were you born and raised here in Atlanta/Kansas City/Rochester/ Milwaukee?
   a. If not, where are you from and when did you move here?
2. How did you come to be involved in public service?
3. How long have you been in this position?
4. What other public-service positions have you held?
5. How many campaigns have you been involved in as the candidate?
6. How many campaigns have you been involved in as staff?
7. Before deciding to run for office, did you volunteer for or work on any other campaigns?
8. What made you decide to run for office?
9. Were there challenges in running for office that you did not anticipate?
   a. If so, what were they?
10. Did you have a paid staff while running?
    a. If so, how did you find/hire them?
11. What about your staff now? How did you find/hire them?
12. Did you rely on volunteers while campaigning, or do you now?
    a. If so, how did/do you recruit them, or did/do they come to you?
13. Have there been challenges to finding volunteers?
    a. If so, what are they?
    b. Has it gotten easier or harder over time, or is it easier or harder at different times (of the year, or while you're campaigning versus while you're in office)?

Community

14. How would you define your community—your neighborhood, your district, your city, all of the above?

15. Has your community changed much in your lifetime?
      a. If so, how?
16. What community issues do you see as most pressing, or which issues
    do you spend most of your time on?
          a. Obviously, this would depend on how community is defined—if
          "all of the above," are there different issues facing neighbor-
          hoods vs. district vs. city, and if so, what are they?
17. Do you think the pressing community issues have changed as the
    community has changed?
      a. If so, how?
18. How do these issues come to your attention—did they motivate you to
    become a public servant, did they emerge during the campaign, are
    they constituent driven, etc.?
19. Do these issues motivate individuals to contact you, work with you, or
    volunteer for you?
20. Have these issues influenced how you work with your constituents or
    neighborhood groups?
21. Have these issues affected your priorities as a councilmember/mayor?
22. Do different issues require different groups of people to come to-
    gether?
23. Have these groups of people changed over time?
24. Do you rely on work with local, citizen leaders to help you accomplish
    your goals for your community/district/constituents?
          a. If so, how?
25. If so, how do you identify these leaders—are they self-identified by
    being president of a local group, or do you seek them out?

Constituents, Contact, Participation, and Voting

26. Whom do you consider to be, or how do you define, your constituents?
27. Do you think there are different constituent groups within your
    district/city?
          a. If so, what are they or how would you define them?
28. Do these different constituent groups have different interests or
    concerns?
          a. If so, what are the various interests/concerns and how are they
          different?

29. Have these constituent groups changed over time?
    a. If so, how?
30. Do your constituents contact you?
    a. If so, how?
31. Do you get contacted regularly and/or often?
32. Why do constituents generally contact you—complaint, question, raise issue, etc.?
33. Are there some individuals or constituent groups that are in contact with you more than others?
    a. If so, why do you think that is?
34. Given that there are varying interests and that different individuals and groups contact you from within your city/district, how do you prioritize or balance these various pressures?
35. Do you ever contact your constituents (individuals) or groups directly?
    a. If so, why?
36. Do you ever contact neighborhood associations, PTAs, or churches?
    a. If so, why?
37. Are there some types of groups (neighborhood associations, PTAs, church groups) that you contact more than others?
    a. If so, why?
38. How would you characterize your relationship with your constituents?
39. How would you characterize your relationship with various community groups and faith-based organizations?
40. Do you work with either constituents or community and faith-based organizations on a regular basis?
    a. If so, why?
    b. Do you work around particular issues, or is it an ongoing partnership?
    c. Who initiates the partnership—the constituent, group, or you?
41. Do you work with individual constituents around times of campaigns?
    a. If so, how?
42. Do you work with organizations/PTAs/churches around times of campaigns?
    a. If so, how?
43. Whom would you say you work with most, individuals or organizations?

44. When it comes to volunteering, either around campaigns or regularly, do constituents or groups contact you, or do you contact them?

   a. Is it different for individuals and groups—i.e., are individuals less likely to contact you for volunteer opportunities while groups are more likely, or vice versa?

45. One of the things I'm interested in is whether or not citizens actually go to the polls. Do you think generally your constituents or residents of your community vote or not?

   a. Do you think this has changed at all over time (as your community has changed)?

46. Do you think there are any challenges to voting facing your constituents or your community?

   a. If so, what are they?

   b. Has this changed at all over your time in public service or in your lifetime?

   c. If so, why do you think that is?

47. If there are challenges to voting, are there ways you try to help them overcome these challenges?

48. Is getting people to vote something you think about regularly?

49. When you think about your campaign and your election, how did you encourage voting?

50. Did you find some strategies more effective?

   a. If so, what worked and what didn't?

   b. If you had to do it again, or when you do it again, what might you do differently?

51. Was it challenging or relatively easy to encourage people to vote?

   a. Why or why not?

   b. Do you think that it has become more or less difficult to encourage people to vote, and why?

52. Do you think that there are some people who are just more likely to vote than others?

   a. If so, why do you think some are more likely?

   b. Do you think this has changed at all or that who is more likely to vote has changed?

53. Do you think there are other forms of political participation that are more important or just as important as voting?

   a. If so, what are they?

54. Do you encourage any other form of political participation?
    a. If so, what and how?
    b. Do you think this has changed at all in your tenure or over your lifetime?

Future

55. Over the next ten years how do you think the community might change?
56. Why do you think these changes will occur—are there citywide changes happening (i.e., new development, new populations, etc.).
57. What do you think will be the most important issues facing your community over the next decade?
58. How do you think individuals, community groups, and politicians can best respond to these challenges and issues—what goals/issues/strategies should they be focusing on?

NOTES

Introduction

1. For good maps on the white and black populations in and around Atlanta in the 1940s, 1950s, 1960s, and 1970s, see Kevin Kruse, *White Flight: Atlanta and the Making of Modern Conservatism* (Princeton, NJ: Princeton University Press, 2005), 16–17. To protect confidentiality all names of respondents have been changed, as has the name of each respondent's organization or church. If the neighborhood has a name that is commonly used, I use it here; if not, I created one for ease of comparison (see Appendix B for more information). In this case West Manor is one name commonly used for this neighborhood in this part of town.

2. Sandra Baker, interview by author, May 15, 2006, digital recording held by author; Shirley Jackson, interview by author, May 18, 2006, digital recording held by author.

3. Kruse, *White Flight*, 16–17.

4. Leroy Perkins, interview by author, May 18, 2006, digital recording held by author.

5. Centre on Housing and Evictions, *Fair Play for Housing Rights: Mega-Events, Olympic Games and Housing Rights* (Geneva, Switzerland: Centre on Housing and Evictions, 2007), http://www.cohre.org/sites/default/files/fair_play_for_housing_rights _2007_0.pdf (accessed on February 26, 2014), 113–25.

6. Ibid.

7. Paul Jargowsky, *Poverty and Place: Ghettos, Barrios, and the American City* (New York: Russell Sage Foundation, 1997); Elizabeth Kneebone, Carey Nadeau, and Alan Berube, "The Re-emergence of Concentrated Poverty: Metropolitan Trends in the 2000s," in *The Metropolitan Opportunity Series* (Washington, DC: Brookings Institution, 2011); Douglas S. Massey and Nancy A. Denton, *American Apartheid: Segregation and the Making of the Underclass* (Cambridge, MA: Harvard University Press, 1993).

8. For more on public choice theory see Charles M. Tiebout, "A Pure Theory of Local Expenditures," *Journal of Political Economy* 64:5 (October 1956): 416–24. For more on the poverty trap see William Julius Wilson, *When Work Disappears: The World of the New Urban Poor* (New York: Vintage, 1996); and Wilson, *The Truly Disadvantaged:*

The Inner City, the Underclass, and Public Policy (Chicago: University of Chicago Press, 1987).

9. Tara Watson, "Metropolitan Growth, Inequality, and Neighborhood Segregation by Income," in *Brookings-Wharton Papers on Urban Affairs: 2006*, ed. Gary Burtless and Janet Rothenberg Pack (Washington, DC: Brookings Institution Press, 2006).

10. Examples of research documenting lower levels of voter turnout among low-income voters include Larry M. Bartels, *Unequal Democracy: The Political Economy of the New Gilded Age* (New York: Russell Sage Foundation, 2008); John D. Griffin and Brian Newman, "Voting Power, Policy Representation, and Disparities in Voting Rewards," *Journal of Politics* 75:1 (January 2013): 52–64; and Sidney Verba, Kay Lehman Schlozman, and Henry E. Brady, *Voice and Equality* (Cambridge, MA: Harvard University Press, 1995).

11. Though some might argue that economic segregation produces only compositional effects in neighborhoods so that locating similar individuals in the same neighborhood will produce trends that are reflective of similarly situated individuals acting in similar ways, the evidence presented here aims to argue otherwise.

12. For more on civic culture see Laura A. Reese and Raymond A. Rosenfeld, *The Civic Culture of Local Economic Development* (Thousand Oaks, CA: Sage, 2002); Ann Swidler, "Culture in Action: Symbols and Strategies," *American Sociological Review* 51:2 (April 1986): 273–86.

13. The myth of free housing choice is similar to the myth of the free market. Just as government decisions and public policy have significant, direct, and lasting effects on economic markets, so too do government decisions have significant, direct, and lasting effects on where people choose to live. For more on this see Peter Dreier, John Mollenkopf, and Todd Swanstrom, *Place Matters: Metropolitics for the Twenty-First Century* (Lawrence: University Press of Kansas, 2001); David Freund, *Colored Property: State Policy and White Racial Politics in Suburban America* (Chicago: University of Chicago Press, 2007); and Kenneth T. Jackson, *Crabgrass Frontier: The Suburbanization of the United States* (New York: Oxford University Press, 1985).

14. Dreier, Mollenkopf, and Swanstrom, *Place Matters*; Colin Gordon, *Mapping Decline: St. Louis and the State of the American City* (Philadelphia: University of Pennsylvania Press, 2008).

15. For more on how this affected individuals and families, see, for example, Wilson, *When Work Disappears*; and Wilson, *The Truly Disadvantaged*.

16. Dreier, Mollenkopf, and Swanstrom, *Place Matters*, 108–109; Freund, *Colored Property*, 185–86; Jackson, *Crabgrass Frontier*, 231–38; Ira Katznelson, *When Affirmative Action Was White: An Untold History of Racial Inequality in Twentieth-Century America* (New York: W.W. Norton, 2005), 121–29.

17. A great deal of research documents the various ways that housing policies developed, evolved, and affected urban landscapes. The following sources include good comprehensive discussions of various facets of housing policy: Gordon, *Mapping De-*

cline, 207–209; Jackson, *Crabgrass Frontier*, 202; Katznelson, *When Affirmative Action Was White*, 121–29; Marc A. Weiss, "Marketing and Financing Home Ownership: Mortgage Lending and Public Policy in the United States, 1918–1989," *Business and Economic History* 18:2 (1989): 109–18.

18. Much scholarship has been produced about the Great Migration of Southern blacks to Northern cities—too much to name here. A recent and acclaimed work on this general subject is Isabel Wilkerson, *The Warmth of Other Suns: The Epic Story of America's Great Migration* (New York: Random House, 2010); examples of other works include Nicholas Lemann, *The Promised Land: The Great Black Migration and How It Changed America* (New York: Alfred A. Knopf, 1991); Joe William Trotter, Jr., ed, *The Great Migration in Historical Perspective* (Bloomington: Indiana University Press, 1991); Stuart E. Tolnay, Kyle D. Crowder, and Robert M. Adelman, " 'Narrow and Filthy Alleys of the City'? The Residential Settlement Patterns of Black Southern Migrants to the North," *Social Forces* 8:3 (March 2000): 989–1051.

19. See, for example, Freund, *Colored Property* (particularly chapter 7), on local efforts to defend largely white communities with tactics, including "Restriction Agreements" in which residents pledged to keep nonwhites out of Dearborn, Michigan, and other restrictionist land-use policies. Kevin Fox Gotham writes about the use of zoning and restrictive covenants in Kansas City, Missouri; for more on Gotham's work on Kansas City see *Race, Real Estate, and Uneven Development* (Albany: State University of New York Press, 2002).

20. Zoning codes are used to classify land use and usually take one of three forms: use-based zoning regulates how a plot of land can be zoned, for example, for residential, agricultural, or commercial activity; form-based zoning codes regulate the physical nature of buildings that can be placed on a particular plot of land, such as specifying single-family housing versus multifamily housing, building height, building location on the lot, building size, etc.; or some combination of the two, so that the zoning code specifies what the land may be used for and what form the structure can take toward that end.

21. Freund, *Colored Property*, 296. For more on how the language of private property served as a proxy for racialized language, see Matthew D. Lassiter, *The Silent Majority: Suburban Politics in the Sunbelt South* (Princeton, NJ: Princeton University Press, 2006).

22. John Iceland and Rima Wilkes, "Does Socioeconomic Status Matter? Race, Class, and Residential Segregation," *Social Problems* 52:2 (2006): 248–73; John Iceland, Daniel H. Weinberg, and Erika Steinmetz, *U.S. Census Bureau, Series CENSR-3, Racial and Ethnic Residential Segregation in the United States, 1980–2000* (Washington, DC: U.S. Government Printing Office, 2002); Watson, "Metropolitan Growth, Inequality, and Neighborhood Segregation by Income."

23. Dreier, Mollenkopf, and Swanstrom, *Place Matters*, 125.

24. For more on the effects of deindustrialization see Wilson, *When Work Disappears*. For more on the residential dislocation in the wake of revitalization and the

attendant emotional and psychological effects of this, see Bernard J. Frieden and Lynne B. Sagalyn, *Downtown, Inc.* (Cambridge, MA: MIT Press, 1994 [1989]).

25. There is a great deal of work on the practice of redlining, its consequences, and the policies created to address redlining, specifically the Community Reinvestment Act. For more on this see Dreier, Mollenkopf, and Swanstrom, *Place Matters*; Margery Austin Turner and G. Thomas Kingsley, *Federal Programs for Addressing Low-Income Housing Needs: A Policy Primer* (Washington, DC: Urban Institute, December 2008); Margery Austin Turner and Felicity Skidmore, eds., *Mortgage Lending Discrimination: A Review of Existing Evidence* (Washington, DC: Urban Institute, 1996); Stephen L. Ross and John Yinger, *The Color of Credit* (Cambridge, MA: MIT Press, 2002); and Mara S. Sydney, *Unfair Housing: How National Policy Shapes Community Action* (Lawrence: University Press of Kansas, 2003).

26. Frieden and Sagalyn, *Downtown, Inc.*

27. There has also been a great deal written about transportation policy. Some important examples are Owen D. Gutfreund, *Twentieth-Century Sprawl: Highways and the Reshaping of the American Landscape* (Oxford: Oxford University Press, 2004); Alan Lupo, Frank Colcord, and Edmond P. Fowler, *Rites of Way: The Politics of Transportation in Boston and the U.S. City* (Boston: Little, Brown, 1971); Raymond A. Mohl, "Stop the Road: Freeway Revolts in American Cities," *Journal of Urban History* 30:5 (July 2004): 674–706; and Jon C. Teaford, *The Rough Road to Renaissance: Urban Revitalization in America, 1940–1985* (Baltimore: Johns Hopkins University Press, 1990).

28. Dreier, Mollenkopf, and Swanstrom, *Place Matters*, 103.

29. Frieden and Sagalyn, *Downtown, Inc.*, 20–25, 27–30.

30. Ibid., 28.

31. See ibid., 29. These numbers reflect numerous examples of this phenomenon across the United States, from Robert Moses and his efforts in New York City, to the development of Baltimore's Interstate 83 through the working-class neighborhood of Fell's Point, to Philadelphia's disjointed freeway planning process, just to name a few. For more on this see Frieden and Sagalyn, *Downtown, Inc.*, 27–30.

32. Clifford Winston, "Government Failure in Urban Transportation," *Fiscal Studies* 21:45 (2000), 403–25.

33. Dreier, Mollenkopf, and Swanstrom, *Place Matters*, 104.

34. For more on income and wealth inequality see Gary Burtless, "Growing American Inequality: Sources and Remedies," in *Setting National Priorities: The 2000 Election and Beyond*, eds. Henry J. Aaron and Robert D. Reischauer (Washington, DC: Brookings Institution, 1999), 137–66; Richard Freeman, "Solving the New Inequality," in *The New Inequality: Creating Solutions for Poor America*, ed. Joshua Cohen and Joel Rogers (Boston: Beacon, 1999); James Kenneth Galbraith, *Created Unequal: The Crisis in American Pay* (Chicago: University of Chicago Press, 2000); Jacob S. Hacker and Paul Pierson, "Winner-Take-All Politics: Public Policy, Political Organization, and the Precipitous Rise of Top Incomes in the United States," *Politics and Society* 38:2

(June 2010): 152–204; Wojciech Kopczuk, Emmanuel Saez, and Jae Song, "Earnings Inequality and Mobility in the United States: Evidence from Social Security Data Since 1937," *Quarterly Journal of Economics* 125:1 (2010): 91–128; Bruce Western, Deirdre Bloome, and Christine Percheski, "Inequality Among American Families with Children, 1975 to 2005," *American Sociological Review* 73:6 (December 2008): 903–20; Edward N. Wolff, *Top Heavy: The Increasing Inequality of Wealth and What We Can Do About It* (New York: New Press, 2002); and Wolff, "The Asset Price Meltdown and the Wealth of the Middle Class," National Bureau of Economic Research, Working Paper No. 18559, November 2012.

35. Hacker and Pierson, "Winner-Take-All Politics," 15–17.

36. Wealth is different from income because it captures all assets (e.g., gross value of an owner-occupied home, other real estate, cash deposits, bond, and money market accounts) minus all economic liabilities, or debt (e.g., mortgage debt, consumer debt, and auto loans). Wealth is an important feature of economic well-being because it is these assets—investments and savings—that families can tap into in times of crisis or leverage for other economic opportunities and gains. In fact, this is why *non-home wealth*, a calculation of wealth that removes the value of homeownership and real estate from the equation, may be more important because real-estate equity is often not as fungible as one would like: in a time of crisis it might not be realistic to sell a home quickly to access that source of money. For more on this see Wolff, "Asset Price Meltdown."

37. Wolff, "Asset Price Meltdown."

38. Tara Watson, "Inequality and the Measurement of Residential Segregation by Income in American Neighborhoods," *Review of Income and Wealth* 55:3 (September 2009): 820–44, see esp. 821. For more in rising levels of economic segregation see also Iceland and Wilkes, "Does Socioeconomic Status Matter?"; Iceland, Weinberg, and Steinmetz, *U.S. Census Bureau, Series CENSR-3.*

39. Lincoln Quillian, "Migration Patterns and the Growth of High-Poverty Neighborhoods, 1970–1990," *American Journal of Sociology* 105:1 (July 1999): 1–37; and Marta Tienda, "Poor People, Poor Places: Deciphering Neighborhood Effects on Poverty Outcomes," in *Macro-Micro Linkages in Sociology*, ed. Joan Huber (Thousand Oaks, CA: Sage, 1999).

40. Watson, "Metropolitan Growth, Inequality, and Neighborhood Segregation by Income," 2.

41. There are many examples of scholarly studies about racial segregation. A few that focus on the political consequences of racial segregation include Cathy J. Cohen and Michael C. Dawson, "Neighborhood Poverty and African American Politics," *American Political Science Review* 87:2 (June 1993): 286–302; John W. Frazier, Florence M. Margai, and Eugene Tettey-Fio, *Race and Place: Equity Issues in Urban America* (Boulder, CO: Westview, 2003); and Karen M. Kaufmann, *The Urban Voter* (Ann Arbor: University of Michigan Press, 2004).

42. See, for example, Dreier, Mollenkopf, and Swanstrom, *Place Matters*; Susan E. Mayer, "How the Growth in Income Inequality Increased Economic Segregation,"

JCPR Working Papers 230, Northwestern University/University of Chicago Joint Center for Poverty Research, 2001; Susan E. Mayer, "How Economic Segregation Affects Children's Educational Attainment," *Social Forces* 81:1 (September 2002): 153–76; Thomas J. Sugrue, *The Origins of the Urban Crisis: Race and Inequality in Postwar Detroit* (Princeton, NJ: Princeton University Press. 2005 [1996]); Wilson, *When Work Disappears*; and Wilson, *The Truly Disadvantaged*.

43. Robert H. Huckfeldt, *Politics in Context: Assimilation and Conflict in Urban Neighborhoods* (New York: Agathon, 1986), 1. For more on this see Margaret Weir, "Politics, Money, and Power in Community Development," in *Urban Problems and Community Development*, ed. Ronald F. Ferguson and William T. Dickens (Washington, DC: Brookings Institution, 1999), 139–92; and Weir, "Mobilizing to Challenge Metropolitan Inequalities," paper prepared for presentation at the Annual Meeting of the American Political Science Association, Washington, DC, August 30–September 2, 2005.

44. The data used in this analysis was compiled by the author from the Neighborhood Change Database and the CQ Voting and Elections Collection from CQ Press (an imprint of SAGE Publications). For more on this, see Urban Institute and GeoLytics, *Neighborhood Change Database*, CensusCD neighborhood change database (NCDB) [electronic resource] : 1970–2000 tract data: selected variables for U.S. Census tracts for 1970, 1980, 1990, 2000; CQ Voting and Elections Collection from CQ Press (an imprint of SAGE Publications), http://library.cqpress.com/elections/index.php (accessed on February 26, 2014). Software programs (I use STATA here) standardize coefficients by creating Z-scores for coefficient, so the mean of each independent variable is zero, with a variance of one. It is important to note that standardizing coefficients does not change the fit of the linear model or even the underlying reality captured in the data. This is simply a way for us to be able to compare the magnitude of the effects of the independent variables. Please contact the author for results using unstandardized coefficients.

45. As these coefficients have been standardized, we would say that in all counties a one standard-deviation change in economic segregation decreases voter turnout by almost half of one standard deviation.

46. Hacker and Pierson, "Winner-Take-All Politics," 44.

47. Joe Soss and Lawrence R. Jacobs, "The Place of Inequality: Non-Participation in the American Polity," *Political Science Quarterly* 124:1 (Spring 2009): 95–125, see esp. 97.

48. Ibid., 123.

49. See, for example, Neil Fligstein, *Going North* (New York: Academic, 1981); Massey and Denton, *American Apartheid*; Stewart E. Tolnay, Robert M. Adelman, and Kyle D. Crowder, "Race, Regional Origin, and Residence in Northern Cities at the Beginning of the Great Migration," *American Sociological Review* 67:3 (June 2002): 456–57; Wilson, *When Work Disappears*; and Wilson, *The Truly Disadvantaged*. See

also Cohen and Dawson, "Neighborhood Poverty and African American Politics"; and Bruce H. Rankin and James M. Quane, "Neighborhood Poverty and the Social Isolation of Inner-City African American Families," *Social Forces* 79:1 (September 2000): 139–64.

50. Jackson, *Crabgrass Frontier*; Massey and Denton, *American Apartheid*.

51. Mark Schneider and Thomas Phelan, "Black Suburbanization in the 1980s," *Demography* 30:2 (May 1993): 269–79.

52. Barbara Jeanne Fields, in "Slavery, Race and Ideology in the United States of America" (*New Left Review* I:181 [1990]: 95–118), supplies a very interesting discussion that is useful here about how race is an ideological construct, created and perpetuated to justify a system of slavery in a democracy founded on ideas of liberty and equality. In this conception of race as ideology, race—and the black-white distinction in particular—has become the language through which Americans talk about all different types of political or social phenomena, when in fact they may actually be talking about something else, such as class and class distinction. As Fields explains, "Nothing so well illustrates that impossibility as the conviction among otherwise sensible scholars that race 'explains' historical phenomena; specifically, that it explains why people of African descent have been set apart for treatment different from that accorded to others. But *race* is just the name assigned to the phenomenon" (100). In other words, what we have been assigning as a racial effect or a racial phenomenon may in fact be due to something else.

53. Census tracts are used as proxies for neighborhoods because census tracts are "small, relatively permanent statistical subdivisions of a county," usually having "between 2,500 to 8,000 persons and, when first delineated, are designed to be homogenous with respect to population characteristics, income status, and living conditions," according to the U.S. Census Bureau, in "Census Bureau Touts New Data Delivery System" (press release, 2001). As is common in the literature, a "poor census tract" is defined here as having a poverty rate between 11 percent and 39.99 percent in 1970 and 1980 and between 13 percent and 39.99 percent in 1990 and 2000, while a high-poverty census tract, also following the literature, is defined as having a poverty rate of 40 percent or above. See for reference Jargowsky, *Poverty and Place*.

54. A high-poverty neighborhood is defined as a neighborhood with a poverty rate of 40 percent or higher (N = 2,059); a highly segregated neighborhood is defined as a neighborhood with an isolation index, a measure of segregation, 40 percent or higher (N = 3,260); a segregated, poor neighborhood is defined as a neighborhood with a poverty rate between 11 percent and 30 percent and an isolation index between 13 percent and 40 percent (N = 1,221); a highly segregated, high-poverty neighborhood is defined as a neighborhood with a poverty rate of 40 percent or higher and an isolation index of 40 percent or higher (N = 88).

55. Segregation is measured by the isolation and dissimilarity indexes, the calculation of which is discussed later in this chapter. As chapters 3 and 4 will discuss, many

civic leaders in these highly segregated, high-poverty neighborhoods talk about residential mobility among residents of their community and the difficulty that this poses for civic and political mobilization. Despite the fact that these data show a relatively smaller percentage of residents who lived in a different home than five years ago, it is possible that the residential mobility that does exist coupled with the very high rates of unemployment, low rates of educational attainment, and other contextual factors discussed in chapters 3 and 4 make mobilization difficult despite relative residential stability.

56. See, for example, Wilson *The Truly Disadvantaged*; Wilson, *When Work Disappears*; Harriet B. Newburger, Eugenie L. Birch, and Susan M. Wachter, *Neighborhood and Life Chances: How Place Matters in Modern America* (Philadelphia: University of Pennsylvania Press, 2011); and Katherine S. Newman, *No Shame in My Game: The Working Poor in the Inner City* (New York: First Vintage/Russell Sage Edition, 1999).

57. See, for reference, Verba, Schlozman, and Brady, *Voice and Equality*; and Raymond E. Wolfinger and Steven J. Rosenstone, *Who Votes?* (New Haven: Yale University Press, 1980), among many, many others.

58. Robert Putnam, *Bowling Alone: The Collapse and Revival of American Community* (New York: Simon and Schuster, 2000); Steven J. Rosenstone and John Mark Hansen, *Mobilization, Participation, and Democracy in America* (Upper Saddle River, NJ: Prentice Hall, 1996).

59. Rosenstone and Hansen, *Mobilization, Participation, and Democracy in America*, 161.

60. For more on this see David E. Campbell, *Why We Vote: How Schools and Communities Shape Our Civic Life* (Princeton, NJ: Princeton University Press, 2006); and J. Eric Oliver, *Democracy in Suburbia* (Princeton, NJ: Princeton University Press, 2001).

61. Robert H. Huckfeldt and John Sprague, "Networks in Context: The Social Flow of Political Information," *American Political Science Review* 81:4 (December 1987): 1197–216; Huckfeldt and Sprague, "Political Parties and Electoral Mobilization: Political Structure, Social Structure, and the Party Canvass," *American Political Science Review* 86:1 (March 1992): 70–86.

62. See Verba, Schlozman, and Brady, *Voice and Equality*; and Bartels, *Unequal Democracy*.

63. For example, in Campbell, *Why We Vote*; and Oliver, *Democracy in Suburbia*.

64. Soss and Jacobs, "The Place of Inequality," 123.

65. Hacker and Pierson, "Winner-Take-All Politics," 154.

Chapter 1. Understanding Civic Engagement in Context

1. For example, Robert Beauregard demonstrates the overall "decline" of American cities in *Voices of Decline: The Postwar Fate of U.S. Cities* (New York: Routledge,

2003). See also U.S. Department of Transportation, "Census 2000 Population Statistics," Federal Highway Administration Office of Planning, Environment, and Realty, http://www.fhwa.dot.gov/planning/census_issues/archives/metropolitan_planning /cps2k.cfm (accessed July 24, 2013); and U.S. Department of Commerce, "2010 Census Urban and Rural Classification and Urban Area Criteria," U.S. Census Bureau, http:// www.census.gov/geo/reference/ua/urban-rural-2010.html (accessed June 28, 2013).

2. Some scholars have already begun to make this point. See, for example Dreier, Mollenkopf, and Swanstrom, *Place Matters*; and Neil Smith, "Gentrification, the Frontier, and the Restructuring of Urban Space," in *Readings in Urban Theory*, ed. Susan S. Fainstein and Scott Campbell (Oxford: Blackwell, 2002).

3. An important note regarding this scholarship is that the effects of rural context and circumstances on political opinion and political behavior are often overlooked. Cynthia M. Duncan has done good work on political behavior in rural areas that is vital for understanding the whole picture of political participation in America (*Worlds Apart: Why Poverty Persists in Rural America* [New Haven, CT: Yale University Press, 1999]). Duncan's work needs to be joined with studies like this one in order to gain a more comprehensive perspective on the political behavior of Americans.

4. This database, originally developed as the Urban Underclass Database by the Urban Institute, has been updated to the year 2010 and is now distributed by GeoLytics, Inc. Here, I used Urban Institute, and GeoLytics, *Neighborhood Change Database*, CensusCD Neighborhood Change Database (NCDB) [electronic resource]: 1970–2000 tract data: selected variables for US Census tracts for 1970, 1980, 1990, 2000.

5. U.S. Department of Commerce, "Geographic Areas—Definitions," U.S. Census Bureau, American Community Survey, http://www.census.gov/acs/www/data_documentation/custom_tabulation_request_form/geo_def.php (accessed July 24, 2013).

6. See, for example, Elijah Anderson, *Streetwise: Race, Class, and Change in an Urban Community* (Chicago: Chicago University Press, 1992); Joe T. Darden, *Detroit: Race and Uneven Development* (Philadelphia: Temple University Press, 1987); Michael C. Dawson, *Behind the Mule: Race and Class in African American Politics* (Princeton, NJ: Princeton University Press, 1995); Frazier, Margai, and Tettey-Fio, *Race and Place*; Sugrue, *Origins of the Urban Crisis*; and Tolnay, Adelman, and Crowder, "Race, Regional Origin, and Residence".

7. In 1988 Douglas S. Massey and Nancy A. Denton published their article "The Dimensions of Residential Segregation" because the authors believed that the field of segregation studies was in a state of "theoretical and methodological disarray" (282). In this article the authors attempt to bring some order to the field by combing the literature and testing twenty separate indicators of segregation then in use. Using factor analysis and principle component analysis, the authors discover five distinct dimensions of segregation and the single best indicator of segregation for each dimension. I use the best indicators for evenness (dissimilarity) and exposure (isolation) here. See "The Dimensions of Residential Segregation," *Social Forces* 67:2 (1988): 281–315, 282–283.

8. Ibid., 284–91.

9. The case-study neighborhoods selected here are within large urban areas, but the calculation of the isolation and dissimilarity indexes are at the county level.

10. It is important to note that the NCDB includes indicators that allow me to calculate dissimilarity and isolation, but the NCDB does not include indicators to construct spatially determined measures of economic segregation, such as centralization or clustering.

11. Massey and Denton, "Dimensions of Residential Segregation," 284.

12. Alan J. Abramson, Mitchell S. Tobin, and Matthew R. VanderGoot, "The Changing Geography of Metropolitan Opportunity: The Segregation of the Poor in U.S. Metropolitan Areas, 1970–1990," *Housing Policy Debate* 6:1 (1995): 24–72, 48.

13. The number of people below the poverty line for each neighborhood is calculated in the NCDB. The Urban Institute and Geolytics calculated this by summing the total number of individuals and individuals in families below the poverty line. The federal poverty lines for families of four in 1970, 1980, 1990, and 2000 were $3,968; $8,414; $13,359; and $17,604, respectively. The federal poverty lines for individuals in 1970, 1980, 1990, and 2000 were $1,954; $4,190; $6,652; and $8,791, respectively. Each dollar amount is adjusted from 1959 dollars to reflect the value of the dollar in that year.

14. Poverty in the United States was 15.3 percent in 2010, up from 11.3 percent in 2000, while income inequality "skyrocketed" in the 2000s after a drop in the 1990s. See Alemayehu Bishaw, "Poverty: 2010 and 2011," *American Community Survey Briefs*, U.S. Census Bureau, September 2012; and Joseph Dalaker, "Poverty in the United States: 2000," *Current Population Reports*, U.S. Census Bureau, September 2001. See also U.S. Congress Joint Economic Committee, "Income Inequality and the Great Recession," September 2010, http://www.jec.senate.gov/public/?a=Files.Serve&File_id=91975589 -257c-403b-8093-8f3b584a088c (accessed on June 28, 2013); and Watson, "Metropolitan Growth, Inequality, and Neighborhood Segregation by Income."

15. The average poverty rate in the average U.S. census tract was 11 percent in 1970 and 1980 and 13 percent in 1990 and 2000. Throughout the text a "high poverty" census tract is defined as one that has a poverty rate of 40 percent or higher, as is common in the literature (see Jargowsky, *Poverty and Place*).

16. This excludes the consideration of Cook County, which is home to Chicago. I deliberately chose not to use Chicago as a case study because of the complexity of racial and economic segregation in the city, and the fact that such a high-profile city warrants a deeper analysis in light of the findings here. In short the complexity and prominence of Chicago make it difficult to compare with other cases. The same is true of other potential options for case-study cities, including Los Angeles and Washington, D.C.

17. In all analyses and in the case-study selection process I only used census tracts that had been established in 1970 or before, had either not changed or had changed in name only, and had populations of two hundred or more in 2000. Figure 1.1 obviously

contains other interesting case-study options for analysis: Chicago (Cook County); Washington, D.C.; and Boston (Suffolk County). San Diego or even Los Angeles would have been reasonable choices as well. But in many ways the politics of these cities have been well covered, and in some cases the scope (San Diego and Los Angeles) or the politics (Washington, D.C.) of the city might complicate the research design. My aim here was to identify the best case studies allowing for geographic and racial variance. Other cases could certainly be used in a confirmatory analysis of the findings offered here.

18. The terms *impoverished* and *prosperous* are used here to evoke not only the economic consequences of increasing poverty or wealth within a neighborhood but to draw attention to broader political and social consequences as well.

19. There are various ways to categorize the literature on racial segregation. To understand the trend of racial segregation broadly see Anderson, *Streetwise*; Camille Zubrinsky Charles, "The Dynamics of Racial Residential Segregation," *Annual Review of Sociology* 29 (2003): 167–207; Reynolds Farley and William H. Frey, "Changes in the Segregation of Whites from Blacks During the 1980s: Small Steps Toward a More Integrated Society," *American Sociological Review* 59 (1994): 23–45; Jargowsky, *Poverty and Place*; Massey and Denton, *American Apartheid*; Gary Orfield and Carol Ashkinaze, *The Closing Door: Conservative Policy and Black Opportunity* (Chicago: Chicago University Press, 1991); Mary Pattillo-McCoy, "The Limits of Out-Migration for the Black Middle Class," *Journal of Urban Affairs* 22 (2000): 225–41; and Sugrue, *Origins of the Urban Crisis*. Other ways to think about racial segregation are to focus on the consequences, of which there are many.

Good scholarship on the political and policy consequences of race, racism, and America's distinct racial history includes Martin Gilens, *Why Americans Hate Welfare: Race, Media, and the Politics of Antipoverty Policy* (Chicago: University of Chicago Press, 1999); Katznelson, *When Affirmative Action Was White*; Jennifer L. Lawless and Richard L. Fox, "Political Participation of the Urban Poor," *Social Problems* 48:3 (2001): 362–85; Jan E. Leighley, *Strength in Numbers? The Political Mobilization of Racial and Ethnic Minorities* (Princeton, NJ: Princeton University Press, 2001); Lee Sigelman and S. Welch, "The Contact Hypothesis Revisited: Interracial Contact and Positive Racial Attitudes," *Social Forces* 71 (1993): 781–95; and Theda Skocpol, Ariane Liazos, and Marshall Ganz, *What a Mighty Power We Can Be: African American Fraternal Groups and the Struggle for Racial Equality* (Princeton, NJ: Princeton University Press, 2006).

Other scholars focus on the consequences of racism and racial segregation for finances and property, education, or public health; some good examples include Hope Landrine and Irma Corral, "Separate and Unequal: Residential Segregation and Black Health Disparities," *Ethnicity and Disease* 19 (Spring 2009): 179–84; Newburger, Birch, and Wachter, *Neighborhood and Life Chances*; Jacob S. Rugh and Douglas S. Massey, "Racial Segregation and the American Foreclosure Crisis," *American Sociological Review* 75:5 (2010): 629–51; Guy Stuart, *Discriminating Risk: The U.S. Mortgage*

Lending Industry in the Twentieth Century (Ithaca, NY: Cornell University Press, 2003).

20. See Gary Goertz and James Mahoney, *A Tale of Two Cultures: Qualitative and Quantitative Research in the Social Sciences* (Princeton, NJ: Princeton University Press, 2012). The real added value of Goertz and Mahoney's work is to clearly articulate the different "cultures" of quantitative and qualitative research and to try to facilitate communication between these two camps, who are often disdainful of the other's work; quantitative scholars see qualitative scholars as lacking rigor, while qualitative scholars see quantitative scholars as bean counters with little to say about the processes and contexts that drive their results. In *A Tale of Two Cultures*, Goertz and Mahoney are trying to further understanding of each type of research, highlighting that the difference between these two approaches to research is not simply about data: it is not that quantitative scholars use hard data and qualitative scholars use case studies, interviews, and archival research. Rather, the difference between these two approaches rests on a fundamental logic of research. Fundamentally, the authors "reject the assumption that a single logic of inference founded on statistical norms guides both quantitative and qualitative research." Instead, the authors argue that "the two traditions are best understood as drawing in alternative mathematical foundations: quantitative research is grounded in interferential statistics (i.e. probability and statistical theory), whereas qualitative research is (often implicitly) rooted in logic and set theory" (2).

21. Goertz and Mahoney, *A Tale of Two Cultures*, 18.

22. Ibid., 20.

23. Alexander L. George and Andrew Bennett, *Case Studies and Theory Development in the Social Sciences* (Cambridge, MA: MIT Press, 2005), 24. One of the main concerns about case-study selection is "selection bias," which is generally understood to occur when the investigator selects cases based on the dependent variable (i.e., in studying revolutions the researchers select cases in which only revolutions occur), which leads to underestimating the effects of the independent variables. What George and Bennett are arguing here is that there is actually much greater risk of and more dire consequences for a researcher selecting on both the dependent and independent variables, which could lead to either understating or overstating relationships. This is why the authors articulate six types of case study research and urge researchers to clearly identify which will be the guiding logic of their case-study selection.

24. George and Bennett, *Case Studies and Theory Development in the Social Sciences*, 25.

25. Ibid., 75.

26. See Stephen van Evera, *Guide to Methods for Students of Political Science* (Ithaca, NY: Cornell University Press, 1997), 79.

27. For a good discussion of the distinction between theory-, method-, and problem-driven political science research, see Ian Shapiro, "Problems, Methods, and Theories

in the Study of Politics, or What's Wrong with Political Science and What to Do About It," *Political Theory* 30:4 (2002): 596–619. But briefly, theory-driven researchers develop research agendas around viable and testable theories and use those theories to try to better understand various phenomena. Method-driven researchers use available methods and develop research agendas to use those methods to understand various phenomena. Problem-driven researchers, however, define a problem or issue; assess how various, previously used theories and methods have failed to address the problem; and only then move onto new theories or methods that might better address the problem or issue.

The focus in problem-driven research is fundamentally rooted in addressing political challenges rather than honing or testing particular methods or theories. This distinction is important to understand here because this study is most interested in understanding the political consequences of the problem of economic segregation, which is undoubtedly complex and very difficult to examine through traditional methodologically or theoretical frames. Yet "if the problems thus placed on the agenda are difficult to study by means of theories and methods that are currently in vogue, an additional task arises that is no less important: to keep them there and challenge the ingenuity of scholars who are sufficiently open-minded to devise creative ways of grappling with them" (Shapiro, 616).

28. Remember, the census tracts I chose for this study have not changed their boundaries from 1970 to the present, so I did not need to account for changes in the census tracts examined here. One critique of this choice might be that it introduces bias into the findings presented because this selection criterion may favor the finding of increased segregation of poverty because older census tracts may be more likely to be located in urban centers, have aging housing stock, and so forth. This, however, is not the case. As the maps in this chapter show and the wealthy case-study neighborhoods exemplify, most cities have very wealthy neighborhoods characterized by stable census-tract boundaries but none of the urban blight plaguing other parts of the city. As a result selecting census tracts that have not changed simply provides a way to control neighborhood boundaries over time and nothing more.

29. In many cases, this interdecade redistricting did not alter the way in which I calculated voter turnout because it was minimal enough or did not affect the specific election districts analyzed here. However, I did locate all maps in order to determine what, if any, changes had been made to the election districts of interest.

30. In some cases boundaries followed census tracts closely enough that percentages of election districts were not required to calculate turnout.

31. There was no available election district breakdown for off-year congressional elections, so I used gubernatorial election results instead of congressional election results to capture voter turnout trends beyond city-level trends. Mayoral elections that fall on the same year as presidential elections are held in the spring, while presidential elections are held in the fall: they are not concurrent.

32. Ruy Teixeira, *The Disappearing American Voter* (Washington, DC: Brookings Institution, 1992). When thinking about voter turnout, it is important to keep in mind that the U.S. Constitution leaves the regulation of voting and elections largely to the states, which means that individual states decide voter eligibility. For example, only two states have unrestricted voting rights for convicted felons, whereas twelve states have laws that could result in permanent loss of voting rights depending on the felony conviction. Moreover, while there are no states that allow noncitizens to vote, the number of noncitizens within each state varies greatly. This means that the population eligible to vote in any given election can vary widely from state to state, which is why the traditional measure of VAP tends to be biased toward lower turnout rates; the denominator is bigger than it should be when calculating turnout. (See also Thomas Holbrook and Brianne Heidbreder, "Does Measurement Matter? The Case of VAP and VEP in Models of Voter Turnout in the United States," *State Politics and Policy* 10 [2010]: 157–79.)

33. Holbrook and Heidbreder, "Does Measurement Matter?" 160. These scholars argue that VAP and VEP are substantially different because the VEP includes only those eligible to vote, removing from the equation noncitizens, convicted felons, and the like. This lowers the total population able to vote when compared with the VAP, or all people over the age of eighteen, thereby increasing turnout rates; the percentage of the VEP that votes is higher than the percentage of the VAP that votes: 54.2 percent to 50 percent, respectively, in 2000, for example. These authors also, note, however that determining VEP for all levels of governance is not possible. See Michael McDonald and Samuel L. Popkin, "The Myth of the Vanishing Voter," *American Political Science Review* 95: 963–74, 963; and Michael McDonald, "Voter Turnout," United States Election Project, http://elections.gmu.edu/voter_turnout.htm (accessed on July 24, 2013).

34. To calculate the VAP, population data from the *Census of Population and Housing: Population and Housing Characteristics for Census Tracts and Block Numbering Areas* from 1970, 1980, and 1990 for each of the case-study census tracts were used. For the year 2000, I used the American FactFinder application, available through the website of the U.S. Census Bureau. This data provides the total population for each census tract from which I subtracted the population younger than twenty-one for years before 1972 and younger than eighteen for 1972 and later. I used linear interpolation to calculate the VAP for the intercensus years.

35. American Political Science Association, Task Force on Inequality and American Democracy, "American Democracy in an Age of Rising Inequality," 2004, 1.

36. Abramson, Tobin, and VanderGoot, "Changing Geography of Metropolitan Opportunity."

37. This is a one-way ANOVA table because I am looking at only one explanatory variable: economic segregation. Another way to do this would be regression analysis, but given the small sample size of the data here, a simpler approach that requires fewer assumptions about the data makes more sense.

38. This was calculated using current dollars, which means that to calculate the number of individuals in households making above the national median income in 1970, I determined the national median income in 1970 dollars and then determined the number of individuals in households making at or above that amount. The national median income was $8,734 in 1970; $17,710 in 1980; $29,943 in 1990; and $41,990 in 2000. Unfortunately, this is a very crude measure, as the data do not allow one to determine the number of individuals in the household who are eighteen and older.

39. Remember that "people participate in electoral politics because someone encourages or inspires them to take part" (Rosenstone and Hansen, *Mobilization, Participation, and Democracy in America*, 161).

40. Jan E. Leighley and Jonathan Nagler, "Class Bias in the U.S. Electorate, 1972–2004," paper prepared for presentation at the Annual Meeting of the American Political Science Association, Philadelphia, August 31–September 3, 2006.

Chapter 2. Public Policy and Civic Environments in Urban America

1. As stated in Chapter 1, civic environments are the context, physical conditions, and surroundings in which citizens develop that cognitive orientation, learn lessons of citizenship, and ultimately act.

2. On progressive urban reformers, see Camilla M. Stivers, *Bureau Men and Settlement Women: Constructing Public Administration in the Progressive Era* (Lawrence: University of Kansas Press, 2002); Allan F. Davis, *Spearheads of Reform* (New York: Oxford University Press, 1967); and Roy Lubove, *The Progressives and the Slums* (Pittsburgh: University of Pittsburgh Press, 1962).

3. U.S. Department of Commerce, "Table 4: Population: 1790 to 1990," U.S. Census Bureau, http://www.census.gov/population/www/censusdata/files/table-4.pdf (accessed July 25, 2013).

4. On the Great Migration of Southern blacks to the North, see Tolnay, Adelman, and Crowder, "Race, Regional Origin, and Residence," 456–57; and Fligstein, *Going North*.

5. Gunnar Myrdal, *An American Dilemma: The Negro Problem and Modern Democracy* (New York: Harper and Row, 1962).

6. Jackson, *Crabgrass Frontier*; Sugrue, *Origins of the Urban Crisis*.

7. Kevin Fox Gotham, "A City Without Slums: Urban Renewal, Public Housing, and Downtown Revitalization in Kansas City, Missouri," *American Journal of Economics and Sociology* 60:1 (January 2001): 285–316; Jackson, *Crabgrass Frontier*.

8. Gotham, "A City Without Slums," 287.

9. Dreier, Mollenkopf, and Swanstrom, *Place Matters*, 103–5; U.S. Advisory Commission on Intergovernmental Relations, *Relocation: Unequal Treatment of People and*

Businesses Displaced by Governments, a Commission Report, January 1965, 66, http://www.library.unt.edu/gpo/acir/Reports/policy/a-26.pdf (accessed March 5, 2014).

10. Though it is important to note that there was considerable disagreement and many court cases and legislative debates over what qualifies as "just compensation" (see Advisory Commission on Intergovernmental Relations, *Relocation*, 4–10), with courts generally ruling in the 1950s and 1960s that "owners and tenants have no constitutional right to compensation for such items as good will, business interruption, costs of moving personal property, loss of rentals due to anticipated taking, and other losses and damages" (5).

11. Advisory Commission on Intergovernmental Relations, *Relocation*, 45.

12. Robert O. Self, *American Babylon: Race and the Struggle for Postwar Oakland* (Princeton, NJ: Princeton University Press, 2003); Douglas A. Massey, Andrew B. Gross, and Kumiko Shibuya, "Migration, Segregation, and the Geographic Concentration of Poverty," *American Sociological Review* 59:3 (1994): 425–45; Massey and Denton, *American Apartheid.*

13. Watson, "Inequality and the Measurement of Residential Segregation by Income."

14. See Freund, *Colored Property*. In his book Freund argues that exclusionary mortgage practices and zoning ordinances, which sought to keep blacks out of white communities, created a racial divide between metropolitan and suburban areas. See also Matthew Lassiter, *Silent Majority*, in which Lassiter makes the argument that a language of class was used as a proxy for race in the South beginning in the 1950s and 1960s, so that white Southerners were able to craft a political agenda that was rhetorically color-blind, even though the ultimate goal was the maintenance of white and black segregation.

15. These numbers come from Martin Anderson, *The Federal Bulldozer: A Critical Analysis of Urban Renewal, 1949–1962* (Cambridge, MA: MIT Press, 1964). To calculate the number of people displaced by urban renewal, Anderson multiplied the number of families affected by urban renewal (427,000) by the average household size at this time (3.65) and then added the number of individuals also affected by renewal. For more on this process see *Federal Bulldozer*, 53–55.

16. Anderson, *Federal Bulldozer*, 54–55; Advisory Commission on Intergovernmental Relations, *Relocation*, 11, 25.

17. Unfortunately, these data are incomplete as they capture the percentage of families that could be located after displacement and similar data do not exist for individuals. Given this, it is very possible that this number is actually much higher.

18. Advisory Commission on Intergovernmental Relations, *Relocation*, 25.

19. Darlene R. Roth, Andy Ambrose, and the Atlanta Historical Society, *Metropolitan Frontiers: A Short History of Atlanta* (Athens, GA: Longstreet, 1996), 65–66.

20. Ibid., 66.

21. Roth, Ambrose, and the Atlanta Historical Society, *Metropolitan Frontiers*.

22. The Great Migration generally refers to rural blacks moving to *Northern* urban centers, but, as is typically the case, Atlanta is somewhat of an exception among other Southern cities. Because of its size and status as an industrial center, rural blacks moved to Atlanta in large numbers during the mid-twentieth century, with a real uptick in "reverse migration," from North to South, beginning in the mid-1960s. For more on this see Dan Bilefsky, "For New Life, Blacks in City Head to South," *New York Times*, June 21, 2011, and Trotter, *Great Migration* (see in particular the foreword by Nell Irvin Painter, viii–x).

23. Report of the Housing Coordinator, "Negro Housing," City of Atlanta, Bureau of Planning, City Range A, A-7, Box 1, Folder 1, August 26, 1960, Atlanta History Center, Kenan Research Center, Atlanta.

24. Roth, Ambrose, and the Atlanta Historical Society, *Metropolitan Frontiers*, 174–78

25. Bureau of Planning, "Urban Renewal—General Description of, clippings pertaining to—1953, 57, 59; 1960, 1961," City of Atlanta, City Range A, A-7, Box 3, Folder 1, Atlanta History Center, Kenan Research Center, Atlanta.

26. *Atlanta Constitution*, "More Push on Renewal Urged Here," February 8, 1960.

27. Ibid.

28. City of Atlanta, *Final Report* 1967, City of Atlanta Online, http://www.atlan taga.gov/government/planning/npu_system.aspx (accessed December 19, 2007).

29. Report of the Housing Coordinator, "Negro Housing," 4; emphasis added.

30. See, for example, *Atlanta Constitution*, "Atlanta Churchwomen Tour 2 Sites for Negro Housing," January 29, 1960.

31. *Atlanta Constitution*, "Urban Renewal Called Hottest Election Issue," February 24, 1960.

32. Perkins, interview by author.

33. Tina McElroy, "Who's Who of Black Atlanta," *Atlanta Journal Constitution*, December 12, 1977, B:12.

34. *Atlanta Constitution*, "25 New Sites Offered in Place of Egleston," March 31, 1960.

35. David Nordan, "Liberal Midtown's Dilemma with Poor," *Atlanta Constitution*, May 8, 1977, A:5.

36. This was occurring at a time when across many cities middle-class blacks were moving out of poor, urban communities to more stable middle-class neighborhoods. However, as Mary Pattillo-McCoy shows us in *Black Picket Fences: Privilege and Peril Among the Black Middle Class* (Chicago: University of Chicago Press, 1999), many of the upwardly mobile, middle-class and wealthier blacks did not move into surrounding white suburbs. Instead, they moved into neighborhoods immediately surrounding the inner-city impoverished communities, which spurred further outmigration from the white residents who had previously lived in these communities. As a result, residential mobility of the black middle class often did not produce racial integration in more prosperous communities; rather, in many cases and in the case of Atlanta specifi-

cally, it created swaths of more prosperous black communities around a core of urban, black poverty, effectively creating a buffer zone between poor urban and mostly black residents and wealthier, white suburban residents. To be sure this does not mean that the residents of these more prosperous black communities were any more accepting of low-income housing, and indeed, upwardly mobile, middle-class, and wealthy African Americans have long sought to distance themselves from poor communities (see *Black Picket Fences*, 25–26).

37. Given the history of racial and economic segregation in Atlanta, it would be ideal if trends from 1940 to 2000 could be mapped, but unfortunately the Neighborhood Change Database (NCDB) only goes back to 1970.

38. The cut points for the second-tier poverty levels are determined by the national average poverty rate; so each map shows areas below the national average for their respective year and areas just above national average to the 20 percent cut point.

39. So while city officials were motivated by some benevolent goals, they were still suspicious of the urban poor and sought to break apart communities that could wield political power (Report of Housing Coordinator, "Negro Housing," 4).

40. Councilman C. T. Martin, interview by author, Atlanta, January 17, 2007.

41. William S. Worley, *Kansas City: Rise of a Regional Metropolis* (Dallas: Heritage Media, 2002), 101–2.

42. Ibid., 88.

43. Ibid., 90.

44. Jackson, *Crabgrass Frontier*, 70.

45. Worley, *Kansas City*, 88.

46. Ibid., 95.

47. There was a slight slump in population numbers in the 1980 and 1990 censuses, but that trend has since reversed, which is why, while there was population loss, it has not been as great here as in other cities. See City Planning and Development Department, "Area Profile: Kansas City, Missouri," March 23, 2012.

48. Worley, *Kansas City*, 105.

49. One of the major infrastructure debates during this time was where to locate a new joint baseball and football stadium. One potential location was downtown, just south of the Municipal Auditorium, and the other was near Leeds, Missouri, just outside of Kansas City to the south and east. The argument for the former site, which ultimately lost, was that this kind of development could help revitalize the downtown economy, attracting restaurants and services for those attending the games. But ultimately, a failure to fully understand the dire economic situation in the downtown area and the efforts of business owners who would have been displaced by the downtown location doomed that site. And, in fact, the end result was two different stadiums—one for baseball and one for football—both built in the suburbs. For more on this see James R. Shortridge, *Kansas City and How It Grew, 1822–2011* (Lawrence: University of Kansas Press, 2012).

50. Gotham, *Race, Real Estate, and Uneven Development*, 78–79.

51. *Kansas City Star*, "Need Master Plan for Area Progress," February 26, 1960, 3; *Kansas City Times*, "Advises That City Hire Urban Expert," September 12, 1961, 3; *Kansas City Times*, "Need for Firm Renewal View," June 6, 1967, 8; *Kansas City Star*, "Redevelopment Policy Lacks Clarity, Vitt Says," December 3, 1974, 6; Gotham, *Race, Real Estate, and Uneven Development*, 81.

52. *Kansas City Star*, "Need Master Plan for Area Progress."

53. Gotham, *Race, Real Estate, and Uneven Development*, 82.

54. *Kansas City Times*, "Homeowners Aggravated by Relocation Snags," March 29, 1973; *Kansas City Star*, "Real Estate Incentives Under Fire," November 17, 1985, 1H:5.

55. Timothy Conlan, *From New Federalism to Devolution: Twenty-Five Years of Intergovernmental Reform* (Washington, DC: Brookings Institution Press, 1998).

56. Lynn Byczynski, "Cost of Tax Breaks for Development Coming into Question," *Kansas City Times*, October 25, 1985, A10:1; Joe Lambe, "State Lawmakers Threaten to Restrict Use of 353 Law," *Kansas City Star*, November 25, 1985, A1:1; Lambe, "Proposal Would Change Tax Abatement Law," *Kansas City Star*, December 5, 1985, A15:3; *Kansas City Times*, "City Wants to Resolve Chapter 353 Problems on Its Own," December 24, 1985, D31:1; Lambe, "Council Will Receive '353' Use Proposals," *Kansas City Star*, January 14, 1986; *Kansas City Times*, "City Hall Can Do It," February 1, 1986, B6:1.

57. John A. Dvorak, "Bill Is OK'd on Developer Tax Breaks," *Kansas City Times*, April 18, 1986, B1:1; Denise Kotula, "City OKs Changes in 353 Use," *Kansas City Times*, September 5, 1986, A1:1. This debate over Missouri's 353 law, and Kansas City's own version of the 353 law, also called attention to the ways in which private developers used the formal classification of "blight" in urban-renewal policies to advance their own agendas. One prominent practice in Kansas City called into question during the 353 debate was the fact that private developers were purchasing perfectly good housing or properties that were within their project area, letting them fall into disrepair to receive the "blight" classification, and then using the tax incentives that came under the 353 law to pursue redevelopment projects (see Lambe, "Of Blight and Right: Concepts of Missouri's 353 Law Shifts," *Kansas City Star*, December 29, 1985, A1:1; *Kansas City Times*, "In Redevelopment, 'Blight' Is What City Says It Is," February 4, 1986, D39:1; James C. Fitzpatrick, "Council Panel Listens to Public's Definition of 'Blight' at Hearing," *Kansas City Times*, February 7, 1986, C1:1; and *Kansas City Star*, "Deliberate Blight Is Not Acceptable," July 25, 1986, A10:1).

58. *Kansas City Times*, "Homeowners Aggravated by Relocation Snags," March 29, 1973.

59. *Kansas City Star*, "Vague Guidelines, Inaction Surround Redevelopment," February 14, 1972, B:1; *Kansas City Star*, "Study Emphasizes Major Setbacks," December 3, 1978, A:1, A:23.

60. Jackson, *Crabgrass Frontier*, 164; Dreier, Mollenkopf, and Swanstrom, *Place Matters*, 104.

61. Dreier, Mollenkopf, and Swanstrom, *Place Matters*, 104; Jackson, *Crabgrass Frontier*, 164.

62. Gotham, *Race, Real Estate, and Uneven Development*, 83. Calculations are based on Anderson's conservative estimates in *Federal Bulldozer*, 53.

63. Jean Hale, "Homeowners Aggravated by Relocation Snags," *Kansas City Times*, n.d. 1973 (the microfilm of this particular story included only the year the story was published).

64. Shortridge, *Kansas City and How It Grew*, 139–45.

65. Quoted in Gotham, *Race, Real Estate, and Uneven Development*, 83.

66. William D. Tammeus, "Families Sue HUD for 'Relocation to Poor Housing,'" *Kansas City Star*, January 22, 1975, 3.

67. Gloria Miller, interview by author, Kansas City, MO, February 15, 2007.

68. John Gurda, *The Making of Milwaukee* (Milwaukee: Milwaukee Historical Society, 1999), 1–58.

69. Ibid., 59–104.

70. Mark Edward Braun, *Social Change and the Empowerment of the Poor: Poverty Representation in Milwaukee's Community Action Programs, 1964–1972* (Oxford: Lexington, 2001), 20.

71. Gurda, *Making of Milwaukee*, 310–11.

72. Braun, *Social Change and the Empowerment of the Poor*, 22.

73. Ibid., 22.

74. Gurda, *Making of Milwaukee*, 325.

75. Ibid., 359.

76. Ibid..

77. Iceland, Weinberg, and Steinmetz, *U.S. Census Bureau, Series CENSR-3, Racial and Ethnic Residential Segregation in the United States*; Bruce Murphy, "'Hypersegregated': It Made Milwaukee Famous," *JSOnline: Milwaukee Journal Sentinel*, January 12, 2003.

78. *Milwaukee Journal*, "Urban Renewal Called on Segregation Cost," January 12, 1957.

79. *Milwaukee Journal*, "Latent Hostility Here to Renewal—Zeidler," March 1957.

80. *Milwaukee Sentinel*, "Zeidler Calls Minority Shifts Serious Problem," March 1957.

81. Part of this similarity may be due to the fact that mayors and members of city councils across the country often traveled to other cities or met with each other at conferences to share ideas and learn from others' approaches to urban renewal. Indeed, in 1958 aldermen from Milwaukee visited Kansas City and "got an eyeful and an earful on the worth of city co-operation with private redevelopment projects to halt downtown deterioration," rather than focusing solely on public investment. The aldermen returned home with a new sense of vigor and interest in incentivizing financial and property interests in redeveloping downtown Milwaukee, though, as time

would tell, these efforts were largely unsuccessful. See *Milwaukee Sentinel*, "Milwaukee Aldermen's Kansas City Trip Seems Most Worth While," n.d. 1958.

82. *Milwaukee Journal*, "Urban Law Legality," June 3, 1959; *Milwaukee Sentinel*, "High Court to Rule on Urban Renewal," April 14, 1959; *Milwaukee Journal*, "Vote Seen Blow to City Renewal," September 5, 1959.

83. Alan J. Borsuk, "City Pays and Pays for Moving," *Milwaukee Journal*, April 10, 1975; Gregory D. Stanford, "It's Difficult to Pull Up Roots," *Milwaukee Journal*, May 15, 1975.

84. *Milwaukee Journal*, "Urban Law Legality"; *Milwaukee Sentinel*, "High Court to Rule on Urban Renewal"; *Milwaukee Journal*, "Vote Seen Blow to City Renewal."

85. Braun, *Social Change and the Empowerment of the Poor*, 35.

86. James W. McCulla, "Nixon 'New Federalism': Let Local Units Do It," *Milwaukee Journal*, February 4, 1973.

87. A prime example of this struggle is the City of Detroit, which at the time of this writing became the largest U.S. city to declare bankruptcy. Though facing a legal challenge, this declaration is evidence that former industrial cities continue to struggle to remake themselves as centers of more modern industry.

88. *Milwaukee Journal*, "Halt Big Project, Perrin Urges City," September 13, 1970; *Milwaukee Sentinel*, "Grant to City Cut by $2.5 Million," January 18, 1982.

89. *Milwaukee Journal*, "Project Would Uproot Thousands in 15 Years," n.d. 1957; *Milwaukee Journal*, "Urban Renewal Called on Segregation Cost."

90. Blake McKelvey, "Rochester in Retrospect and Prospect," *Rochester History* 23 (1961): 3; Though Rochester did have access to the Erie Canal, which aided in shipping product, it was never considered a major transport hub the way the other cities here were.

91. Blake McKelvey, "The Population of Rochester," *Rochester History* 7 (1950): 4.

92. Lou Buttino and Mark Hare, *The Remaking of a City: Rochester, New York, 1964–1984* (Dubuque, IA: Kendall/Hunt, 1984); McKelvey, "The Population of Rochester"; McKelvey, *Rochester on the Genesee: The Growth of a City* (Syracuse, NY: Syracuse University Press, 1973).

93. Richard S. Sterne, Barry Kaufman, and Gerald Rubenstein, "Relocatees' Perceptions of Urban Renewal," City of Rochester, Prepared for City of Rochester, Department of Urban Renewal and Economic Development, October 30, 1970. City of Rochester Records Management, City Manager Subject Files, Box 22n, Bin X0325, File: Dept. of Urban Renewal.

94. *Times Union*, "In City: 72% of Homes Pre-1920; In Suburbs: 14% Census Shows," June 2, 1953.

95. Bill Beeney, "Area Seen Lacking Rental Housing for Under-$4,500 Class," *Rochester Democrat and Chronicle*, June 4, 1955; *Times Union*, "Close the Housing Gap in Metropolitan Rochester," June 12, 1970, 14A.

96. William D. Tammeus, "House Need Acute for Displaced," *Times Union*, April 29, 1968.

97. William D. Tammeus, "The Third Ward and Renewal," *Times Union*, January 5, 1970; Buttino and Hare, *Remaking of a City*, 96.

98. Sterne, Kaufman, and Rubenstein, "Relocatees' Perceptions of Urban Renewal."

99. City of Rochester. *Annual Report, Rochester New York: Progress That Reflects Economical Management and Sound Planning*, 1952, 10.

100. Report of Survey of Hanover Houses, For the Citizens Advisory Committee to the Rehabilitation Commission, Rochester, NY, June 8, 1958, 3, City of Rochester Municipal Archives and Records Center, Rochester, NY.

101. Ibid., 4.

102. Ibid., 6.

103. Ben Douglas, interview by author, digital recording, Rochester, NY, April 18, 2007.

104. Steve Knowlton, "3 Top City Officials See Ghetto 'Like It Is,'" *Democrat and Chronicle*, January 24, 1970.

105. *Times-Union*, "Close the Housing Gap in Metropolitan Rochester."

106. Knowlton, "3 Top City Officials See Ghetto 'Like It Is.'"

107. Paula Musto, "A Fight for the 'Old' in 16th Ward," *Democrat and Chronicle*, July 19, 1976; Linda K. Wertheimer, "Local Area Among Most Segregated," *Democrat and Chronicle*, November 11, 1991.

Chapter 3. Economic Segregation and the Mobilizing Capacity of Voluntary Associations

1. There is a long and well-documented debate about the fundamental nature of America's founding and the ideals embodied by American political institutions and the polity; are we fundamentally a liberal or a republican nation? Many scholars argue that at its core America is a liberal nation, a nation of people motivated by individual freedom, private property, and limited government. Others argue that we are in fact a nation of citizens, driven by discovering and securing the public good through active civic participation and building institutions that both promote participation and privilege the public over the private. Many scholars argue that these impulses are not mutually exclusive, but that each plays an important role in America's founding and in shaping the actions and behaviors of the American people. I do not attempt to weigh in on the debate over which theory—classical liberalism or republicanism—is most important for understanding contemporary American politics. I do draw on the theory of civic republicanism here, though, to contextualize this study by indicating that scholars have long noted the American propensity for civic engagement. For more on this see Gerald Gamm and Robert Putnam, "The Growth of Voluntary Associations in America, 1840–1940," *Journal of Interdisciplinary History* 29:4 ("Patterns of Social Capital: Stability and Change in Comparative Perspective: Part II") (Spring 1999): 511–57; Gregory B. Markus, "Civic Participation in American Cities," Institute for Social

Research, University of Michigan, February 2002, http://www-personal.umich.edu /~gmarkus/markus2002.pdf (accessed January 31, 2014); James Morone, *The Democratic Wish: Popular Participation and the Limits of American Government* (New Haven, CT: Yale University Press, 1998); Putnam, *Bowling Alone*; Arthur M. Schlesinger, "Biography of a Nation of Joiners," *American Historical Review* (1944) L:1: 1–25; and Theda Skocpol, *Diminished Democracy: From Membership to Management in American Civic Life* (Norman: University of Oklahoma Press, 2003). For more on the debate about the meaning of these terms, see Daniel T. Rodgers, "Republicanism: the Career of a Concept," *Journal of American History* 79:1 (June 1992): 11–38; and Louis Hartz, *The Liberal Tradition in America: An Interpretation of American Political Thought Since the Revolution* (New York: Harcourt, Brace, and World, 1955).

2. Putnam, *Bowling Alone*, 338.

3. For more on how organizational and church membership can translate into heightened social capital and civic skills, see Putnam, *Bowling Alone*, 19; and Verba, Schlozman, and Brady, *Voice and Equality*. There are also some good books on the relationship between religion, church membership, and American politics more broadly, including Robert D. Putnam and David E. Campbell, *Amazing Grace: How Religion Divides and Unites Us* (New York: Simon and Schuster, 2010); and Clyde Wilcox and Carin Robinson, *Onward Christian Soldiers: The Religious Right in American Politics* (Boulder, CO: Westview, 2000).

4. Verba, Schlozman, and Brady, *Voice and Equality*, 304; Putnam, *Bowling Alone*, chapter 1.

5. Anthony Downs, *An Economic Theory of Democracy* (New York: Harper and Row, 1957); Leighley, *Strength in Numbers?*; and William H. Riker and Peter C. Ordeshook, "A Theory of the Calculus of Voting," *American Political Science Review* 62:1 (March 1968): 25–42.

6. For a good discussion of this, see Rosenstone and Hansen, *Mobilization, Participation, and Democracy in America*, in which the authors summarize this strategy nicely when they say that that "people participate in electoral politics because someone encourages or inspires them to take part" (161).

7. Scholars have long been interested in the problem of the validity of self-reported voter turnout. The origins of this research stem from the fact that survey results often indicate much higher voter-turnout rates than actually occur in any given election, and this phenomenon occurs within many advanced democracies, not just in the United States. Researchers have found many reasons for this, but the leading factors contributing to overreporting seem to be faulty memory and, most important, social desirability, or the desire of the respondent to be seen as socially and civically responsible by the person giving the survey. Supporting the social desirability understanding of overreporting is the fact that the effect of this impulse varies by electoral context so that high-turnout elections are also elections that produce higher rates of overreporting. There are ways to mitigate this tendency in survey respondents, namely, question wording, allowing respondents to report secretly whether they voted, or changing to

delivery of the survey from in-person or over the phone to the Internet. The point here is that there are many factors to motivate people to vote (or to lie about voting), one of which is purely social. For more on this, see Brian Diff, Michael J. Hanmer, Won-Ho Park, and Ismail K. White, "Good Excuses: Understanding Who Votes with an Improved Turnout Question," *Public Opinion Quarterly* 71:1 (Spring 2007): 67–90; Allyson L. Holbrook and Jon A. Krasnick, "Social Desirability Bias in Voter Turnout Reports: Tests Using the Item Count Technique," *Public Opinion Quarterly* 74:1 (2010): 37–67; and Jeffrey A. Karp and David Brockington, "Social Desirability and Response Validity: A Comparative Analysis of Overreporting Voter Turnout in Five Countries," *Journal of Politics* 67:3 (August 2005): 825–40.

8. When thinking about increased professionalism within organizations, what I mean is the increased reliance on professional staff, bureaucratic structures and processes, and a reliance on "checkbook participation" instead of grassroots participation by members. For more on this, see Skocpol, *Diminished Democracy*. Though Rosenstone and Hansen, in *Mobilization, Participation, and Democracy in America*, did note that part of the explanation of trends in civic and political participation since the 1960s has been declining mobilization, they do little to explore what this means. See also Leighley, *Strength in Numbers*, and Robert Kleidman, "Volunteer Activism and Professionalism in Social-Movement Organizations," *Sociology and Criminology Faculty Publications*, Paper 4 (1994), for a review of this literature.

9. See Skocpol, *Diminished Democracy*; and Verba, Schlozman, and Brady, *Voice and Equality*.

10. There are notable exceptions to this, especially Leighley's *Strength in Numbers*, which specifically examines the political and social context of elite mobilization of various racial and ethnic groups and finds that these contexts matter. Leighley argues that the racial-ethnic context shapes the mobilization of racial-ethnic groups and does so differently for different groups, but that racial-ethnic context has no independent effect on mobilization of Anglo voters. This is important to keep in mind here, for while I do not focus on race, but rather focus on economic segregation and context, the discovery that context can alter elite mobilization is important for my story. Other scholars examine individual political behavior in politically and economically heterogeneous and homogeneous contexts but do so by examining larger units of analysis than the neighborhood-level analysis offered here. For these studies, see, Campbell, *Why We Vote*; and Oliver, *Democracy in Suburbia*.

11. See Rosenstone and Hansen, *Mobilization, Participation, and Democracy in America*; and Putnam, *Bowling Alone*.

12. For more on this, see Putnam, *Bowling Alone*, chapters 3 through 6. See also Steven Greenhouse, "Union Membership in the U.S. Fell to a 70-Year Low Last Year," *New York Times*, January 21, 2011, http://www.nytimes.com/2011/01/22/business/22union.html?_r=0 (accessed October 24, 2013).

13. For more on the role of local organizations in civic life, see Everett Carl Ladd, *The Ladd Report* (New York: Free Press, 1999). For more on the new style of associa-

tionalism, including indirect contact through mail, or e-mail, by organizations and different forms of individual participation in organizations, which include check or letter writing, see Skocpol, *Diminished Democracy*.

14. Extensive data on national union membership and metropolitan union membership can be found at "Union Membership and Coverage Database from the CPS," http://www.unionstats.com/ (accessed October 25, 2013). There is no shortage of literature on labor unions, but for a good, broad history of unionism in the United States, see Nelson Lichtenstein, *State of the Union: A Century of American Labor* (Princeton, NJ: Princeton University Press, 2002).

15. The data source for this analysis came from InfoUSA. In the analysis presented in Figure 3.1, religious organization does not refer to a church but rather any ministry or religiously affiliated support or service enterprise. Across all communities there were many churches, although there is no tract-level data that allows me to explore the nature of congregational life in these communities. According to pastors Martin Jefferson and Benjamin Paisley, interviewed by the author in Rochester on April 17, 2007, and in Milwaukee, on April 24, 2006, respectively, accessing the many churches within these neighborhoods can be difficult because safety is a concern, and the ability of clergy in these churches to build a relationship with residents of the impoverished communities was greatly hampered by high levels of residential mobility.

16. Soss and Jacobs, "The Place of Inequality," 123.

17. See Appendix B for more on the interview methodology, the interview schedule, and my decisions regarding attribution, or contact the author for more information about the interview process. I changed the names of all organizational and church leaders to protect confidentiality.

18. See Verba, Schlozman, and Brady, *Voice and Equality*.

19. Perkins, interview by author.

20. Perkins, interview by author; Harold Painter, interview by author, Atlanta, GA, January 24, 2007, digital recording held by author.

21. Perkins, interview by author.

22. Ibid.

23. Ibid.

24. Ibid.

25. Miller, interview by author.

26. Roy Turner, interview by author, Rochester, NY, March 22, 2006, digital recording held by author; Miller, interview by author.

27. The source for this data is the 2005–2009 American Community Survey, conducted by the U.S. Census Bureau. American Community Survey data can be found at http://www.census.gov/acs/www/ (accessed on March 6, 2014).

28. Eric Bryant, interview by author, Milwaukee, WI, April 25, 2006, digital recording held by author.

29. Bryant, interview by author.

30. Benjamin Paisley, interview by author, Milwaukee, WI, April 24, 2006, digital recording held by author.

31. Tamara Thompson, interview by author, Rochester, NY, April 12, 2007, digital recording held by author.

32. Ibid.

33. Turner, interview by author.

34. Ibid.

35. Thompson, interview by author.

36. Harriet Taylor, interview by author, Rochester, NY, April 17, 2007, digital copy held by author.

37. Shirley Jackson, interview by author.

38. While Kevin Kruse, in *White Flight*, documents white activism in this part of town against black encroachment, the economic class of all residents on this side of Atlanta was much higher than in other parts of town. So while initially neighborhood activism was about keeping out blacks, more recent iterations of this activism are about keeping out the poor.

39. Jackson, interview by author; William Howard, interview by author, Atlanta, GA, January 19, 2007, digital recording held by author.

40. Jackson, interview by author; Charles Kerns, interview by author, Atlanta, GA, January 19, 2007, digital recording held by author.

41. Christopher Ingram, interview by author, Kansas City, MO, February 10, 2007, digital recording held by author. This example is important because it highlights that the prosperous case-study neighborhoods and the impoverished case-study neighborhoods are not identical, despite similar prosperous and impoverished contexts. It also shows that these civically important features combine differently in different places but that some combination of each is necessary to sustain a lively civic environment and civic engagement.

42. Ingram, interview by author.

43. Danielle Hines, interview by author, Milwaukee, WI, March 12, 2007, digital recording held by author.

44. Robert Williamson, interview by author, Milwaukee, WI, March 12, 2007, digital recording held by author; Hines, interview by author.

45. Williamson, interview by author.

46. The data presented in the tables in the Chapter 2 indicate average neighborhood income. Current and 2000 median income statistics can be found on the U.S. Census Bureau's American FactFinder website; see http://factfinder2.census.gov/faces/nav/jsf/pages/index.xhtml.

47. Patrick Logan, interview by author, Rochester, NY, April 16, 2007, digital recording held by author.

48. Jeanette Keane, interview by author, Rochester, NY, April 17, 2007, digital recording held by author.

49. See Verba, Schlozman, and Brady, *Voice and Equality*, 28; emphasis added.

50. See Putnam, *Bowling Alone*.

51. Baker, interview by author; Jackson, interview by author.

52. Kerns, interview by author.

53. The data on median income used here is drawn from American FactFinder on the U.S. Census website; see http://factfinder2.census.gov/faces/nav/jsf/pages/index .xhtml. It is important to note that I cite *median* income here, which is higher than the *mean* (or average) income discussed in Chapter 2 and shown in Table 2.1 in that chapter, which accounts for the discrepancy between incomes levels discussed in these two chapters.

54. See Verba, Scholzman, and Brady, *Voice and Equality*; Kenneth Miles, interview by author, Atlanta, GA, January 17, 2007, digital recording held by author.

55. Ingram, interview by author.

56. Again, the data on median income used here is drawn from American Fact-Finder on the U.S. Census website (see http://factfinder2.census.gov/faces/nav/jsf /pages/index.xhtml) and uses median as opposed to mean income.

57. Perkins, interview by author.

58. The data on the distribution of population by age used here is drawn from American FactFinder on the U.S. Census website; see http://factfinder2.census.gov /faces/nav/jsf/pages/index.xhtml.

59. The number of residents with no high school diploma is an aggregate of the percentage of sixteen- to nineteen-year-olds in the neighborhood who are neither enrolled in nor have graduated from high school, and the percentage of residents twenty-five and older who have some years of schooling in high school but no diploma.

60. The data on median income used here is drawn from American FactFinder on the U.S. Census website; see http://factfinder2.census.gov/faces/nav/jsf/pages/index .xhtml. See U.S. Census Bureau, "Poverty Thresholds, 2000," http://www.census.gov /hhes/www/poverty/data/threshld/thresh00.html (accessed on August 16, 2013).

61. Councilwoman Carla Smith, interview by author, Atlanta, GA, January 17, 2007, digital recording held by author. The names of public officials have not been changed.

62. George Lawson, interview by author, Rochester, NY, March 24, 2006, digital recording held by author.

63. Ibid.

64. Shared economic experience was important for shaping the prosperous and impoverished neighborhoods of Atlanta as well. In our interview Shirley Jackson in Atlanta pointed out that many in her neighborhood worked together as educators or in the government offices of downtown Atlanta, indicating that similar work experiences and sharing free time brought families in prosperous neighborhoods together as well. Similar neighborhood features were discussed by other community leaders in the other prosperous case-study neighborhoods, specifically by Pastor Williamson. Moreover, the stability of the population in segregated, prosperous neighborhoods has

made it easier to maintain the stability of these economic ties. It is also important to note that much of the damage to the civic environment by declining union membership and strength had been done by the time of the study so that by 2000 those interviewed did not recognize labor unions as key players in associational life within their communities.

65. The data on the distribution of population by education, by age and median income used here is drawn from American FactFinder on the U.S. Census website; see http://factfinder2.census.gov/faces/nav/jsf/pages/index.xhtml. The information about unemployment is drawn from the Neighborhood Change Database and is presented in Chapter 2.

66. The data on the distribution of population by age used here is drawn from American FactFinder on the U.S. Census website; see http://factfinder2.census.gov /faces/nav/jsf/pages/index.xhtml. Interestingly, the number of youth in the prosperous Milwaukee neighborhoods is also quite high; 2,338 of the 3,306 neighborhood residents are under the age of twenty-five, but the bulk of this population is between the ages of fifteen and twenty-four.

67. Thompson, interview by author; Martin Jefferson, interview by author, Rochester, NY, April 17, 2007, digital recording held by author.

68. Thompson, interview by author.

69. Ibid.

70. Jane Jacobs, *The Death and Life of Great American Cities* (New York: Vintage, 1992 [1961]), 29.

71. Perkins, interview by author.

72. Miller, interview by author.

73. Rita Blake, interview by author, Kansas City, MO, May 24, 2006, digital recording held by author.

74. Miller, interview by author.

75. Ibid. It is important to note that according to Miller, by the mid-2000s, with help from a grant from the Kauffman Foundation, the Bank of America, and the Hall Family Foundation, the Ivanhoe Community Organization had a paid staff of five, including an executive director (Miller), a fundraiser, a community mobilizer, and two program coordinators, and that the neighborhood was no longer in the top ten for neighborhood crime in the city. But it should also be noted that this is the result of a major influx of capital, a key neighborhood resource missing in the majority of segregated, impoverished urban neighborhoods.

76. Paisley, interview by author.

77. Jacobs, *Death and Life of Great American Cities*, 56.

78. Thompson, interview by author.

79. Jefferson, interview by author.

80. Thompson, interview by author.

81. Logan, interview by author.

82. Howard, interview by author.

83. The basic idea of "postmaterialism," advanced primarily by Ronald Inglehart, is that in advanced Western democracies the majority of citizens have attained a certain level of economic security that allows them to think about issues beyond ameliorating economic need and scarcity, such as social or environmental issues (see "The Silent Revolution in Europe: Intergenerational Change in Post-Industrial Societies," *American Political Science Review* 65:4 [December 1971], 991–1017). And, indeed, in the 1960s and 1970s a number of social movements—civil rights, women's rights, students' rights, and environmental movements—emerged in the United States and other advanced democracies, providing some evidence for this claim.

84. Bartels, *Unequal Democracy*; Burtless, "Growing American Inequality."

85. See especially Putnam, *Bowling Alone*; and Rosenstone and Hansen, *Mobilization, Participation, and American Democracy*.

Chapter 4. Economic Segregation, Political Parties, and Political Mobilization

1. See, for example, Walter Dean Burnham, *Critical Elections and the Mainstream of American Politics* (New York: W. W. Norton, 1987); Carol Cassel, "The Nonpartisan Ballot and the Decline of American Parties: A Contextual Effect?" *Political Behavior* 9:3 (1987): 246–56; and Frances Fox Piven and Richard A. Cloward, *Why Americans Don't Vote* (New York: Pantheon, 1988).

2. At the turn of the century urban political machines and ward bosses largely controlled major urban centers. These political machines created social networks for citizens in each district that served certain latent social functions, such as job placement, financial support, and the dissemination of political information. These networks were often run in accordance with a statewide political agenda directed by a state-level political boss who planned party strategy from the elected position of senator or congressman. The initial focus of Progressive Era reforms was almost entirely on initiatives that sought to protect "public interest," which is assumed to be harmed by the political corruption and patronage of urban machines and bosses. In other words the Progressives sought to protect the local political process and city government from the whims of popular opinion, the effect of statewide or national party influence, and potentially corrupt(able) politicians. These reforms sought to promote a system of efficient governance designed to make governing more "businesslike," with governments run by managers and experts as opposed to popular will and elected politicians. Political parties and their candidates were the focus of these reforms, and the party- and candidate-constituent relationship changed over time as a result. What was once a party-centered political system has become a candidate-centered system in which the politics and characteristics of individual candidates drive campaigns and electoral outcomes as much as parties, if not more so. For more on this see Edward Banfield and J. Q. Wilson, *City Politics* (Cambridge, MA: Harvard University Press, 1963), 125–26; John F. Bibby, "State and Local Parties in a Candidate-Centered Age," in *American*

State and Local Politics: Directions for the 21st Century, ed. Ronald E. Weber and Paul Brace (Chatham, NJ: Chatham House, 1999), 194–211; Richard Hofstadter, *The Age of Reform* (New York: Knopf, 1955); Theda Skocpol, *Protecting Soldiers and Mothers: The Political Origins of Social Policy in the United States* (Cambridge, MA: Belknap Press of Harvard University Press, 1992), 78, 100; Lincoln Steffens, *The Shame of the Cities* (New York: S. S. McClure, 1904); Alan Ware, "Anti-Partisan and Party Control of Political Reform in the United States: The Case of the Australian Ballot," *British Journal of Political Science* 30:1 (January 2000): 1–29; and Martin P. Wattenberg, *The Rise of Candidate-Centered Politics: Presidential Elections of the 1980s* (Cambridge, MA: Harvard University Press, 1991).

3. See Jeffrey M. Stonecash, Mark D. Brewer, and Mack D. Mariani, *Diverging Parties: Social Change, Realignment, and Party Polarization* (Boulder, CO: Westview, 2003), 132.

4. See David R. Mayhew, *Congress: The Electoral Connection* (New Haven, CT: Yale University Press, 1974).

5. Rosenstone and Hansen, *Mobilization, Participation, and Democracy in America*, 218.

6. Using multiple data points about citizens—where they shop, what websites they visit, what magazines they subscribe to and what TV shows they watch—to target specific political messages is a practice called microtargeting. Because of the wealth data available to campaigns, the use of microtargeting in elections has increased dramatically. For more on recent uses of microtargeting see Allison Brennan, "Microtargeting: How Campaigns Know You Better Than You Know Yourself," November 5, 2012, http://www.cnn.com/2012/11/05/politics/voters-microtargeting/ (accessed March 7, 2014); and James Surowiecki, "Calculating Campaigns," *New Yorker*, September 24, 2012, http://www.newyorker.com (accessed March 7, 2014).

7. See Appendix C for more on the interview methodology, the interview schedule, and my decisions regarding attribution, or contact the author for more information about the interview process. I did not change the names of elected officials but did change the names of unelected mayoral and city staff.

8. Typically, scholars see one of two situations occurring within cities, both fundamentally rooted in elite power. Urban regime theory posits a "privileged position of business interests in the formation of municipal socioeconomic policies," while urban growth machine theory focuses "less on policy outcomes than on the process of urban redevelopment itself," paying attention to the interests that operate in the formation coalitions around various urban redevelopment issues. For more on this see Neil Brenner, "Is There a Politics of 'Urban' Development? Reflections on the U.S. Case," in *The City in American Political Development*, ed. Richardson Dilworth (New York: Routledge, 2009), 123. The analysis here does not attempt to wade into the debate over which theory best captures urban political systems, but the idea of governing coalitions playing an important role in urban politics is important for the analysis here. It is important for two reasons. First, focusing on which interests have a seat at the table

forces us to home in on the process of politics: who is let in and who is kept out. Second, a study of governing coalitions and interest representation is really a study of political winners and losers, and economic segregation creates both. Therefore, it is helpful to keep the framework of interest representation and governing coalitions in mind as we look at how the process of economic segregation included or excluded certain interests, thereby creating vicious and virtuous feedback cycles. For more on urban growth machine theory see John Logan and Harvey Molotoch, *Urban Fortunes: The Political Economy of Place* (Berkeley: University of California Press, 1987); and Brenner, "Is There a Politics of 'Urban' Development?" 121–40. For more on urban regime theory see Clarence N. Stone, *Regime Politics: Governing Atlanta, 1946–1988* (Lawrence: University Press of Kansas, 1989).

9. The possibility that *economic* segregation might be contributing to growing "class bias" in American politics is discussed in Soss and Jacobs, "The Place of Inequality," quote on 123.

10. See, among others, Alan S. Gerber and Donald P. Green, "The Effects of Canvassing, Telephone Calls, and Direct Mail on Voter Turnout: A Feld Experiment," *American Political Science Review* 94:3 (September 2000): 653–63; and Donald P. Green and Alan S. Gerber, *Get Out the Vote: How to Increase Voter Turnout*, 2nd ed. (Washington, DC: Brookings Institution, 2008).

11. Martin, interview by author.

12. Perkins, interview by author.

13. Perkins, interview by author; Smith, interview by author.

14. Smith, interview by author.

15. Perkins, interview by author; Painter, interview by author.

16. Perkins, interview by author.

17. Smith, interview by author; Martin, interview by author.

18. Baker, interview by author.

19. Jackson, interview by author; Baker, interview by author.

20. Councilman Troy Nash, interview by author, Kansas City, MO, February 8, 2007, digital recording held by author.

21. Ibid.

22. This finding is borne out by other studies that show contact by a friend or acquaintance has a greater effect of spurring civic action than contact by a stranger, although contact by a stranger is better than no contact at all. For more on this see Gerber and Green, "The Effects of Canvassing"; and D. Sunshine Hillygus, "Campaign Effects and the Dynamics of Turnout Intention in Election 2000," *Journal of Politics* 67:1 (February 2005), 50–68.

23. This complicates our understanding of Rosenstone and Hansen, *Mobilization, Participation, and Democracy in America*; if contact from a candidate, for example, an invitation to attend a campaign event that is free and provides free food, is not enough to motivate voters to get to the polls, the quality and context of the contacting may matter in ways not previously recognized.

24. It should be noted that 501(c)3 status is different from the professionally staffed, service organizations discussed in Chapter 4 and by Skocpol in *Diminished Democracy*. These are not service providers. They are neighborhoods groups that need 501(c)3 status in order to fundraise and secure municipal and private grants.

25. Miller, interview by author.

26. Smith, interview by author.

27. Judie Callahan, interview by author, Kansas City, MO, February 7, 2007, digital recording held by author.

28. Ibid.

29. Alderman Michael D'Amato, interview by author, Milwaukee, WI, March 5, 2007, digital recording held by author.

30. Ibid..

31. Rebecca Jones, interview by author, Milwaukee, WI, March 12, 2007, digital recording held by author.

32. Douglas, interview by author.

33. Frances Coleman, interview by author, Rochester, NY, April 11, 2007, digital recording held by author.

34. Councilwoman Lois Geiss, interview by author, Rochester, NY, April 18, 2007, digital recording held by author.

35. Perkins, interview by author; Douglas, interview by author; Smith, interview by author; Geiss, interview by author.

36. E. E. Schattschneider, *The Semisovereign People: A Realist's View of Democracy in America* (New York: Harcourt Brace Jovanovich, 1975 [1960]), xix.

37. Roth, Ambrose, and the Atlanta Historical Society, *Metropolitan Frontiers*, 207; City of Atlanta, *Final Report* 1967, City of Atlanta Online, http://www.atlantaga .gov/government/planning/npu_system.aspx (accessed December 19, 2007).

38. Stone, *Regime Politics*, 86.

39. Ibid., 82–85

40. Melinda Williams, interview by author, Atlanta, GA, January 17, 2007, digital recording held by author.

41. Roth, Ambrose, and the Atlanta Historical Society, *Metropolitan Frontiers*, 207–209.

42. Stone, *Regime Politics*, especially chapter 9.

43. Ibid., 89.

44. Roth, Ambrose, and the Atlanta Historical Society, *Metropolitan Frontiers*, 207.

45. Martin, interview by author.

46. Ibid.

47. This said, the potential for change in the West Manor neighborhood is high, given that according to the U.S. Census, the average age in Councilman Martin's district is sixty-two and housing ownership has begun to shift as a result of generational turnover. As these shifts occur, it is possible that the stability in this community and

therefore its political power might also change. Moreover, while not explicitly a part of this study, it is interesting to note that part of the reason this demographic and residential transition would destabilize political power in this neighborhood is that zoning laws regulating housing on the south side of Atlanta are not as strong as those on the north, and largely white, side of Atlanta. In this way the historical development of local zoning laws is vital to this analysis.

48. Nash, interview by author.

49. Gotham, *Race, Real Estate, and Uneven Development*, 40–43.

50. Nash, interview by author; Gotham, in *Race, Real Estate, and Uneven Development*, also presents data to this effect. The 1968 Housing Act included Section 235, which was a program to help the poor secure mortgages for homeownership and which could help disperse low-income families throughout the city. And yet between 1969 and mid-1972, 475 low-income families bought homes in the existing housing located in the impoverished, eight-square-mile area east of Troost Avenue.

51. See Gotham, *Race, Real Estate, and Uneven Development*.

52. I have chosen to keep the names of mayoral staff confidential as well. See Appendix C for more information about source attribution.

53. Jonathan Wright, interview by author, Kansas City, MO, February 13, 2007, digital recording held by author.

54. Katharine Edwards, interview by author, Kansas City, MO, February 13, 2007, digital recording held by author. In Kansas City each district has two representatives: one within district, elected by members of that district, and one at large, who represents a particular council district but is elected by citizens of the entire city.

55. Wright, interview by author. As evidence of difficulty recruiting good representation, Edwards (interview by author) explained that in 2007 one of the two sitting council members representing this district was under indictment.

56. Gail Fletcher, interview by author, Kansas City, MO, February 8, 2007, digital recording held by author.

57. Cited in Gurda, *Making of Milwaukee*, 346.

58. See gmconline.org/about/overview (accessed July 16, 2013).

59. Margo Anderson and Victor Greene, *Perspectives on Milwaukee's Past* (Urbana/Chicago: University of Illinois Press, 2009), 321.

60. Ibid., 322.

61. Brian Larson, interview by author, Milwaukee, WI, March 13, 2007, digital recording held by author.

62. D'Amato, interview by author.

63. Verba, Schlozman, and Brady, *Voice and Equality*, 227.

64. One way that segregated wealth also makes contact and mobilization easier is that so many more residents in these types of communities have access to the Internet. Councilman D'Amato said that the nature of his work has changed as a result of the increased use of e-mail by his constituents to contact him. On the one hand, this makes

it easier for constituents to convey preferences and grievances to their elected representatives and easier for these elected representatives to mobilize their constituents through on-line resources. On the other hand, this may contribute even further to the class gap because broadband access is not evenly or equally distributed. Indeed, more recent research shows that there is a widening digital divide between the "haves" and the "have-nots." For more on the digital divide and its consequences see Karen Mossberger, Caroline J. Tolbert, and Mary Stansbury, *Virtual Inequality: Beyond the Digital Divide* (Washington, DC: Georgetown University Press, 2003); or for a more comparative work and one that develops an Internet engagement model, see Pippa Norris, *Digital Divide: Civic Engagement, Information Poverty, and the Internet Worldwide* (Cambridge: Cambridge University Press, 2001).

65. Paisley, interviewed by author.

66. Michael Robinson, interview by author, Milwaukee, WI, April 24, 2006, digital recording held by author.

67. Douglas, interview by author.

68. Ibid.

69. Ibid.

70. Smith, interview by author.

71. American Political Science Association, Task Force on Inequality and American Democracy, "American Democracy in an Age of Rising Inequality," 1.

72. Abramson, Tobin, and VanderGoot, "The Changing Geography of Metropolitan Opportunity."

73. Owing to missing records in the Fulton County Board of Election, I do not have data for the 1970 congressional election, the 1972 presidential election, the 1974 congressional election, and the 1978 congressional election.

74. Hal Gulliver, "Now That the Voting Is Over," *Atlanta Constitution*, October 20, 1977, 4-A; Stone, *Regime Politics*.

75. Owing to missing data the congressional elections of 1970 and 1978 are not included.

76. Miller, interview by author; Blake, interview by author.

77. Gurda, *Making of Milwaukee.*

78. I use gubernatorial results here because congressional results were not available. While not directly comparable, I wanted to include races in which presidential coattails would not be a factor.

79. Blake McKelvey, "Rochester's Political Trends: An Historical Review," *Rochester History* 14:2 (1952), 11–22; Buttino and Hare, *Remaking of a City*, chapter 7.

80. I was unable to locate voter-turnout data for midterm congressional elections after 1994.

81. For more on the elected-mayor debate in Rochester see Buttino and Hare, *Remaking of a City*, chapter 14.

82. See Richard F. Fenno, *Home Style: House Members and Their Districts* (Boston: Little, Brown, 1978). In his study Fenno starts with the same premise as many other

scholars, that members of Congress are driven by electoral politics and the desire to get reelected. But where other scholars examine what this means for a member of Congress's behavior in Washington, D.C., Fenno focuses on the politician/candidate-constituency relationship. He argues that when members of Congress are in their home districts, they cultivate a "home style," which includes an allocation of their personal resources and those of their office, their presentation of self, and their explanation of their Washington activity. This is an important contribution to our understanding of representational politics and important for the study here because it draws our attention to the on-the-ground, day-to-day mobilization and outreach activities elected officials and candidates engage in to garner electoral support.

83. An example of such thinking is seen in Edward Blackwell, "In the Inner City," *Milwaukee Journal*, November 2, 1976, Accents, 1. He wrote about the anticipated low turnout of low-income citizens in the 1976 elections and cited Eddie N. Williams, then president of the Joint Center for Political Studies (now the Joint Center for Political and Economic Studies). In this article Williams is quoted as saying, "They are casting doubt on their continuing commitment to self-determination and to use every available means, including politics, to achieve their goals and aspirations. . . . To practice political abstinence is to commit political suicide."

84. See, for example, Rosenstone and Hansen, *Mobilization, Participation, and Democracy in America*.

Conclusion

1. In some instances voter turnout in segregated, prosperous communities dipped in the early 1970s, perhaps as a result of Watergate, but in all cases turnout rebounded to similar or higher levels than before the short period of decline.

2. Soss and Jacobs, "Place of Inequality."

3. Ibid., 124.

4. Jacob S. Hacker and Paul Pierson, *Winner-Take-All Politics: How Washington Made the Rich Richer—and Turned Its Back on the Middle Class* (New York: Simon and Schuster, 2010).

5. Martin Gilens, *Affluence and Influence: Economic Inequality and Political Power in America* (Princeton, NJ: Princeton University Press, 2012), 81. See also Bartels, *Unequal Democracy*. Though in this case it is important to note that while Bartels finds general unresponsiveness to the policy positions of the poor, he also examines this by political party, finding that Republicans appear less responsive than Democrats and that part of the problem may stem from voters themselves. In many cases "the actual working of American democracy also reflects the profound difficulties faced by ordinary citizens in connecting specific policy proposals to their own values and interests" (27), indicating that elected officials may also be receiving incoherent or mixed messages from their constituents.

6. For example, Paul Pierson, "When Effect Becomes Cause: Policy Feedback and Political Change," *World Politics* 45 (July 1993): 595–628; Suzanne Mettler, "Bringing the State Back in to Civic Engagement: Policy Feedback Effects of the G.I. Bill for World War II Veterans," *American Political Science Review* 96:2 (June 2002): 351–65; and Mettler, *Soldiers to Citizens: The G.I. Bill and the Making of the Greatest Generation* (New York: Oxford University Press, 2005).

7. James Rodgers, interview by author, Kansas City, MO, February 16, 2007, digital recording held by author.

8. Edwards and Wright, interviews by author.

9. Rodgers, interview by author.

10. Skocpol, *Protecting Soldiers and Mothers*, 22.

11. Margaret Weir, *Politics and Jobs: The Boundaries of Employment Policy in the Unites States* (Princeton, NJ: Princeton University Press, 1992), 168–69.

12. Anne Schneider and Helen Ingram, "Social Construction of Target Populations: Implications for Politics and Policy," *American Political Science Review* 87:2 (June 1993): 334–47.

13. Martin, interview by author.

14. Mark L. Joseph, Robert J. Chaskin, and Henry S. Weber, "The Theoretical Basis for Addressing Poverty Through Mixed-Income Development," *Urban Affairs Review* 42:3 (2007): 369–404, esp. p. 369.

15. Urban Land Institute, *Mixed-Income Housing: Myth and Fact* (Washington, DC: Urban Land Institute, 2003).

16. Joseph, Chaskin, and Weber, "Theoretical Basis for Addressing Poverty," 370.

17. Margery Austin Turner, "Moving Out of Poverty: Expanding Mobility and Choice Through Tenant-Based Housing Assistance," *Housing Policy Debate* 9:2 (1998): 373–94. See also Ingrid Gould Ellen and Margery Austin Turner, "Does Neighborhood Matter? Assessing Recent Evidence," *Housing Policy Debate* 8:4 (1997): 833–66.

18. Critics of mixed-income housing claim that the theory behind economically integrated communities promotes the notion that low-income citizens need to be taught how to behave by wealthier citizens, which is at best patronizing and at worst a bit like contemporary, urban colonization—the white man's burden played out in American cities.

19. Putnam, *Bowling Alone*, 22–23.

20. U.S. Department of Housing and Urban Development, "About HOPE VI," http://portal.hud.gov/hudportal/HUD?src=/program_offices/public_indian_housing/programs/ph/hope6/about (accessed July 23, 2013).

21. U.S. Department of Housing and Urban Development, "About HOPE VI." In other words successful mixed-income housing rests on attracting market-rate renters, providing enough market-rate units so that there is no difference between the units offered owing to income disparity, and developing other strategies to promote

upward mobility among low-income residents, such as skills training or employment resource centers and job opportunities. Another challenge identified in studies of HOPE VI is that these developments tend be built in low-income neighborhoods. The result is that the neighborhood environments tend to be poor, which makes it difficult to attract market-rate renters and economic opportunities for low-income families remain low. Some studies examine the development of social ties, which have implications for the creation of social capital, and indicate that relocating low-income families to mixed-income communities breaks already established ties, albeit weak ties in segregated, impoverished neighborhoods, which are not reestablished in new communities. For more on this see Paul C. Brophy and Rhonda N. Smith, "Mixed-Income Housing: Factors for Success," *Cityscape: A Source of Policy Development and Research* 3:2 (1997): 3–31.

This and other studies bring to the fore two problems with mixed-income housing policies as they are currently being implemented. First, one of the key components for promoting upward mobility is providing economic opportunity. Locating mixed-income housing developments in inner cities, with notoriously bad public transit to the suburbs where the majority of jobs are located, creates a spatial mismatch between a population that needs work and where the work is actually done. Without providing increased access to these jobs, the possibility for upward mobility will remain low. Second, placing mixed-income housing in segregated, impoverished communities without a plan to also develop the surrounding areas will do little to attract middle- and upper-income residents to the neighborhood, and only serves to continue the relocation process of low-income residents from one impoverished neighborhood to another. As Brophy and Smith point out, the key to successful mixed-income housing is attracting all income levels, not just providing affordable housing to low-income residents. For more on this see Susan Clampet-Lundquist, "HOPE VI: Moving to New Neighborhoods and Building New Ties," *Housing Policy Debate* 15:2 (2004): 415–47.

22. Heather L. Schwartz, Liisa Ecola, Kristin J. Leuschner, and Aaron Kofner, *Is Inclusionary Zoning Inclusionary? A Guide for Practitioners* (Santa Monica, CA: RAND Corporation, 2012). The first inclusionary zoning laws were established in Montgomery County, Maryland, in 1974 and are used widely throughout the United States to address housing needs for low- and moderate-income families.

23. Freund, *Colored Property*, 179, 221–226.

24. Schwartz, Ecola, Leuschner, and Kofner, *Is Inclusionary Zoning Inclusionary?*

25. See http://portal.hud.gov/hudportal/HUD?src=/program_offices/comm_plan ning/economicdevelopment/programs/rc (accessed on March 7, 2014).

26. See for more information Gerry Riposa, "From Enterprise Zones to Empowerment Zones," *American Behavioral Scientist* 39:5 (March–April 1996): 536–51; and Deirdre Oakley and Hui-Shien Tsao, "A New Way of Revitalizing Distressed Urban

Communities? Assessing the Impact of the Federal Empowerment Zone Program," *Journal of Urban Affairs* 28:5 (2006): 443–71.

27. Oakley and Tsao, "A New Way of Revitalizing Distress Urban Communities?"

28. Lawrence Jacobs and Theda Skocpol, *Inequality and American Democracy: What We Know and What We Need to Learn* (New York: Russell Sage Foundation, 2007), 1.

INDEX

American Community Survey, 127, 219n5
American Institute of Architects, 79–80
American Taxpayer Relief Act (2012),
    191
analysis of variance (ANOVA) tests, 50, 52,
    224n37
Anderson, Martin, 81
anti-Semitism, 8
Atlanta, Ga., 62–76; Comprehensive
    Development Plan of, 159; deindustrial-
    ization in, 132–33; demographics of, 74;
    dispersion of voting blocs in, 66, 75;
    Economic Development Corporation of,
    159–60; educational levels in, 63, 74, 75,
    131; and Great Migration, 64, 227n22;
    history of, 62–63; Kansas City versus, 78,
    82, 88; maps of, 69–72; Metropolitan
    Planning Commission of, 66; Neighbor-
    hood Planning Unit system of, 158–61;
    neighborhood political involvement in,
    75–77, 120–22, 126–27, 130–33, 139,
    148–54; Olympic Games in, 2; poverty
    rates in, 35, 69, 70, 73, 74; public housing
    projects in, 1–4, 62, 67–68; redlining
    practices in, 64; Strategic Action Plan,
    159; union membership in, 116; urban
    revitalization of, 65–68; voter turnout in,
    45–51, 148–54, 157, 167–71

Baltimore, Md., 9, 214n27
Barrett, Mark "Tom," 155–56
Bartels, Larry M., 186,
Bausch and Lomb Corporation, 99
blockbusting practices, 64
Boston, Mass., 211n17
Brockey, Harold, 159
Bush, George H. W., 191

Callahan, Judie, 154
case-study selection, 28–41, 222n23
census tracts, 28–29, 217n53; and election
    districts, 42–43

"checkbook participation," 113, 123, 124n8,
    128–29
Chicago, Ill., 76, 89, 99, 211n17
civic environments, 3–7, 13–24, 54–61, 109,
    165–84; definition of, 4, 23, 225n1; and
    public spaces, 120, 135–39; and safety,
    115, 135–40; and social assets, 130–35,
    140; and voluntary organizations, 110–20.
    See also political involvement
civil rights movement, 1, 67, 68, 167, 239n83.
    See also race
"class gap," 4–6, 17–18, 55; in Atlanta, 73;
    and Internet access, 243n64; in Kansas
    City, 162; and political involvement, 110,
    117–18, 185–88. See also economic
    segregation
Clinton, Hillary, 125
Comprehensive Development Plan
    (Atlanta), 159
Cookingham, L. P., 77
Country Club Plaza, Kansas City, 8, 77, 161
Crescent neighborhood. See Rochester

D'Amato, Michael, 154–55, 163–64,
    243n64
deindustrialization, 9, 28, 140; in Atlanta,
    132–33; in Milwaukee, 92, 163; in
    Rochester, 133, 165
Denton, Nancy A., 30
Detroit, Mich., 99, 231n87
disciplined configurative case studies, 40
dissimilarity index, 29–34
Douglas, Ben, 156, 164–65
Duffy, Robert "Bob," 156

Eastman Kodak Company, 99, 133
Economic Development Corporation
    (Atlanta), 159–60
economic segregation, 3–7, 142–46;
    consequences of, 185–88; and "free"
    choice, 3, 7; measurement of, 217n55,
    219n7; origins of, 7–13, 56; and political

ACKNOWLEDGMENTS

This book began as a small kernel of an idea when I was working at Mercy Housing, Inc., in San Francisco. As an event planner and fundraiser for an organization that develops low-income housing and programming for its residents, I spent a lot of time with community organizers in various economically segregated and struggling neighborhoods. It was during this time that I became interested in housing policy and patterns of residential segregation. Without this experience I never would have started this project. And once I began, I could not have finished without the assistance of many institutions and individuals, and the support of friends and family.

The Horowitz Foundation for Social Policy provided financial assistance with a small research grant early in the project. The Maxwell School of Citizenship and Public Affairs at Syracuse University, the Dean's Office of the Maxwell School, and the Syracuse University Political Science Department supported this research through numerous research grants and awards. The National Archives and Records Administration in College Park, Maryland, was a great place to work for a time while I was traveling to do research and while I was writing; it provided flexibility in scheduling and camaraderie among friends and colleagues, and I learned a lot about what Americans think about their federal government. Finally, a Research Fellowship in Governance Studies at the Brookings Institution provided the invaluable resources and space to write the first draft of what became this book.

In addition to financial support many individuals made the burden of research lighter with their generosity and assistance. Suzanne Mettler provided constant guidance and insightful advice. I have learned a great deal from her and am truly grateful for having had the opportunity to work with Suzanne. I also have to thank all those who spent time with me in all four case-study cities and allowed me to interview them. Quite literally, without their assistance this project would never have been completed. Aside from everything I document in the book, my time in these different communities taught me that we are not as different from one another as we often think and that the perception of others can be a major obstacle in forging a sense of community and shared fate.

There were several families and individuals who allowed me to stay with them while researching in each of the four cities I visited. McGee and Anne Young and their children opened their home to me and provided great company during my time in Milwaukee, Wisconsin. In Kansas City, Missouri, Rebecca Landewe took me in for two weeks on only the good word of my sister-in-law; she made me feel welcome and helped me celebrate my thirtieth birthday. And Michael and Jamie Krafic graciously let me stay with them while I was researching in Atlanta, Georgia, and for that I am grateful.

The staff at the Rochester Municipal Archives opened their office and their stacks to me, helped me track down hard-to-find documents, and provided office equipment and support to aid my research. The staff of the Kansas City Election Board and the staff of the Monroe County Board of Elections in Rochester, New York, went above and beyond assisting me in tracking down voter-turnout records. I would particularly like to thank the staff in Kansas City who let me roam their caves—actual caves that house some of Kansas City's archived records—to track old electoral district maps and voter-turnout records. The archivists and librarians at the Kenan Research Center at the Atlanta History Center provided a welcoming space to conduct research. The staff of the Government Documents and Maps Department at University of Maryland's McKeldin Library, and in particular Kim Ricker and Claire Schnitzer in the Geographic Information Systems (GIS) office, provided support early in the project. My student assistants at Arcadia University, especially Erin Moran, Kate Slenzak, and Rich Baker, have provided crucial research support in the final stages of this project. Michael Sullivan gave me detailed and much-appreciated feedback and constructive criticism during the final stages of the project. I owe my gratitude to Peter Agree at the University of Pennsylvania Press and Rick Valelly for supporting this work and providing great guidance and encouragement along the way. And finally, the reviewers of this manuscript gave invaluable feedback, and one in particular went above and beyond expectations by giving thoughtful, insightful, and extremely helpful feedback.

Writing a book is a long and often challenging process, and a strong personal support system is vital for sustaining oneself over the years. I have many colleagues who provided much needed encouragement, support, and professional advice along the way. At California State University, Long Beach, where I started my academic career, I would especially like to thank Chuck Noble and Terri Wright for their advice and guidance, Kevin Wallsten for his camaraderie, and Chris Dennis for his endless encouragement. I would like to thank my colleagues in my new academic home, Arcadia University, for providing friendship and a welcoming and supportive work environment. And while I have never worked in the same department as Richardson Dilworth, he has proven a good and kind colleague, providing honest feedback and advice when it was not his obligation to do so.

Finally, my family—parents and grandparents, siblings, aunts, uncles, and cousins—and close friends have given me constant love, made homecomings fun and revitalizing, and always cheered me on, even when they were not quite sure what I was up to. I especially have to thank my mom, Kim Dowsett, for always being a quick phone call away, and for reminding me not to sweat the small stuff (it won't matter ten years from now anyway). Alexandra Sullivan and the many friends I made in graduate school provided the support, humor, and distractions that were necessary to maintain a sense of humor while writing this book. My daughters, Avila and Sidra, were born during the course of this project, and I thank them for making me stop and play and for keeping me grounded and focused on the present. Finally, I thank my husband, Jeremy Sullivan, for everything from reminding me that life is a journey for us to enjoy to reading just one more draft. His incisive insight and unwavering love, patience, and encouragement made the completion of this project possible. For this and so much more, thank you.